Armageddon Ost
The German Defeat on the Eastern Front 1944-5
Nik Cornish

Ian Allan
PUBLISHING

This book is dedicated to my children Charlotte and Alex and to Ann for her patience and support. Thanks are due to Dmitry Belanovsky and Norbert Hofer for their assistance.

Picture credits

Nik Cornish at Stavka:

Pages 1, 6(both), 7, 8(middle), 9(top), 10 (middle), 11, 18, 20(top), 25(top), 27(top), 28(bottom), 30, 33(both), 36, 37(top), 38(top), 41, 43(top), 44, 45, 46, 47(both), 50(bottom), 51(both), 52(bottom), 58(top), 61, 62(both), 64, 68(both), 72, 75(both), 77(both), 78, 81(bottom), 82, 85, 87, 88(bottom), 90(top), 91, 92(top), 99, 100, 101(both), 105, 109, 110, 112, 114, 115, 116, 120, 124, 128, 129, 131, 132, 137, 138, 139(both), 145(top), 151(top)

Central Museum of the Armed Forces, Moscow:

Pages 3, 4, 5(bottom), 8(bottom), 9(bottom), 14, 15, 16, 17, 19(both), 21, 22, 23, 24(both), 25(bottom), 26(both), 27(bottom), 28(top), 29, 31, 35(both), 37(bottom), 38(bottom), 39, 40(both), 42, 48(both), 49(both), 50(top), 52(top), 53, 56, 58(bottom), 60, 63, 65(both), 66(both), 67(both), 69, 74, 76(both), 80(both), 81(top), 84, 86, 89, 90(bottom), 92(bottom), 93, 94, 95(both), 96, 97, 98, 102, 103, 104, 106, 107, 108(bottom), 111, 113(both), 118, 119, 121, 122, 127, 130, 134, 140, 141, 142(top), 148(bottom), 149, 150, 151(bottom)

From the Fonds of the RGAKFD at Krasnogorsk:

Pages 5(top), 10(top and bottom), 13, 20(bottom), 34, 43(bottom), 54, 59, 70, 73, 88(top), 108(top), 125, 126, 133, 135, 142(bottom), 143(both), 144, 145(bottom), 146, 147(both), 148(top), 152 (both), 153, 154

First published 2006

ISBN (10) 0 7110 3036 7
ISBN (13) 978 0 7110 3036 7

Published by Ian Allan Publishing

an imprint of Ian Allan Publishing Ltd, Hersham, Surrey KT12 4RG.
Printed in England by Ian Allan Printing Ltd, Hersham, Surrey KT12 4RG.

Code: 0606/B

Visit the Ian Allan Publishing website at www.ianallanpublishing.com

Title page:
German mountain troops in action. The artillery piece is the 75mm Model 1936 mountain gun that had a range of 9,150 metres (10,000 yards). The shield was often omitted to allow for greater mobility. These weapons broke down into six loads for mule transport and weighed 726kg (1,600lb). A skid chassis for use in snow could replace the wheels.

Opposite:
Crossing the border into the Reich, a Soviet infantry platoon headed by a political officer (in soft cap), moves forward. By late 1944 Moscow was gradually reasserting the Communist Party's influence across the state, particularly in the newly liberated regions where years of occupation had caused the populations to consider political and economic alternatives to Communism.

Contents

Introduction

The purpose of this book is to bring together a collection of mostly unseen images from both Russian and German sources and a straightforward narrative that covers the major actions of the period. Much has been written (for example, Cornelius Ryan's *The Last Battle* and Anthony Beevor's *Berlin: The Downfall 1945*) regarding elements of the Red Army's behaviour first in East Prussia and then across Germany, particularly with reference to Berlin, therefore I have made little reference to this or the plight of the refugees from the east in 1944–5.

The Eastern Front during this period was dominated by the Red Army which was to drive the forces of the Axis back from the outskirts of Leningrad to the heart of Berlin. However, this was not a tale of unalloyed success. Although, by early 1944, there was

little doubt of the outcome there were still 12 months of heavy fighting to come. During April–May 1944 it was still possible for Axis troops to look at a map showing the Eastern Front stretching from the Baltic to the Black Sea and for them to travel home on leave to families for whom the war was still very far away.

As Finland, Hungary, Slovakia and Romania had all contributed troops to the fighting as allies in one way or another of Germany the fighting was not to stop at their borders, whatever their governments may have hoped. Retreating German units were to be followed and dealt with even as the politicians discussed the niceties. Governments driven out by the Nazis or politicians out of step with the regimes in their homelands before the war viewed the Red Army's advance with a mixture

of trepidation and hope. The exiled governments of Czechoslovakia, Poland, Greece and Yugoslavia were all locked in negotiations with the USSR, Britain and the USA regarding the nature of their post-war regimes. Just who was going to take power when the fascist or pro-fascist governments fell was a moot point. Certainly in Poland the prospect of liberation by the Russians was viewed as a very mixed blessing.

As the Red Army advanced across the Baltic states, Poland, Hungary, the Balkans and Germany itself millions of refugees, former POWs and collaborators sought a place away from the fighting spurred on by fear of retribution, hunger and death.

Paradoxically the last fighting took place between two groups of Russians in Prague after the surrender of Berlin. This fratricidal

Above: The architects of Soviet victory during 1944–5. To the right Marshals G. K. Zhukov and K. K. Rokossovsky converse as I. S. Konev waits in the background. All three had risen through the ranks of the Red Army. Rokossovsky frequently wore spurs, as he had been a cavalry officer during the Civil War.

action was mirrored elsewhere in eastern and central Europe as pro- and anti-Soviet forces had clashed in Yugoslavia, Hungary, the Ukraine and the Baltic states. Although the arrival of the Soviet troops was greeted with jubilation across much of the region as it brought relief from years of Nazi oppression it rapidly became clear that independence was not a real option.

From his sanctum in the Kremlin Stalin exercised control over an ever-growing Red Army that included colossal fleets of aircraft and tanks.

During the three years of war Stalin had grown to trust his generals more and more, allowing them to discuss and even argue with his strategic decisions. The Soviet High Command, *Stavka*, had learned many lessons during the years following the invasion of the USSR, though paying a price in human suffering that was unparalleled in history. From 1943 onwards those lessons had been applied, with increasing confidence, by men such as Zhukov, Rokossovsky and Konev who had all but driven the Axis forces from their country.

Hitler, conversely, had grown less and less trusting of his generals and more reliant on his own strategic genius. When the Red Army began its 1944 summer offensive Hitler issued an increasingly fantastical stream of orders to an ever-diminishing army that was itself

Above: A pair of T-34/76 tanks with their complement of 'tank desant' infantry prepare for the off. The T-34's turrets were provided with grab rails for their riders to hang on to when the charge was underway. The task of keeping the enemy's positions suppressed was left to the tank's secondary armament.

becoming less than eager to share their Führer's vision of Armageddon. As his empire shrank Hitler placed his faith in officers whose loyalty to him often outweighed their abilities in the field and in the 'wonder weapons' under development by his scientists that would snatch victory at the eleventh hour.

However, in the final analysis it would be the men who had stopped the 'master race' at Stalingrad who would raise their arms in victory and Hitler who would take his own life as the Soviet artillery beat a Wagnerian tattoo in the grounds of his last refuge in the Berlin bunker.

Above: The legacy of Stalingrad, a field of Axis corpses. The city can be seen in the background as a Soviet-produced GAZ lorry delivers yet more bodies. The loss of Sixth Army was a grievous blow to Hitler's ambitions in the USSR and a huge fillip to Soviet morale.

Chapter 1

'Barbarossa' to 'Bagration'

'We shall not capitulate, no never. We may be destroyed, but if we are we shall drag a world with us — a world in flames.' By 1944 these prophetic words, spoken by Adolf Hitler in 1933, seemed to have more than hollow bombast to them.

The final year of World War 2 on the Eastern Front was an incredible period in military history. Battles of unimaginable magnitude raged across the steppes of the Ukraine, the forests and wetlands of Belorussia, the Carpathian Mountains, the river valleys of Yugoslavia and the plains of Hungary and Poland. By the time that the echoes of the last shot had faded away in May 1945 millions of men, women and children had died, been maimed or were on the move. Great cities from Kiev and Minsk to Warsaw, Budapest and Berlin lay in smouldering ruins, torn apart by the vicious fighting waged in defence of one man's dream of world domination. The roads to Moscow and beyond resounded to the shuffling feet of Hitler's defeated armies as they tramped into captivity — the men of the Wehrmacht penetrating deeper into the USSR now as prisoners than they had as invaders. Streaming west were the displaced, former POWs and the recently liberated inmates of the concentration camps. Watching these columns were the men and women of the Red Army, some of whom had fought their way from the gates of Moscow or the banks of the Volga River at Stalingrad to the heart of the Third Reich and the final victory. Behind them lay Eastern Europe where countries that had sided with or been overrun by Germany adjusted themselves to their altered circumstances.

Allies and Supporters

To gain a clearer understanding of the 12 months leading up to the defeat of Germany it is necessary to consider the countries in which the fighting took place and their relationship with Germany.

The first of Hitler's acquisitions, albeit an apparently willing one, was Austria which was absorbed into what became Greater Germany in 1938. From the end of World War 1 a vocal group of Austrians had been agitating for unification with Germany and now that wish was granted. Austria became a German state like Bavaria or Saxony and the Austrian Army was absorbed into the Wehrmacht.

Above: Hungarian gendarmes, identifiable by the black cockerel feathers in their hats, guard a supply train during the summer of 1943. By this stage of the war the Hungarian forces in the USSR were mainly relegated to security duties behind the lines.

A less simple process was undergone by Czechoslovakia which was dismembered in 1938–9. The Sudetenland was incorporated into Greater Germany, Bohemia-Moravia became a German protectorate and Slovakia an unoccupied, German puppet state led by Monsignor Jozef Tiso with its own small army. Both Hungary and Poland were granted parts of Slovakia.

In September 1939 Hitler's territorial ambitions led him to invade Poland and World War 2 broke out. With Poland's defeat and division between the Soviet Union and Germany the country effectively ceased to exist but for the government in exile. Stalin, ever eager to increase the buffer zone around the USSR, imposed 'mutual defence agreements' on the Baltic states of Lithuania, Latvia and Estonia, which provided bases for the Soviet armed forces.

A similar agreement was offered to Finland but negotiations broke down and the USSR invaded Finland on 30 November 1939. After a series of humiliating defeats the Red Army finally overcame Finnish resistance and on 12 March 1940 peace was agreed. However, the Finns were looking to the future and an opportunity to regain their lost territories near Leningrad and in Karelia. The lacklustre performance of the Red Army during its war with Finland did not pass unnoticed by the Germans.

Above: A Romanian infantryman in winter kit poses for the camera behind the lines of Army Group South. The Romanian Army was ill equipped for the armoured battles of 1943–4 but fought tenaciously in defence and earned the respect of its German allies. When Romania changed sides in 1944 the army was issued with a mixture of German and Soviet equipment alongside that domestically produced.

The campaigns of 1940 saw Norway, Denmark, the Low Countries and France all defeated and the British driven out of continental Europe. While Hitler was fighting in the west, Stalin, still smarting from his Pyrrhic victory over the Finns, occupied the Baltic states and the Romanian provinces of Bessarabia and Bukovina. By these acquisitions Stalin had advanced the USSR almost to the old borders of the tsars.

On 27 September 1940 Germany, Italy and Japan signed the Tripartite Pact dividing the world into spheres of influence, Europe, the Mediterranean and East Asia respectively. Hungary and Romania became members of the Pact at the same time. During October the Soviet Union was invited to join but, such was Stalin's list of requirements, the offer lapsed. Several weeks later Hitler declared that, 'Russia must now be smashed.' Planning for the projected invasion of the Soviet Union went ahead apace under the code name of Operation 'Barbarossa'.

Admiral Miklós Horthy, who enjoyed the title of Regent, ruled Hungary. Horthy was staunchly anti-Communist but also less than enamoured with Hitler; however, he was not averse to adding to Hungarian territory by hanging on to the Führer's coat-tails. Having gained land from Slovakia and Poland, Horthy raised the question of Transylvania, a part of Romania since 1920 but prior to that a part of the Austro-Hungarian Empire. Acting as the 'honest brokers' in this matter Germany and Italy granted half of Transylvania to Hungary. This further loss of territory, only months after the Soviet Union's action, was a source of deep resentment in Romania. During September 1940 King Carol II was forced to abdicate and his son Michael was crowned in his stead. However, power rested in the hands of General, later Marshal, Ion Antonescu who assumed the title 'Conducator'. A strong German military mission was sent to Romania later that winter.

Mussolini, Hitler's partner, had declared war on France and Britain on 10 June 1940 and in late October invaded Greece from Italian-occupied Albania. However, Italian troops failed to achieve anything in the face of stout Greek resistance and were driven back to their start lines. To counter the possibility of British aid to Greece Hitler had ordered the preparation of Operation 'Marita', the invasion of Greece. Operation 'Marita' required the compliance of Yugoslavia, Hungary, Romania and Bulgaria to be speedily executed. On 1 March 1941 Bulgaria joined the Tripartite Pact followed by Yugoslavia on 25 March. Almost immediately the German Twelfth Army crossed into Bulgaria.

Although an unwelcome diversion of forces from the build-up to Operation 'Barbarossa', the conquest of Greece was seen as an essential

Above: The de facto ruler of Romania, Marshal Ion Antonescu (left), with Field Marshal Walther von Brauchitsch (centre) in Bucharest in 1943. The defection of the Romanian Army in August 1944 left the southern wing of Germany's Eastern Front in total disarray.

move to prevent the British from bombing the Ploesti oilfields in Romania, on which the Germans depended for almost their entire supply of fuel. Both Hungary and Romania were happy to allow the passage of German troops to Greece. But, much to Hitler's chagrin, a coup (27 March) in Yugoslavia resulted in a new government which dissociated itself from the pro-Axis stance of its predecessor. In a matter of hours plans were made to invade Yugoslavia — Operation 'Punishment'. Belgrade was bombed on 6 April as troops from Hungary, Italy, Bulgaria and Germany poured into Yugoslavia from all directions. Within two weeks Yugoslavia had been defeated. To satisfy his allies Hitler carved Yugoslavia up, all bar Romania receiving a portion of this multi-ethnic, multi-faith kingdom. Croatia emerged as an 'independent state' in the manner of Slovakia. The dismemberment of Yugoslavia resulted in three years of merciless internal warfare between the various ethnic, religious and political groupings that presaged the situation in the late 20th century. The fall of Greece resulted in the further enlargement of Bulgaria. The majority of the garrisons occupying Yugoslavia and Greece were Italian, an arrangement which was to create problems when Italy surrendered in 1943. With the Balkans organised to his satisfaction, Hitler could now return, without distraction, to what he perceived as his great mission — the destruction of the USSR.

Operation 'Barbarossa'

The Axis invasion of the Soviet Union began on 22 June 1941. Three army groups were formed to complete this huge undertaking. Army Group North (AGN), deployed across a front from the Baltic Sea to Suwalki and commanded by Field Marshal von Leeb, was to march on Leningrad and 'liberate' the Baltic states. Army Group Centre (AGC) covered the line from Suwalki to the Pripyat Marshes. It was commanded by Field Marshal von Bock and would advance towards Moscow. Army Group South (AGS) held the front from the Pripyat Marshes to the Black Sea. It was commanded by Field Marshal von Rundstedt with the task of advancing into the Ukraine towards Kiev. The Third and Fourth Romanian Armies and a corps each from the Slovakian and Hungarian Armies were subordinated to AGS. Including reserves and the units advancing from Norway against Murmansk well over 150 divisions were committed to the Eastern Front.

Finland, not formally an ally, but a *de facto* one, began operations on 10 July. Having achieved their objectives by restoring the territory lost in 1940 the Finns halted outside of Leningrad just as the Germans cut the city off in September 1941. During August Mussolini's contribution, the Italian Expeditionary Corps in Russia, joined AGS.

Although the advance into the Soviet Union was spectacularly fast, the failure to take

Above: The optimism of the Wehrmacht prior to the start of Operation 'Barbarossa' was understandable following the experiences in Poland and the west. This Wehrmacht coach bears the legend Suwalki–Moscow and the date 15/6/41 but it did not reach its destination. The eastern campaign was to prove no tourist excursion.

Above: Soviet infantrymen surrender in the Ukraine during 1941. Of the millions of Red Army men captured few survived the brutal treatment meted out to them in POW camps. Almost outlawed by Stalin, their return to the USSR was frequently an unpleasant experience. The tank burning to the rear of the photo is a Soviet BT-7 with its conical turret.

Above: Soviet infantry march to the front in the spring of 1942. The inspirational placard quotes from a speech by Molotov declaring that, 'Our cause is right, the enemy will be defeated and victory will be ours.' Appeals to the men's patriotism as opposed to party formulas became more acceptable during 1942.

Moscow and the Wehrmacht's subsequent retreat showed Hitler that the war in the east would last longer than anticipated. The Axis summer campaign of 1942 at first repeated the successes of the previous year on a reduced scale but the disaster at Stalingrad demonstrated that victory was not easily within Germany's grasp. The failure of the ill-conceived offensive at Kursk during July 1943 clearly proved to those who chose to see that the Red Army was a very different force to that which had been hounded and herded across the steppes of the USSR two summers before.

Although part of a speech made in November 1941, when the Wehrmacht was at the gates of Moscow, the following words of Josef Stalin were more than apposite by early 1944. 'Another few months, another half year . . . And Hitler's Germany is bound to burst beneath the weight of its crimes.'

Driving the Wehrmacht and its Axis satellites back from the Moscow suburbs almost to the Soviet borders of 1940 had taken three years of hard, vicious fighting with untold losses. To the west the combined weight of the USA, the British Commonwealth and Free France stood ready to launch the long-awaited Second Front. The announcement of the Second Front went someway to alleviate the sense of isolation felt by the Soviet Union during the three years when it believed, with considerable justification, that it was shouldering the greatest burden of the struggle with the Axis. Suspicion of American, and in particular British, motives was rooted in the days of the Russian revolutions and civil war when Churchill had been the prime mover behind anti-Communist intervention. Stalin had never forgotten or forgiven this policy and was very careful to ensure that the Soviet Union's efforts and achievements were not in vain. The regimes that were to be established in Eastern Europe at the war's end would be, at the very least, sympathetic to Stalin's requirements.

Kursk to the Crimea

In the wake of its victory at Kursk in July 1943 the Red Army had, by November of that year, liberated Kharkov and Kiev. Next, in operations reminiscent of the Wehrmacht's thrusts into the Soviet Union in 1941, the Red Army advanced across the snow-covered steppe between December 1943 and April 1944. The Germans, with their Hungarian and Romanian allies, found it almost impossible to stem the Russian advance. It was unfortunate for the German forces on the Eastern Front that Hitler issued Directive 51 in early November. In this he stated that the Western Front would now have priority in the allocation of arms, men and equipment to halt any attempt by the Western Allies to open a second front in Europe.

Above: The Italian forces in the USSR fought exclusively in the south. Here a machine-gun team moves into position to the north of Stalingrad during September 1942. Within the next year the 200,000 men of Italy's CSIR (Expeditionary Corps in Russia) had been withdrawn from the Eastern Front.

Above: The shattered remains of Panzer III tanks on the battlefield at Kursk during July 1943. This offensive proved to be the last occasion on which the Wehrmacht was able to launch a major operation on ground of its own choosing with some hope of success. The added side armour on the Panzer III had proved to be of little use in these cases and the type was withdrawn from front-line service shortly after this time.

As compensation, commanders in the east would be allowed, '. . . to lose ground, even on a large scale, without a fatal blow being dealt to the nervous system of Germany'. So, although deprived of resources, it looked as though Germany's officers were to be allowed to conduct the sort of mobile defence that had proved so formidable in the past. No longer would they have to fight to the last man and the last bullet for the sake of some

symbolic piece of real estate that lacked any real strategic or tactical value. Unfortunately for the generals this promise of operational freedom was illusory and very quickly Hitler began to repeat his old mantra of not a step backwards.

In January 1944 the Russian 2nd Ukrainian Front (a front was a group of armies) trapped significant German forces in the Korsun-Shevchenkovsky pocket. Some

30,000 troops were extricated with difficulty but this was of little consolation to the Wehrmacht as it was forced ever further westwards. The final hours of the Germans trapped in the Korsun-Shevchenkovsky pocket took on something of the quality of a nightmare. Herded like sheep by Soviet T-34 tanks, thousands of German and Western European Waffen-SS volunteers were brought up short by the recently thawed Gniloy Tikich River, roughly 8 metres (25 feet) wide. Crossing this barrier proved too much for hundreds of hungry, exhausted and freezing men who drowned making the attempt. A Soviet officer, Major Kampov, graphically described this episode:

'The Germans ran in all directions. And for the next four hours our tanks raced up and down the plain crushing them by the hundred. Our cavalry, competing with the tanks, chased them through the ravines . . . Hundreds and hundreds of cavalry hacked at them with their sabres and massacred the Fritzes as no one had been massacred by cavalry before . . . It was the kind of carnage that nothing could stop until it was over.'

On 26 March the 2nd Ukrainian Front reached the Pruth (Prut) River which marked the 1940 border between the USSR and Romania. To celebrate the event Stalin ordered a salute of 'the first category, 24 volleys from 324 guns'. At 21:00 hours the rockets announcing the victory salute lit up the sky over Moscow. It was to be the first of many such celebrations over the course of the next 12 months.

On 4 March 1944 the 1st, 2nd and 3rd Ukrainian Fronts began a series of attacks aimed at pushing the Germans out of the Ukraine before the *rasputitsa*, the rains and floods of the spring thaw, brought an end to the chance of mobile warfare. Within three weeks the borders of Poland had been reached and AGS was in tatters.

The 4th Ukrainian Front was given the task of liberating the Crimea. Attacked across the land bridge and through the shallow waters of the Sivash lagoons, the Axis defences crumbled. Following hot on the heels of their retreating enemies, the Red Army stormed through the peninsula. Sevastopol, taken by the Axis at such cost in 1942, fell with barely a whimper during the first week of May. Although over 100,000 German and Romanian troops were evacuated by sea, all their heavy equipment was lost. Again the celebratory guns boomed out in Moscow. However, it was the summer of 1944 that was to witness the most spectacular advances of the Red Army and the greatest defeat suffered by Hitler's Wehrmacht.

Above: As a Panzer VI Tiger burns, a T-34/76 transports an infantry section across a main road during the winter of 1943–4. Frozen ground such as this made excellent going for armoured vehicles. To speed the advance in the absence of lorries or personnel carriers infantry were often transported by tank.

Preparations for Operation 'Bagration'

During May the Red Army paused for breath; the speed of the advance and the condition of the road and rail links were such that supply lines were tenuous and in desperate need of refurbishment, as were the men and machines at the front. It was at this time that the Soviet fronts were given the titles by which they would be known until the end of the war. From north to south there were 12 fronts: Karelian Front, Leningrad Front, 3rd, 2nd and 1st Baltic Fronts, 3rd, 2nd and 1st Belorussian Fronts, 1st, 2nd, 3rd and 4th Ukrainian Fronts. Stalin and the *Stavka* could afford to be ambitious in their planning. Increasingly Stalin was granting his team of front commanders greater freedom of operation whilst Hitler was assuming an even more domineering role as his faith in his commanders diminished.

The Axis also reorganised its command structures in the east. AGN occupied the line from the Baltic Sea to the Dvina River just north of Vitebsk. From there to just south of the Pripyat Marshes was controlled by AGC. Army Group South had been replaced by two commands. The first of these was Army Group North Ukraine (AGNU) whose position ran from south of the Pripyat Marshes into the Carpathian Mountains where it joined Army Group South Ukraine (AGSU), which ended on the Black Sea. Only Romania, Hungary and Finland of Germany's allies still maintained forces on the Eastern Front; Italy and Slovakia had withdrawn theirs.

Soviet Planning

Soviet planning in previous years had set unrealistic goals way beyond the capacity of its men, machines and logistics. The summer offensive of 1944 was to be a more carefully planned affair that broke down into three phases. The first blow was to fall on Finland; this would be followed by phase two, an attack directly into the front of AGC, straight down the Moscow–Minsk highway, one of the few all-weather roads in the USSR. The third phase was aimed at the northern Ukraine and was dependent on the success of phase two in drawing off the reserves to

Above: Wearing his trademark 1940 pattern field cap Field Marshal Erich von Manstein, pictured here in 1942, commanded Army Group South from February 1943 until March 1944. Although a master of mobile defence Manstein was dismissed by Hitler for over-realistic assessments of Germany's future prospects.

Above: A T-34/76 Model 1943 during early 1944. This tank was the most commonly used during the last year of the war. When not in combat the fug and noise generated by the crew and the engine was relieved by driving with all hatches open to ventilate the interior. The boxes on the side are for spare ammunition.

support AGC. The offensives anticipated nothing less than the reincorporation of the Baltic states into the USSR, the removal of Finland from the war, the liberation of Belorussia and the destruction of AGC. The code name for the attack on AGC was Operation 'Bagration', after a Russian hero of the Napoleonic Wars. The fronts involved in Operation 'Bagration' were the 1st Baltic and 1st, 2nd and 3rd Belorussian. Over the front commanders were placed *Stavka* 'co-ordinators': Marshal G. K. Zhukov oversaw 1st and 2nd Belorussian Fronts and Marshal A. M. Vasilevsky 1st Baltic and 3rd Belorussian Fronts.

The great strength of the Red Army lay in its tank formations that were expected to exploit the holes made in the Axis defences by the artillery, air force and infantry. By driving as far and as fast as possible the tankers were to allow the Germans no opportunity to rebuild their shattered lines. Mopping up and dealing with strong pockets of resistance were to be left to the other arms.

On the German side of the line an offensive on the Eastern Front was anticipated with dread. Since November 1943 the Wehrmacht's forces in the west had been given priority of reinforcements and equipment. Consequently the formations in the east were both under-manned and under-equipped. Although the previous nine months' fighting had sapped the strength of both sides, by 1944 Soviet industrial capacity far outstripped that of Germany, particularly in the critical matters of artillery and tanks. Added to these, immense numbers of lorries and half-tracks supplied by the USA and Great Britain increased the mobility of the Red Army dramatically. Despite the best endeavours of Albert Speer, Hitler's Minister for War Production, Germany was far behind in the race. It is little wonder that the leaders of the Wehrmacht were more than concerned at the prospect of a Soviet offensive.

Above: Waffen-SS grenadiers of an unidentified unit pause for a smoke in the Ukraine during the early months of 1944. The man to the rear is carrying the legs for an 81mm mortar. By this date the Germans were generally well prepared to face the rigours of a Russian winter as the dress of these men testifies. However, the metal studded boots were not ideal footwear.

German Planning

German planning was based on assumptions that were, in the event, to prove false. The Soviet offensive against AGS earlier in the year had led Hitler to believe that Stalin's objectives were Romania's oilfields at Ploesti, Bucharest, the rest of the Balkan peninsula up to and including the old imperial Russian objective of Istanbul and control of the sea lane between the Black Sea and the Mediterranean. Ploesti provided the oil that fuelled the Panzers and the Luftwaffe and was therefore essential to the war economy of the Axis. The bombing of the Reich's synthetic fuel plants during 1944, which destroyed much of their production capacity, increased this dependency. But such an offensive would be open to counter-attack into its right flank

from AGNU. Another possibility available to the Soviets was an attack on AGNU aimed at cutting it off from AGC and AGN by advancing from the Ukraine across Poland to the shores of the Baltic Sea. This scenario was the one anticipated by Hitler and OKH (Oberkommando des Heeres — Army High Command) which was responsible for the war in the east. This operation presented the hope of Soviet reversals on a significant scale, a hugely appealing vision for Hitler who, by this stage of the war, had adopted wishful thinking as a substitute for facing unpalatable facts. In Hitler's mind the USSR was on the verge of collapse; he was convinced that the Red Army was at the end of its strength and that Germany would be victorious. Such are the delusions of megalomaniacs.

But, tragically for his soldiers, such dreams dominated his strategic thinking. Therefore, as well as removing seven armoured divisions from the Eastern Front, he also insisted that the bulk of the remaining tank formations in the east be placed under the control of AGNU. During the fighting of the previous months AGC had withdrawn steadily and effectively, bloodying the nose of the Red Army on several occasions. However, AGC's positions in June 1944 were weak. To bolster them Hitler had ordered, on 8 March, the creation of 'fortified areas', *feste Plätze*. The Führer order of that day stated, 'Their task is to prevent the enemy from seizing centres of decisive strategic importance. They are to allow themselves to be encircled so as to engage as many of the enemy as possible.

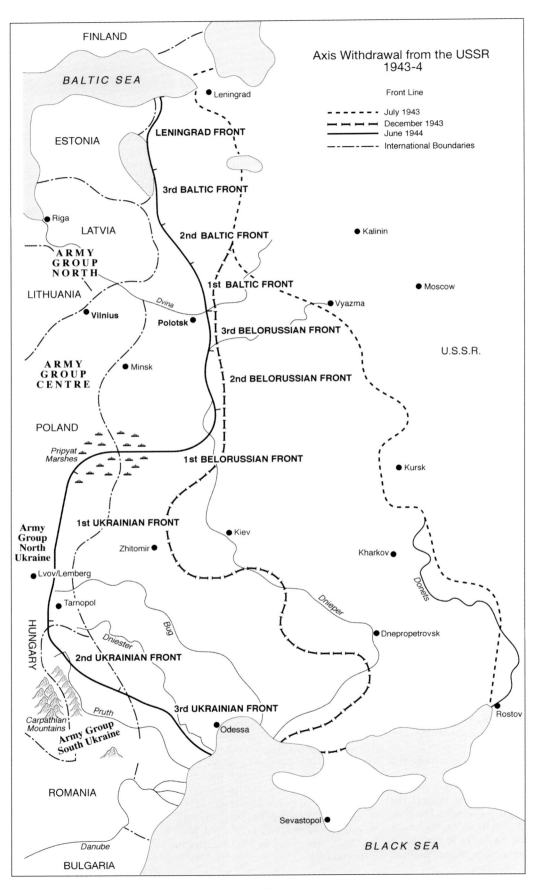

Axis Withdrawal from the USSR
1943-4

Front Line

- - - - - - July 1943
- ▪ - ▪ - ▪ December 1943
——————— June 1944
- · - · - · International Boundaries

FINLAND

BALTIC SEA

Leningrad

ESTONIA

LENINGRAD FRONT

3rd BALTIC FRONT

Riga

LATVIA

2nd BALTIC FRONT

Kalinin

ARMY GROUP NORTH

LITHUANIA

1st BALTIC FRONT

Moscow

Vilnius

Dvina

Polotsk

Vyazma

3rd BELORUSSIAN FRONT

U.S.S.R.

ARMY GROUP CENTRE

Minsk

2nd BELORUSSIAN FRONT

POLAND

Pripyat Marshes

1st BELORUSSIAN FRONT

Kursk

Army Group North Ukraine

1st UKRAINIAN FRONT

Zhitomir

Kiev

Kharkov

Lvov/Lemberg

Dnieper

Donets

Tarnopol

Bug

Dniester

2nd UKRAINIAN FRONT

Dnepropetrovsk

HUNGARY

Pruth

3rd UKRAINIAN FRONT

Carpathian Mountains

Army Group South Ukraine

Odessa

Rostov

ROMANIA

Sevastopol

Danube

BLACK SEA

BULGARIA

Above: The effect of the sun and camouflage netting are shown on this heavy gun during the summer of 1944. The weapon itself is a 203mm B-4 Model 1931 howitzer that has just completed its loading cycle. It was capable of firing one 100-kg (220-lb) shell every two minutes.

They are to create opportunities for fruitful counter-attacks.' How these fortified areas were to be supplied was a unclear. As no new units were sent east to garrison the fortified areas troops were instead to be withdrawn from the field armies to man them. The major fortified areas within AGC were Vitebsk on the Dvina River, Mogilev and Orsha on the Dnieper River and Bobruisk on the Berezina River. Field Marshal Busch, commander of AGC, overruled those officers who criticised this policy. Indeed, during May, Hitler dismissed a general who suggested withdrawing to the Berezina River to shorten the line and create a reserve as, 'another of those generals perpetually looking backwards'. Fortified areas were to loom large in Hitler's defensive strategy during the last year of the war, as were cowardly and untrustworthy generals.

On 6 June 1944 the long anticipated nightmare that had stalked Hitler since at least 1942 became a reality — the Western Allies launched the invasion of France, the second front had become a reality. Now Nazi Germany was faced with a two-front war just at the time when the Soviet Union was clearly on the point of carrying out its own summer offensive.

The Red Army Prepares

To camouflage their troop movements during the build-up to Operation 'Bagration' the Red Army had mounted a deception operation, known in Russian as a *maskirovka*. General K. K. Rokossovsky, commander of 1st Belorussian Front, described these operations in the following manner:

'All headquarters were required to maintain constant air and ground control over the effectiveness with which all activities at the Front were concealed from the enemy. He was to see only what we wanted him to see. Troops deployed and regrouped under cover of night, while in the daytime trainloads of dummy tanks and guns travelled from the front to the rear. In many places we built fake crossings and roads. Guns were concentrated on secondary lines, from which they launched artillery attacks and were then removed to the rear, dummies being left in their place on the firing positions. General Malinin, my Chief of Staff, was inexhaustibly inventive in this respect.'

Rokossovsky also pointed out the specialist training that was undertaken to prepare the men for the swampy terrain in which many of them would be fighting:

'Men learned to swim, cross swamps and rivers with any available means and find their way through woods. They made special 'swamp shoes' to cross the bogs, and built boats, rafts and platforms for trundling machine guns, mortars and light artillery. The tankmen also underwent training in the art of marsh warfare. General Batov once showed me such a 'tankodrome' in the Army rear area. For more than an hour we watched machine after machine drive into the swamp and cross it to the other end. Helped by engineers, the crew provided each tank with faggots, logs, and special triangles for crossing wide ditches.'

Such training would prove invaluable in the vast trackless woods and swamps that made up much of this part of the war zone. The river lines and the swampy areas alongside and around them were integral to the German defences. The rapid crossing of such obstacles would keep casualties low and afford the Germans no respite from the momentum of the offensive.

Genuine radio traffic was to be kept to a minimum, but messages organising fake deployments and transport arrangements were transmitted freely. However, the identity of front-line formations was almost impossible to disguise as German patrols brought in prisoners for interrogation and, remarkably, the flow of deserters continued even at a time when the Red Army was enjoying unprecedented success. Despite their best efforts the sheer volume of movement behind the Russian lines was well nigh impossible to conceal.

Strengths and Weaknesses

The condition of AGC immediately prior to the beginning of Operation 'Bagration' was poor. However, it was not expected to be the major Soviet target. Busch, AGC's commander, had 34 infantry divisions, one Panzer division, two Panzergrenadier divisions, two Luftwaffe field divisions, seven security divisions and some Hungarian formations at his disposal. Only the two Panzergrenadier divisions were anywhere near full strength; the security troops were not equipped for front-line combat; and the Luftwaffe divisions were made up of men surplus to requirements due to lack of planes and were short on training, experience and heavy weapons. In total there were some 400,000 combat troops of varying degrees of efficiency and a similar number of non-combatants. The armour consisted of 480 assault guns and 70 tanks including 29 of the redoubtable Panzer VI Tiger. The ratio of assault guns to tanks reflected Hitler's thinking that AGC would be fighting a fairly static battle. Artillery strength is believed to have been some 9,000 guns of all calibres and a variety of mortars. The air support was in an even more parlous condition. Sixth Air Fleet, AGC's air asset, had some 40 fighters, 300 bombers and 100 ground-attack aircraft on its inventory.

On the other side of the line lay four Soviet fronts deploying 118 infantry divisions, 8 tank and mechanised corps, 14 anti-aircraft divisions, 13 artillery divisions and 6 cavalry divisions — over 1,500,000 men. The armoured units included 2,700 tanks and 1,300 assault guns — approximately six times the number available to the Wehrmacht. The majority of the tanks were T-34s armed with a 76mm gun, but there were diesel-engined M4A2 Shermans, T-34s with 85mm guns and 85 IS-2 Stalin tanks with 122mm guns which were the most powerful on the Soviet roster and more than capable of taking on the Tiger. Specialist engineer units were issued with flame-throwing and mine-sweeping tanks to

Above: A Belorussian partisan group poses for the camera proudly displaying recently awarded medals. Youngsters such as the two boys shown here were often orphans who had no other family than the band to which they belonged. Following the liberation of the area in which they operated such groups were usually drafted into the Red Army.

clear the extensive minefields and fortifications. The need to bridge the swamps and rivers that criss-crossed the area had led to the training of engineers who were to deal with these obstacles. Planking for corduroy roads and wicker hurdles for negotiating swamps had been stockpiled close to the front line. The superiority in artillery was nearly as great as that in armour — 10,500 guns, 11,500 mortars, 4,000 light anti-tank guns and over 2,000 multiple rocket launchers — the *Katyusha*. The Red Air Force could field over 2,000 fighters, 2,000 bombers and 1,700 *Shturmovik* ground-attack aircraft, a superiority of seven to one.

Partisans

Behind the Axis lines were the partisans. The Belorussian swamps and forests were home to the largest group of partisan bands that operated on the Eastern Front. Recruited from Red Army stragglers left behind in the wake of Operation 'Barbarossa' and civilians alienated by the racial and economic policies of the Nazi administration, the partisan strength was estimated at over 250,000, organised in brigades or smaller units. Roughly 15 per cent of the manpower at the disposal of Army

Group Centre was engaged in a vicious, no-holds-barred anti-partisan war right up to the eve of Operation 'Bagration'. By June 1944 the partisans controlled the countryside, forests and marshes; only the towns and lines of communication were in the hands of the Axis. However, German supply columns travelling by road and rail were always under threat and intelligence could be gathered easily and radioed back to Moscow. Supplies were provided by air drop or glider as were specialist personnel. Although weakened by several major anti-partisan sweeps during May and June 1944, the partisan forces were too resilient to be written off. Tightly controlled both politically and militarily from Moscow, the partisans were to carry out their greatest blow against the Wehrmacht on the night of 19/20 June, the original date for the start of Operation 'Bagration'. According to the sketchy remains of German records over 9,000 acts of sabotage were carried out that night. These ranged from shooting German sentries at bridges to blowing up sections of railway line. Whatever the physical results of these acts, the fear and insecurity that the partisans generated amongst their opponents was great. The limited and primitive road network in the area behind the German lines was a very dangerous place for the unwary and set to become more so in the days that followed.

Finland

Starting on 9 June, the Leningrad Front pounded the Finnish lines with 500 aircraft, 5,500 pieces of artillery and 800 rocket launchers for two days. Three Soviet infantry divisions broke the Finns' first line of defence and forced them back to the VT Line. Despite counter-attacks and the arrival of reinforcements rushed south from Karelia, the Finns were driven back to their second line of defence, the VKT Line, on 18 June; it was at this point they requested help from Germany. Hitler's response was speedy and generous. Anti-tank weapons, 80 assault guns, 70 Stuka dive-bombers and an infantry division were dispatched across the Gulf of Finland. On 20 June the city of Viborg (Viipuri) was captured, its Finnish defenders fleeing before T-34 tanks which they had no means of stopping. However, with the arrival of the German aid, Finnish resistance stiffened and on 11 July *Stavka* called off the offensive.

The Destruction of Army Group Centre

Prepared thoroughly and provided with all the weapons that Soviet industry could pour out, the fronts that would be involved in Operation 'Bagration' could look forward to the offensive with optimism. However, due to road and rail congestion in the assembly areas, the start date was postponed from 19 until 23 June. Three years and one day after the Axis invasion of the Soviet Union, the Red Army was poised to sweep the Wehrmacht and its allies from Russian soil.

The offensive was staggered with 1st Baltic Front opening the proceedings followed by 3rd, 2nd and 1st Belorussian Fronts over the next two days. This method left the Germans uncertain about the main direction of the attack and confused as to where to deploy their reserves. An artillery barrage of unparalleled ferocity devastated the German defences and shattered the early morning tranquillity of 23 June. Infantry attacks followed the artillery storm and, as the Germans reported, '. . . behind the assault groups, undisclosed until needed, lay tanks to

follow on and break through'.

The Soviet tidal wave crashed over the German lines, sweeping everything before it. The 3rd Belorussian Front and 1st Baltic Front surrounded Fortress Vitebsk and by 25 June Soviet armoured forces had reached the Smolensk–Minsk road and rail lines, cutting the line of retreat of the German Fourth Army. At roughly the same time several of Rokossovsky's 1st Belorussian Front's armoured columns encircled Fortress Bobruisk, trapping 70,000 men, whilst others raced westwards. Orsha and Vitebsk Fortresses fell on 27 June and Mogilev the following day. With three out of four of his much-vaunted *feste Plätze* washed away like sandcastles, Hitler was forced to concede that the attack on AGC was more than a feint. On 28 June Hitler replaced Busch with Field Marshal Walther Model and authorised the transfer of several divisions from AGN and AGNU to plug the gaping hole torn in the front.

The Soviet IX Tank Corps crossed the Berezina River on 27 June and several German divisions were thus trapped on its eastern bank. At this point Rokossovsky released

Above: Guarded by cavalry and infantry of the NKVD, German POWs are marched through Moscow as proof of the successes of the Red Army during the summer of 1944. An eyewitness recalled that the event provoked feelings of sympathy for the prisoners and many civilians threw bread and cigarettes to their former enemies.

I Guards Cavalry Corps and I Mechanised Corps to take Baranovichi, an important rail junction 120km (75 miles) south-west of Minsk. Minsk was the headquarters of AGC, the capital of Belorussia and a vital communications and transport centre and *Stavka* wanted it captured as rapidly as possible. To add to AGC's troubles, on 29 June Bobruisk fell. *Ad hoc* formations broke out but the majority of the 40,000 troops caught inside were killed or captured. Now it was the turn of Minsk. Despite a series of fine defensive actions north of the city, during which 5th Panzer Division claimed to have destroyed almost 300 of Fifth Guards Tank Army's tanks, Hitler granted permission to evacuate the city on 2 July. During the early hours of the next morning the streets resounded with the noise of T-34s of the 4th Guards Tank Brigade crushing the shambolic German rearguard. Over the course of the next few days Soviet infantry and partisans systematically eliminated pockets of German stragglers as they tried desperately to evade death or capture in the flight west.

Baranovichi fell on 8 July and Rokossovsky's men crossed the pre-war Polish border on 18 July. Five days later Lublin was taken followed by Brest-Litovsk. Finally, on 31 July, elements of 1st Belorussian Front's Second Tank Army reached the outskirts of Praga, a heavily fortified suburb of Warsaw, on the eastern bank of the Vistula River (Wisla).

The Baltic States

1st Baltic Front (General I. Kh. Bagramyan) was to protect the forces advancing on Minsk from interference by AGN. To achieve this its advance was to be inclined to the north-west towards Dvinsk (also known as Daugavpils). The offensive began on 23 June and within days the Dvina River (Daugava) had been crossed and the Soviets were threatening Polotsk. Despite heavy infantry casualties and severe depletion of his tank forces Bagramyan forged ahead and Polotsk fell in early July. The Red Army had crossed the 1939 border into Latvia.

Between AGC and AGN a 70km (44-mile) gap had opened up. Desperately, Model hurled divisions almost straight from the march into the path of the advancing Russians in an attempt to seal what Hitler called 'the hole in the Wehrmacht'.

The next Soviet target was Kaunas in Lithuania to be followed by a drive into south-eastern Latvia as 3rd Belorussian Front (General I. D. Chernyakhovsky) pushed towards Vilnius. Chernyakhovsky was under orders to take Kaunas by the first week of August. Assisted by members of the Polish resistance Vilnius was cleared of Germans on 13 July. Two days later 3rd Belorussian Front crossed the Niemen River (Nemunas) and

Above: A combined attack along a tributary of the Berezina River east of Minsk during Operation 'Bagration' in July 1944.

reached Kalvarija, 24km (15 miles) from the East Prussian border. Kaunas had fallen by 1 August with its garrison fleeing north-westwards closely pursued by motorcyclists and cavalry. Germany was now in sight. However, German resistance began to stiffen and the Soviets were unable to sustain their momentum.

Meanwhile, Bagramyan was instructed to cut AGN's communications with East Prussia. Anticipating that Riga at the mouth of the Dvina River on the Baltic coast would be the logical point to aim for, Bagramyan drew up his plans to move in that direction. If the Soviets took Riga AGN would be trapped north of the Dvina and could be finished off by 2nd and 3rd Baltic Fronts. However, *Stavka* viewed the situation differently. Stalin and his staff were not anxious to repeat the mistakes of past offensives when their goals had been too ambitious; therefore they erred on the side of caution, fearing a German attack into their flanks from the west or the north-east. Consequently 1st Baltic Front was to cut off AGN further to the south whilst covering the flank of 3rd Belorussian Front as it advanced on Warsaw. The remaining Baltic Fronts and Leningrad Front (General L. A. Govorov) were tasked with clearing Estonia and Latvia.

Bagramyan's men attacked on 5 July with Sixth Guards Army spread across 160km (100 miles) of front. Progress was slow as the Soviets ran into solid defence lines which were held with much determination; furthermore 1st Baltic Front was reaching the limit of its supply lines.

Five days later 2nd Baltic Front (General A. I. Yeremenko) swung into action. Although

the front was weak in tanks, a hole 80km (50 miles) wide by 17km (10 miles) deep had been made within two days and at the end of a week the Latvian border had been reached. As 2nd Baltic Front plodded on through swamp and forest, Bagramyan requested permission to attack Riga but was refused. Now it was the turn of 3rd Baltic Front (General I. I. Maslennikov) to enter the fray which it did on 12 July, achieving such success that *Stavka* ordered it to take Valga and cut the Germans in Estonia and northern Latvia off from Riga. By late July the position of AGN looked critical with Dvinsk threatened and Narva under pressure from Leningrad Front. It was at this point that Vasilevsky, the *Stavka* co-ordinator, gave Bagramyan permission to strike at Riga with the first objective being Mitau (Jelgava). The attack began in the early hours of 28 July. Supplementary orders from Stalin whilst approving Vasilevsky's decision, called for an advance in the direction of the port of Memel (Klaipeda) on the German–Lithuanian border.

Although the attack was partly bogged down in heavy fighting around Mitau, Soviet motorised forces dashed ahead and secured Tukkum on 30 July and later that day they arrived on the Baltic coast south of Riga. AGN was now isolated.

To the north, following several days of vicious fighting, Dvinsk (Daugavpils) fell on 27 July and central Latvia was now open to 2nd Baltic Front. Very swiftly *Stavka* ordered Yeremenko to undertake 'a decisive thrust' towards Riga.

Leningrad Front unleashed its offensive towards Narva on 25 July. The plan involved

Above: The crew of a 45mm Model 1942 anti-tank gun prepares to give covering fire to an infantry section off camera advancing through a town in one of the Baltic states during the early autumn of 1944. The armour-piercing capabilities of this weapon were marginal at anything over 500 metres (550 yards). However, it was still useful in the infantry support role and against soft-skinned targets.

crossing the Narva River and outflanking the strongly held positions in and around the city itself. Following an 80-minute barrage and accompanied by the loudly amplified strains of recordings of patriotic and martial tunes, the Soviet troops began their crossing. Despite murderous fire a foothold was established and pontoon bridges for the tanks were assembled. By midday on 26 July Narva itself had fallen and its defenders withdrew to their new positions in the Tannenberg Line, which covered the approaches to the Estonian capital, Tallinn.

AGN's 30 divisions, commanded by General Ferdinand Schörner, were thus isolated. Hitler's refusal to evacuate AGN from the region was based on the premise that it would lead to the defection of Finland; furthermore the Baltic was important to the Kriegsmarine which used it to test new types of U-boat.

Army Group North Ukraine

The attack on AGNU that Hitler had anticipated began on 13 July, spearheaded by Konev's 1st Ukrainian Front. This front was the most powerful striking force of the Red Army, with 1,600 tanks and assault guns, over 15,000 guns, rocket launchers and heavy mortars and 2,800 aircraft. AGNU, its strength depleted by the transfer of units to AGC, was still a formidable opponent with 900 tanks and assault guns, 6,000 guns and mortars and 700 aircraft. Despite holding the initial Soviet attacks, AGNU was pushed back and then its front was broken. A planned German counter-attack ended in disaster, as recalled by Major General von Mellenthin,

'Eighth Panzer [Division] was caught on the move by Russian aircraft. Long columns of tanks and lorries went up in flames, and all hope of a counter-attack disappeared.'

On 16 July Konev pushed two tank armies through the Koltov Corridor and 24 hours later they had reached the gates of Lvov. 1st Belorussian Front's southern wing joined in with the attack on 18 July, heading for the Bug River and Polish city of Lublin. In rapid succession Brody, Lvov and Przemysl were taken.

The destruction of AGC had cost the Wehrmacht between 25 and 30 divisions, approximately 300,000 men, and with them almost 300 armoured fighting vehicles and 1,300 guns. To celebrate this triumph 57,000 POWs were marched in procession along the avenues of Moscow to give tangible evidence to the people of the full extent of the Red Army's victory. It is notable that eyewitnesses recall the event not as triumphalist but as almost pitiful and many of the onlookers gave food and drink to the bedraggled soldiers of the Third Reich.

But there was to be no let up in the momentum that the Soviet offensive had built up. The Wehrmacht was to be allowed no rest in its graceless exit from the USSR and other occupied lands. Rokossovsky summed up the mood of the *Stavka* in an interview during July 1944:

'It is no longer important to capture such and such a position. The essential thing is to give the enemy no respite. The Germans are running to their deaths.'

The Bomb Plot

As the Eastern Front collapsed in chaos, a bomb exploded at the Wolf's Lair, Hitler's command post in East Prussia, on 20 July. Although several staff officers were killed or wounded, Hitler, the real target, was virtually unscathed. The so-called 'Bomb Plot' had been the work of a group of Wehrmacht officers who wanted to remove Hitler before negotiating peace. The conspirators signally failed and brought down the wrath of the Führer who indulged in an orgy of revenge, including a series of show trials and executions. The net result was a further reduction of Hitler's faith in his senior officers and a greater reliance on his own genius and the SS.

The Soviet offensive had proved to be successful beyond imagining. By 1 August the Red Army had driven the Axis out of the USSR, beyond the frontiers of 1939. However, although there was no question that the USSR would reoccupy all the territory it had gained in 1939–40, beyond those borders were other groups who wished to demonstrate their national independence.

With AGN effectively cut off and AGC and AGNU fighting desperately to hold some sort of line the Red Army had pushed the front forward by as much as 560km (350 miles) and the ultimate goal, Berlin, was less than 650km (400 miles) away. When the offensive had run its course the Soviet advance halted along the Vistula River and the East Prussian border. The Carpathian Mountains shielded Slovakia and Hungary and, as yet, Romania had been spared.

Chapter 2

Warsaw Rising: August 1944

'. . . militarily against the Germans and politically against the Russians . . .'
H. von Krannhals, German historian

Romania

The situation in the Balkans was a strange one. The kingdoms of Romania and Bulgaria were allied to Germany but only Romania had committed troops to the Eastern Front. Romanian soldiers had fought alongside the Germans in the advance across the Ukraine and suffered heavy casualties during the Stalingrad battles. But, now that the tide had turned clearly in the favour of the Red Army, Romania was looking for a way out of its partnership with Germany. However, the oilfields of Ploesti were an asset that Hitler was not prepared to give up easily. When the Red Army arrived at the Romanian border in April 1944 Romania's head of government, Marshal Ion Antonescu, was offered an armistice by the USSR; the offer had been refused. Since that time Romanian partisans had been parachuted into the country and had carried out pro-Soviet propaganda work. Antonescu visited Hitler's headquarters at Rastenburg in East Prussia during the first week of August 1944. Alarmed at the situation on the Eastern Front, Antonescu suggested a withdrawal to a shorter, more defensible line even though it would cost Romanian territory. General Otto Friessner, commander of AGSU, agreed with this proposition, as did Hitler but he imposed the proviso that the retirement could not take place until there was clear evidence of a serious Soviet attack in the region.

The intelligence arriving at Rastenburg from Romania was contradictory. On the one hand Friessner expressed a distinct lack of faith in the Romanian troops under his command, doubting not only their loyalty to the cause but also their combat efficiency. Friessner's concerns over the Soviet build-up and the reliability of the Romanians caused him to report on 3 August, 'If these symptoms of insecurity among the Romanian troops go on for long it will be necessary to order an immediate retirement behind the Prut [River] on the Galati–Focsani–Carpathian line.' On the other hand German diplomats and politicians in Bucharest reported, 'Situation absolutely stable. King Michael guarantees the alliance with Germany.' Someone was incorrect in his analysis. Lower down the

Above: A Romanian machine-gun nest on the banks of the Dniester River. The weapon is the Czech-made ZB-53 Model 37. An extremely efficient and robust weapon, this belt-fed 7.92mm gun had a rate of fire of over 500 rounds per minute.

social strata Soviet propaganda had been at work to undermine the will of Romania's soldiers to continue the fight and plans for a communist coup were put in motion.

Romania's position had been made clear in April 1944 through diplomatic channels when the Romanians were informed that the USSR required the return of Bessarabia and northern Bukovina to Soviet control. Romanian offers to withdraw from the war were hedged around by the requirement that none of the Allies, particularly the USSR, interfere with Romania's domestic situation. No such guarantee was forthcoming and, as the summer drew on, wrangling and mistrust between the Allies and Romania's distrust and fear of the USSR led Stalin to order 2nd Ukrainian Front (General R. K. Malinovsky) and 3rd Ukrainian Front (General F. I. Tolbukhin) to launch themselves into Romania. Malinovsky was a native of Odessa and for him the operation was something of a homecoming.

Facing the Soviets was AGSU, which had been considerably weakened as men and tanks had been siphoned off to shore up the front to the north. AGSU was split into two

commands: Group Wohler (German General O. Wöhler) and Group Dumitrescu (Romanian General P. Dumitrescu). Group Wohler held the line from the junction with AGNU to the Prut River and consisted of Third and Fourth Romanian and Eighth German Armies. To their left, guarding the Carpathian passes into Transylvania, was Romanian First Army. From the Prut to the Black Sea lay Group Dumitrescu with Third Romanian and Sixth German Armies. Other German units were scattered throughout Romania guarding the ports and the all-important oil fields at Ploesti. Everywhere along the 885km (550-mile) front line German and Romanian formations alternated to encourage the resistance of the latter in the event of a Soviet offensive. Earlier in the year, in an attempt to bolster the Romanians' armoured forces and encourage their loyalty to Germany, 100 Panzer IVs and StuG III assault guns, along with other German equipment, had been delivered to Romania. This tank force along with the couple of hundred tanks and assault guns at Friessner's disposal, was considerably weaker than that available to the Soviet fronts which had a

Above: A Soviet 82mm PM41 mortar team on the point of firing. A well-trained crew of six could deliver 25–30 bombs within a minute to a maximum range of 3,040 metres (3,325 yards). The shoulder straps, *pogoni*, reintroduced in late 1942 were a throwback to the days of the Imperial Army.

combined strength of 1,800 tanks. Of these 1,200 were in 2nd Ukrainian Front which was generally the stronger of the two.

No date had been set for the Soviet offensive but reserves were moved into the area during early August. Special attention was paid to the preparations of the Soviet Black Sea Fleet and the recently created Danube Flotilla. The *Stavka* co-ordinator for the region was Marshal S. K. Timoshenko. The Soviet plan was for both fronts to undertake a series of enveloping movements with the aim of destroying the Axis forces on the Bendery–Jassy line. This would be followed by an advance on Focsani, the capture of which would open the way to central Romania and considerably more open ground giving freedom of manoeuvre to the south and west.

While the staffs of both fronts planned the details a concentrated training programme was undertaken to turn the 250,000 new recruits that 2nd Ukrainian Front had called up from the area immediately to its rear into soldiers. Particular attention was given to the men's political education, stress being laid on their role as representatives of 'Soviet dignity' and respect for the lives led by Romanian peasants.

Above: Soviet infantry advancing through the remains of a Polish village during the summer of 1944. The rifleman is armed with the standard Red Army rifle, the 7.62mm Mosin Nagant Model 1891/30. A very reliable 'soldier-proof' weapon, it saw service with many armies until the late twentieth century. The bayonet was always fixed in the combat zone.

Above: An early production Panzer VI Tiger I moves into a defensive position in central Poland. The Tiger I was the mainstay of the heavy tank formations of both the Waffen-SS and Heer. This is an early model as evidenced by the style of the commander's cupola.

The Soviet attack

At 06:00 hours on 20 August 1944 2nd Ukrainian Front's artillery barrage began, followed by that of 3rd Ukrainian Front two hours later. By midday the German third line of defence north of Jassy had been penetrated, German Eighth Army's whole position was breaking up as Romanian units that were short of anti-tank weapons saved themselves. Friessner was given permission to withdraw by Hitler but once again it was too late.

To carry out this operation the Russians fielded over 90 infantry divisions and seven armoured or mechanised corps. The superiority in tanks and assault guns of more than 5 to 1 was matched, at least at the points of attack, in men, guns and aircraft. Part of the reserve allotted to 2nd Ukrainian Front was the 1st Volunteer Division *Tudor Vladimirescu* which had been formed in 1943 from Romanian troops captured during the Stalingrad fighting. The Soviet monthly return noted that the *Tudor Vladimirescu* Division was well equipped, numbering, '9,500 men, it had 98 guns and 160 mortars of various calibres, almost 500 light machine guns and more than 110 heavy machine guns'.

Within 48 hours Malinovsky's armour was 80km (50 miles) inside Axis lines and advancing to join up with 3rd Ukrainian Front which had enjoyed similar success. Jassy was abandoned and German Sixth Army fell back. Unfortunately it found its path south blocked by Soviet forces. When two Soviet mechanised corps hit Sixth Army's rear it too began to disintegrate.

Above: Lend-Lease in action. An American manufactured Sherman M4A2 covers the advance of an infantry section. Armed with the long 76mm gun and powered by a reliable diesel engine the *Emcha* was the most popular foreign tank to serve with the Red Army.

By 23 August the entirety of AGSU was faced with a catastrophic situation as fighting raged around the town of Husi near which lay the bridges across the Prut River that were the only viable means of escape. Senior German officers rallied the stragglers and formed a defensive area to await events. To the east Romanian Third Army and a mixed bag of five German corps were surrounded. On the same day King Michael ordered his men to cease fire and surrendered unconditionally to the Allies. Marshal Antonescu was arrested. With AGSU in tatters there was virtually nothing left to stop the Red Army as the Romanian troops obeyed their king's order. Hitler's reaction to the defection of Romania was swift, German troops in Bucharest were ordered to restore the situation and efforts were made to defend the Ploesti region. Bucharest was bombed on 24 August by 150 German aircraft by way of retaliation for the king's betrayal of his partners. The bombing of their capital decided the loyalty of many Romanians who viewed the advance of the Soviets with some misgiving. That day *Stavka*, caught out by the speed of events, reacted. Malinovsky and Tolbukhin were ordered to press ahead but to allow Romanian soldiers to keep their weapons as long as they fought against the Germans. This was a very acceptable idea to the bulk of the Romanian troops and on 26 August Romania declared war on Germany.

Malinovsky was now instructed to go west towards the Carpathian Mountains and to move rapidly to Focsani. Meanwhile behind Soviet lines thousands of German stragglers had achieved some sort of cohesive structure and were attempting to break out across the Prut. Indeed they were remarkably successful and some 70,000 men headed for the relative safety of the Carpathians and Hungary. Although many did succeed in escaping by the end of August, AGSU had ceased to exist and Sixth Army, resurrected after Stalingrad, was written off once again. German forces in Romania, mainly the rump of Eighth Army, conducted a fighting withdrawal into Transylvania pursued by the 2nd Ukrainian Front.

By 29 August Tolbukhin's front had reached Constanza near the Bulgarian border. With Romanian assistance the 2nd Ukrainian Front captured the Ploesti oilfields and later that day King Michael sued for peace. However, no move against Bucharest was made. It had been decided that a formal parade, with flags and bands would mark the Red Army's entry into the city on 31 August. *Stavka*'s orders for 2nd Ukrainian Front were now to move towards the Yugoslav, Hungarian and Bulgarian borders, linking its right flank with the left of 4th Ukrainian Front and its left with 3rd Ukrainian Front that was moving towards Bulgaria along the

Above: An interesting view of a 280mm mortar BR-5 Model 1939. Using the same tracked chassis as similar heavy artillery there were 48 of this type of weapon in the Soviet inventory of 1945. Even with a 15-man crew only two rounds per minute were possible. This piece appears to be operating at almost the maximum elevation of 60 degrees.

Black Sea coast. However, a problem arose almost immediately with the Sherman tanks used by some of the Soviet armoured formations. The Sherman had a rubber-coated track and rollers that made for excellent handling on hard surfaces. Unfortunately one unit, having driven over 100km (62 miles) in one day with temperatures exceeding 30 degrees Celsius, found that the rubber began to peel off and jam the tracks. This resulted in the entire corps grinding, quite literally, to a halt. Moscow was informed of the situation and new parts were dispatched promptly. Nevertheless several days were lost, three of which were spent repairing the vehicles.

An unforeseen consequence of the occupation of Romania was social. Many German POWs were found to have several contraceptives on them. The political officers made considerable propaganda from this, claiming that the Germans were intending to rape any Russian woman they found. However, prostitution was common in Romania at the time, a situation which many

Soviet troops took full advantage of, but the pre-invasion pep talks had not included the avoidance of venereal diseases and consequently infection spread rapidly. Indeed so great was the epidemic that the authorities had to set up a special hospital to deal with the soaring casualty rate.

Hungary Wavers

The advance towards the Carpathians galvanised the Hungarians into action. Hungary's regent, Admiral Horthy, had seen his country lose much of its independence in March 1944 when a pro-Nazi government was installed. During August Horthy began quietly to remove the more extreme members of his cabinet and attempts were made to sound out the Allies regarding their terms for Hungary's defection. To this end contact was made with the Western Allies but Horthy was told that he must negotiate with the USSR. This was not an attractive option for the Hungarians and the matter was shelved. The hopes of the Regent and his supporters now revolved around the remote chance that the

Western Allies would land troops on the Dalmatian coast and liberate Yugoslavia. The next step, so they hoped, would be the occupation of Hungary and the establishment of a protectorate that would spare them the anticipated excesses of a Soviet invasion. Although Churchill had floated the possibility of a Dalmatian expedition it remained nothing more than one of several ideas.

Guderian recalled his visit to Budapest where Hitler had sent him to deliver a letter and, 'form his own impression of' Horthy's attitude. The Regent's first words to Guderian were sufficient to convey a clear picture, 'Look, my friend, in politics you must always have several irons in the fire.' Having granted Horthy's request for the return of Hungarian forces to Hungary, Guderian returned to Germany.

In the meantime, as the Soviets advanced, there appeared no alternative for Horthy but that he approach Stalin. First Hungarian Army was covering the Carpathian passes and eight divisions from it combined with five German divisions to launch a spoiling attack against the advancing 2nd Ukrainian Front.

Above: Troops of the Third Ukrainian Front roll into Sofia, the capital of Bulgaria, to passing interest from the onlookers. The tank is a Lend-Lease British-manufactured Valentine Mark 9 armed with a 57mm (6-pounder) gun. The Valentine enjoyed a reputation for reliability and durability with its Soviet crews.

Above: Although very clearly posed, this image catches the elan of a Soviet cavalry charge. The badge of an elite Guards formation is just visible on the right pocket of several of the men. Charges such as this were clearly obsolete by 1944 but this branch of service proved valuable for escort and patrol duties in the wilder parts of Central and Eastern Europe.

Model's Counter-Attacks

In late July Model had attempted a counter-attack aimed at recapturing Siedlce, an important road and rail town between Warsaw and Brest-Litovsk. The operation had failed and the tank formations were withdrawn to be used south of Warsaw. The two main bridgeheads that the Soviets had managed to throw across the Vistula River in this area needed to be dealt with swiftly and effectively if the Germans wished to regain the advantage of the river as a part of their defence system.

The Sandomierz Bridgehead

1st Ukrainian Front's bridgehead at Sandomierz, established on 30 July, posed the greater threat as it was larger and beyond it lay good tank country but it was over 160km (100 miles) south of Warsaw. Model gathered his forces to make a serious attempt to dislodge the Soviets, who were digging in as fast as possible to allow their engineers time to construct bridges capable of taking the weight

of heavy tanks. The dry, sandy soil made entrenching and tank manoeuvre difficult.

To support AGNU reinforcements had been sent from AGSU and the interior of the Reich including the *Hermann Göring* Panzer Division, 3rd SS Panzer Division *Totenkopf,* 5th SS Panzer Division *Wiking* and the *Grossdeutschland* Panzergrenadier Division. Amongst the resources that Model received was the 501st Heavy Tank Battalion equipped with the new Tiger II, the King or Royal Tiger, which had not yet seen action on the Eastern Front. These 70-ton giants were to be committed at Sandomierz. The Tiger II had only gone into production during the previous winter and was, as yet, unproven.

Konev was well aware that the Germans would try and push his men back across the Vistula and made his preparations accordingly. The bridgehead was to be defended in depth and in many respects the operation came to resemble a miniature version of the Battle of Kursk. The Germans would be attacking an obvious target in an

attempt to straighten the line and the Soviets knew they were coming. Both sides would be deploying strong forces in what was to be a crucial engagement. However, there were significant differences between this action and Kursk. The Red Army had only enjoyed a brief time to prepare its defences at Sandomierz but was considerably more experienced and undoubtedly more confident than in 1943. Minefields had been laid and anti-tank gun positions sited and camouflaged. Bridges had been built that were capable of carrying the heaviest equipment so that over 180 tanks were on the west bank, some of which were dug in whilst others were held in reserve. The Germans had been chased out of the USSR and were nowhere near as strong as they had been a year earlier. Nor did the Luftwaffe enjoy more than the occasional period of air superiority as the Red Air Force had improved out of all recognition during the previous 12 months.

The Germans spent a day or two jockeying for position and then launched a major attack on 11 August. German tanks advanced in a manner designed to expose the Soviet positions, particularly the anti-tank guns. The more mobile Panzer IVs would drive ahead supported by infantry while the heavier Tigers

Above: A sight that became more common as 1944 drew on, a T-34/76 driving through the streets of a newly liberated town in eastern Europe showing the flag. The Red Army maintained the traditions of the Tsar's army by carrying flags into the combat zone. Axis accounts often record infantry attacks being led by standard bearers.

would remain hull-down some distance in the rear. Unfortunately for the Soviets the greater number of their anti-tank guns were 76mm ZIS-3 weapons which required a special shell to deal with Tigers and these were in short supply. The problem for the Soviet anti-tank crews was when to open fire and it became a test of nerves. If they fired on the Panzer IVs too soon then they would expose themselves to the accurate fire of the Tigers. However, if they waited too long the infantry would overrun them. The solution was that no one fired until the Panzer IVs, by luck, blocked the Tigers' line of sight and then only at the last minute to be sure of a kill and covering smoke from the burning victim. The infantry could be dealt with by Soviet machine gunners.

Soviet tank assets in the bridgehead included 71st Independent Guards Heavy Tank Regiment with a dozen IS-2 (Josef Stalin) tanks. These were the most powerful tanks in the Soviet inventory at the time and, armed with a 122mm gun, were more than capable of taking on the Tiger I or II. The Germans had first encountered them in May 1944 and were aware of their capabilities.

Above: This Tiger II was captured in the fighting around the Sandomierz bridgehead. The tactical number, 502, can be seen on the turret side. The inscription on the side reads, 'Captured 13-8-44 by tank brigade commanded by Arhipov'. The turret is the later Henschel type and the framework around the commander's cupola is an AA machine-gun mounting.

Above: A Waffen-SS battlegroup.

Above: A Guards artillery unit mans its 76mm regimental gun. If the six-man crew worked efficiently this gun was capable of 12 rounds per minute. The camouflage scheme appears to be brown, green and buff.

These types were to clash on 13 August near the village of Staszow on the south-western face of the bridgehead.

The Tiger IIs advanced out of the early morning mist followed by Panzergrenadiers in their half-tracks and supported by Panzer V Panthers. Overhead German and Soviet aircraft battled for supremacy. Well camouflaged Soviet tanks waited in ambush positions, refusing fire until the Germans had approached to within 800 metres (875 yards). Within minutes the IS-2s had destroyed several Tigers and the German attack began to falter. Although several attempts to regain momentum followed, the ambush had caught the Germans unawares and their attack failed. Although there were further efforts during the next couple of days the Soviet defences held up well and the fighting died down.

The Magnuszew Bridgehead

Rokossovsky's 1st Belorussian Front had crossed the Vistula at Magnuszew, only 32km (20 miles) from Warsaw on 1 August. However, much of the ground on the west bank was marshy and, while suitable for defence, it was a weak position from which to advance further. Nor were there any bridges. Eighth Guards Army was holding the bridgehead and was attempting to consolidate its position. But detachments had weakened Chuikov's forces and it had little or no air cover, as there was an acute shortage of aviation fuel.

The main German attack began on 5 August. For the next three days the Soviet positions were subjected to continual pressure from tanks of the *Hermann Göring* and 19th Panzer Divisions, supported by artillery and air strikes. On occasions the Soviet position look precarious; nevertheless they held on, fighting in trench positions that came to resemble those of World War 1. With their backs to the river and only a small area in which to operate the Soviet Guardsmen had little option but to defend for all they were worth. Some of them had doubtless experienced something similar when they fought at Stalingrad where their heroic conduct won their formation the distinction of being named a guards army.

Although quite well provided with armour, the Germans were weak in infantry. The two infantry formations involved here were both

Volksgrenadier (People's Grenadier) units which were a recent innovation dreamt up by SS chief Heinrich Himmler who had assumed command of the Training and Replacement Army following the Bomb Plot. The prefix *Volks* was included in an attempt to bolster morale as the age for volunteers for military service had been lowered to 16 and men were being further combed out from jobs in the rear. The total or virtual destruction of regular infantry divisions during Operation 'Bagration' had led the Germans to allocate men to the remains of the various divisions as speedily as possible, often at the cost of training time. By way of compensation for the age and lack of experience of these new troops they were supposed to be more heavily armed to take on defensive roles. In practice this was seldom the case. Although there was sometimes a good, reliable core of veterans in such units the new men had little time to 'shake down' before they were in action. Consequently the armoured troops were poorly supported on the ground and had difficulty retaining any gains they made against determined counter-attacks.

Above: The advance of the Red Army meant that fewer damaged vehicles were abandoned to the enemy. Here a damaged SU-152 is being recovered for repair. Developed as a support weapon for the infantry, the SU-152 was a pairing of the KV-1 chassis and a 152mm ML-20 gun.

Above: A machine-gun team moves forward carrying a Maxim Model 1910 7.62mm gun, the standard weapon for such groups. The terrain has obviously been judged too rough to pull the gun on its wheeled carriage.

The Magnuszew bridgehead held out and was reinforced from 8 August onwards with elements of Second Tank Army diverted from the fighting east of Praga. Meanwhile another crossing point had been taken by Sixty-Ninth Army some 24km (15 miles) to the south. Although there were to be further attacks on the Soviet bridgeheads the moment at which they were most vulnerable had passed and they continued to grow in strength.

Rokossovsky commented that, 'We succeeded in holding it because the defence was led by General Chuikov, Commander of the Eighth Guards Army, who remained in the very midst of the inferno all through the fighting.' As the man who led the defenders in Stalingrad itself there could not have been a more fortuitous choice of commander for the position at Magnuszew than Chuikov.

The northern edge of the bridgehead was held by the Soviet-sponsored First Polish Army (General Zygmunt Berling) and these troops were almost within earshot of the Warsaw Rising. What their feelings were is impossible to imagine.

Warsaw

Warsaw in July 1944 was a city in chaos. The Polish capital with its million or so inhabitants now lay a few miles from the front line. Its position astride the Vistula River and at the centre of north–south and east–west road and

Above: The final large-scale use of the Panzerjäger Elefant took place at the Sandomierz bridgehead in August 1944. Only 90 of these tank destroyers were built. A highly successful weapon in the ambush or long-range anti-tank role it was less successful in attack as the gun lacked traverse. It was particularly vulnerable to determined infantry tank hunting squads.

Above: The size of the rivers of Eastern Europe made the employment of gunboats worthwhile. Here a Soviet vessel is seen on the Vistula south of Warsaw in the summer of 1944. Usually finished in battleship grey and manned by men of the Red Navy they were armed with one or two tank turrets with a 20mm AA gun atop the wheelhouse.

Above: A remarkable shot of a very heavily armed group of young Polish partisans in the suburb of Praga taken during the early hours of the Warsaw Rising. The men only have armbands in the Polish national colours of white over red to identify themselves as combatants. The interesting array of weapons carried appears to include an anti-tank rifle, an automatic rifle and a light machine gun.

Above: A German gunboat on the Pripyat River. This type of improvised vessel was used to provide mobile fire support against the Soviet partisan groups that operated in the vast wetlands of Belorussia. The gun is a captured Soviet 76.2mm Model 1902/31 field piece that retains its wheeled carriage possibly for use with landing parties.

Above: A team of Polish artillery spotters pass information back to their batteries in Praga. These men are part of General Zygmunt Berling's First Polish Army. Raised and equipped by the Soviet Union, Berling's forces were attached to Rokossovsky's 1st Belorussian Front. The field cap is the traditional square topped Polish *rogatywka*.

rail links made it a place of vital importance. Four bridges, three road and one rail, crossed the Vistula in Warsaw, all of which were in continual use. Defensively the Vistula was of great value as the western bank was higher than the eastern and, although the river was only 320–370 metres (350–400 yards) wide in the city, beyond it was double that.

The population, who had endured almost five years of Nazi occupation, anticipated liberation at the hands of the USSR as a mixed blessing. The Polish government in exile in London now had a communist rival, the so-called Lublin Committee. Established in Lublin on 24 July 1944, the Lublin Committee had received backing from Stalin and would later be formally recognised by the Soviets as the legal representatives of Poland. The Polish partisan movement itself was also divided into those who wished for an independent nation and those who wanted to be a satellite of the USSR. For some time the future of Poland had generated considerable diplomatic wrangling between Britain, the USSR and the USA. Now, with the Soviets already inside Poland's 1939 borders and Polish resistance forces considering an uprising, the situation was becoming more and more complex by the day. At the end of

July Stalin had put any discussion of Poland on hold for several days, as he was 'preoccupied with military matters.'

As the shattered remains of German units, accompanied by a stream of refugees, plodded despondently through Warsaw the commander of the largest partisan group in the city, General, Duke Tadeusz Komorowski, met with his staff to consider the situation. Komorowski, code-named Bor, led the Polish Home Army, the *Armija Krajowa*, better known as the AK. The resistance in Poland was the largest in occupied Europe but was divided along political lines roughly into communist and non-communist factions; the AK was non-communist.

The speed of the Soviet advance had taken everyone by surprise. Komorowski, anticipating further German reverses and hoping to free his nation's capital before the Soviets arrived, declared to the Polish authorities in London on 25 July, 'We are ready to fight for the liberation of Warsaw at any moment . . .' He also called for support

from the Western Allies in the form of the bombing of German airfields and the dropping of Polish paratroops to support the rising. However, the situation outside the capital had changed because Model's counter-attacks had succeeded in holding Rokossovsky's advance.

Events in Warsaw now overtook the Allies. On 27 July the new German commander in the city, acting under the orders of General Guderian (from 21 July Chief of the OKH General Staff) mobilised 100,000 Polish civilians to work on improving Warsaw's defences. Plainly the Germans were going to fight for the city despite their apparent weakness. Although they had received no real answers to his requests for assistance Komorowski and his staff decided the moment had come to act before the Germans grew any stronger.

The Warsaw Rising

At 17:00 hours on 1 August the AK attacked. Divided into combat groups and armed with a

Above: With mosquito nets at the ready, a Waffen-SS patrol moves out in one of the marshier regions of the Finnish front in 1944. The nets were used as facial camouflage as well as protection against insects. The machine gun nearest the camera has not been identified.

variety of weapons, the Polish partisans numbered some 10,000 men and women. Their targets included points such as barracks, arsenals and administrative buildings but particularly the bridges so vital if Soviet support was to be forthcoming. The Old Town and the city centre were to be the main areas of fighting but they were heavily populated and the AK therefore had to be careful to avoid civilian casualties. The bridges were attacked from both sides of the river but, despite fierce attacks, none were captured so, from the outset, the AK was divided. Although several important buildings were captured and hundreds of Germans killed, the initial attacks had proved disappointing with casualties in the region of 2,000. Ironically a clothing depot had been taken and many of the Poles now outfitted themselves with Waffen-SS camouflage jackets, which was to cause a degree of confusion. The Germans had been expecting something to happen and were to an extent prepared which accounted for the Poles' lack of success.

From the early hours of 2 August Komorowski's HQ, in a factory near the ruins of the Jewish ghetto, issued a series of communiqués to London informing the authorities of the situation and requesting help. Moscow was also told of the rising. However, the radio links were not perfect and within days the intelligence flow became confused. Communications within AK lines were also problematic and runners, often children, were soon the most reliable means of passing orders and information. The same day the AK began to erect barricades and battle lines formed inside the perimeter where isolated groups of Germans defended themselves as best they could. Rokossovsky, himself of Polish descent, climbed a factory chimney and saw the city in flames.

The German Response

Hitler's response to the rising was unequivocal, ending with the phrase, 'Wipe them out.' Himmler was given responsibility for crushing the rising and delegated the job to Obergruppenführer Erich von dem Bach-Zelewski who had considerable anti-partisan experience. Bach-Zelewski sent all the troops he could muster to Warsaw, arriving himself on 5 August. Amongst the earliest arrivals were two SS units, the Russian Assault Brigade RONA (Brigadeführer Bronislav Kaminski) and a penal formation commanded by Oberführer Oskar Dirlewanger. In addition a collection of Ukrainian, Azerbaijani and Cossack troops was drafted in giving Bach-Zelewski some 12,000 men. During early August German troops were in the minority and the bulk of Bach-Zelewski's force was made up of former Soviet citizens. This led the AK to lump them together as Ukrainians. Historically, relations between Poles and Ukrainians had been awful and consequently the fighting in Warsaw took on the aspect of a brutal, no-quarter-given struggle with few prisoners taken on either side.

The first serious German operation began on 5 August with an attack, spearheaded by Dirlewanger's men supported by tanks, that aimed to advance 5km (3 miles) across the city centre to divide the AK position in two. Some progress was made but the havoc wreaked by Dirlewanger's troops on the civilians sheltering in their apartments was appalling. Rape, murder and drunkenness were the order of the day as this scum drove the AK back. Himmler's order, 'Every inhabitant of Warsaw is to be shot. Prisoners will not be taken; the town is to be razed to the ground', was taken literally and with apparent relish. Other SS and German police units were equally

Above: Soviet infantrymen advancing at the run into a town in one of the Baltic states during the summer of 1944. They are all lightly equipped other than the man on the left who has his greatcoat rolled around his back and chest and kit bag with mess tin on his back. All are wearing the *pilotka* side cap.

enthusiastic in carrying out these orders on what became known as 'Black Friday'. However, when Bach-Zelewski arrived later that day he ordered his men to behave in a more civilised manner but by then it was too late and Polish resistance became much firmer.

Moscow and London debated what should be done. Stalin announced that he would 'do everything possible' within two or three days due to 1st Belorussian Front's other commitments. On 9 August Bach-Zelewski's men reached the Vistula but the attacks bogged down in the rubble created by the artillery and air strikes that were becoming an increasingly deadly feature of everyday life for the Poles, AK and civilian alike. The German field commanders were beginning to regain some control over Kaminski's and Dirlewanger's men but were so horrified at the growing tally of atrocities that they demanded their removal. However, this did not happen and the slaughter and rape remained ghastly features of any operations these men were engaged in. For the next week the fighting continued and by the middle of August, despite some local successes, the AK's position was deteriorating. A major German attack was launched towards the Old Town

about 15 August. It was supported by a powerful artillery and rocket barrage, which achieved little but to improve the Pole's defences. Both sides were suffering terrible casualties. Despite some supplies being parachuted in by the Western Allies, the Poles were running short of medicines. A handful of anti-tank weapons had made the German armour more vulnerable to attack and the Poles even captured a couple of tanks. Tragically, supply flights were rare as the Soviets withheld permission for the RAF and USAF to land and refuel in Soviet-held territory. As the AK's perimeter shrank, Komorowski made preparations to withdraw from the Old Town to the city centre through the sewers.

Stalin's next pronouncement on the matter was made on 22 August when he denounced the 'handful of power-seeking criminals who launched the Warsaw adventure'.

AK combatants, often only differentiated from civilians by a red and white brassard on their arms, had learnt the art of street fighting in a very short space of time and practised it to great effect. But they lacked any answer to the Germans' greater firepower, supplemented in late August by super-heavy artillery such as the

540mm mortar 'Thor', flame-throwers, assault guns and remote-controlled demolition vehicles. Such technology sapped the defenders' morale as did the sufferings of the thousands of civilians trapped in the pockets.

Finland

To the north the position of Finland was becoming increasingly parlous. The Soviet offensive that had paused in July had brought matters there to crisis point with Helsinki itself in danger. Germany had lent some support but the Finnish government was discussing ways of ending the war and avoiding Soviet occupation. On 1 August Finland's President R. H. Ryti resigned and Marshal C. G. Mannerheim, the army commander, took his place. Mannerheim, a former officer in the tsarist army, had one aim: to lead Finland out of the war as easily as possible.

Near the Arctic Circle were the 200,000 men of German Twentieth Mountain Army (General L. Rendulic) which had spent the war in splendid isolation having failed to advance much beyond the Norwegian–Soviet border or capture Murmansk. The Germans had foreseen the likelihood of Finland signing a separate peace and two plans were in place to deal with this eventuality. Operation 'Birch Tree' provided for Twentieth Army to retreat to Norway and Operation 'Pine Tree' involved the Kriegsmarine taking control of several islands off the Finnish coast to contain the Soviet Baltic Fleet.

Field Marshal Wilhelm Keitel, the chief of the OKW (Oberkommando der Wehrmacht — High Command of the Armed Forces) representing Hitler, visited Mannerheim on 17 August in an effort to persuade him to continue fighting. Mannerheim was having none of this and told Keitel, 'Even if fate did not favour German arms, Germany could continue to exist. Nobody could say the same for Finland.' It was now clear that Finland was going to ask for terms from the USSR and it did so on 25 August through the embassies in neutral Stockholm. Stalin had only two conditions: that Finland break off diplomatic relations with the Third Reich and that German troops leave Finland by 14 September or become Soviet POWs. A short period to consider this offer was allowed.

The Baltic States
In early August Chernyakhovsky's 3rd Belorussian Front kept up the pace it had set earlier, Kalvarija had fallen and the Niemen River had been crossed at several points. The German border and the province of East Prussia were now within reach. Inevitably there were those in the Soviet ranks who remembered the fate of the last Russian armies that invaded East Prussia in 1914 and the disaster of Tannenberg that had become a case study at the USSR's military academies. Indeed it was almost as if following an historical precedent that the Germans launched a counter-attack near Kaunas which, having surprised and almost destroyed a Soviet armoured corps, forced them to pull back. However, *Stavka* had ordered on 28 July that Insterburg (Chernyakhovsk) in East Prussia was a target to be achieved.

Elsewhere on its line 3rd Belorussian Front secured an immense propaganda coup by being the first Soviet formation to cross the German border. At 05:30 hours on 17 August men of the 184th Rifle Division planted the Red Flag inside East Prussia; it may have only been a few metres over the border but nonetheless it was Germany. No further significant incursions were made, as the area was known to be strongly fortified. Indeed Chernyakhovsky was fully occupied clearing up pockets of German stragglers behind the front who posed a significant threat to his tenuous supply lines. This was a common problem during this period when there was really no such thing as a front line. Once the T-34s broke through they headed for their objectives with orders to ignore groups of defenders which were to be

mopped up by the infantry. In Belorussia such work had devolved on the partisans who combed the woods and river valleys, using their unrivalled local knowledge to round up the Wehrmacht's waifs and strays in their hundreds and thousands. However, in Latvia and Estonia there was a much smaller partisan movement as the population, if not pro-German, was certainly anti-Soviet. Therefore when the tanks of 3rd Belorussian and 1st Baltic Fronts had raced ahead, their infantry had been slowed considerably by having to fight and risk heavy casualties or wait for artillery support. Such operations never worked perfectly as the Germans had occupied these lands for three years and knew the terrain quite well. Therefore the chance of catching them all rapidly was negligible and the risk that such groups would emerge to play havoc with the columns of supply trucks and hold matters up even more was considerable. Ammunition and fuel were at a premium and a couple of burning tankers in the rear could mean the difference between success and failure. Therefore it was essential to have a period of consolidation before rushing headlong towards the next goal. Nor was it only a matter of logistics; the vehicles and the men themselves had been in action for long periods and would need routine repairs, maintenance and rest, gun barrels would have to be cleaned and tracks cared for. To re-tension a track on a T-34, for example, took three men, a sledge-hammer and considerable brute force. Again, unlike in Belorussia, there were few men to conscript therefore the numbers of infantry fell and replacements took their time to arrive as there were few railways and the roads were poor.

AGN had been cut off from the rest of the Eastern Front in July. However, Guderian wished to restore the land route and recognised that the most direct way was through 1st Baltic Front's south-western and northern flanks, which were held mainly by armoured troops. Therefore a strong force of tanks and infantry was assembled and by early August the Germans were ready. An attack was launched against the left flank of the salient by over 100 German tanks on Forty-Third Army's position in an attempt to pin down the Soviet forces. The second attack came on 16 August and was again designed to force the Soviets to commit their reserves but in this it failed. The main attack followed 24 hours later and this time 300 tanks and assault guns pushed deep into the Soviet lines in the direction of Jelgava. Supplementary German efforts, although weaker, also began to bite into the Soviet positions. Bagramyan shuffled his reserves to counter these incursions and after four days of bitter fighting the Germans were stopped and a line established. But almost simultaneously the Germans broke

through on the shores of the Baltic and once more AGN had a land connection with the rest of the front. On 21 August Bagramyan ordered his men to withdraw and Tukkum was surrendered to the enemy. The corridor to AGN was only 40km (25 miles) wide and its creation had occupied a considerable amount of armour. These precious assets were all that stood between Schörner's AGN and total isolation. As the fighting died down towards the end of August *Stavka* ordered plans to be laid that would cut AGN off permanently.

AGN's north-eastern sector had retreated from Narva to the Tannenberg Line before Tallinn at the end of July. At the same time Yeremenko's 2nd Baltic Front was advancing towards Riga from the east but again the terrain favoured the defender with swamps and dense forests that channelled the Soviet attacks into well-defined areas which the Germans turned into artillery killing zones. 3rd Baltic Front (Maslennikov) was faced with similar difficulties when its offensive recommenced on 10 August. But, despite horrendous casualties, the Red Army inexorably pushed AGN backwards and the pocket became smaller week by week.

Obviously this was not good tank country and the armour of both sides sometimes played a deadly game of hide and seek. The Soviet self-propelled artillery units that operated the SU-76 had developed a tactic, which they used with deadly effect. Operating in pairs, one would act as bait to entice the German tank from cover, reveal itself briefly, fire a round and reverse. If the German followed up the second SU-76, positioned at right angles to its partner, would wait in cover until the side armour of the German came into view and then fire, preferably from a range of less than 400 metres (440 yards). Tank side armour was always thinner and from that range not even a Tiger I was safe.

Evacuation of Greece
As the Soviet columns spread out across Romania, the position of the German garrison in Greece, its islands and Albania began to look decidedly precarious. Over 250,000 German troops were scattered across the region as Army Group E (General Löhr). When Romania's cease-fire became operative Löhr was ordered to pull his men out of the islands and mainland Greece and fall back to the north. Assembling the ships and aircraft to evacuate the islands would take time and organisation and the movements on the mainland would have to run the gauntlet of the increasingly aggressive partisan forces.

Three Bulgarian divisions, whose attitude to the Germans was becoming more ambivalent by the day, occupied part of Greece. Although Bulgaria had not declared

war on the USSR, the tanks of the Red Army were almost at the Romanian–Bulgarian border. There was now the possibility that the Bulgarians would turn on the Germans as the Romanians had done.

As Germany's partnerships began to fall apart, Guderian attempted to create a network of fixed defences behind the existing front. He resurrected the Fortifications Department and drew up plans that Hitler grudgingly approved. A considerable amount of work was carried out over the next few months by civilian labour. Trench systems, anti-tank ditches, artillery positions and bunkers were constructed to connect rivers and other natural features. However, such was the shortage of infantry that providing even skeleton garrisons was well nigh impossible. Equally difficult was extracting artillery of any type as the terms of Directive 51 were still applied which gave priority of supply to the Western Front where similar work was being done to upgrade the West Wall, the so-called Siegfried Line. Dreadful as the summer had been for Hitler in the east, the collapse in the west had been similarly catastrophic, as the Allies had raced across France liberating Paris on the way.

Above: Two Waffen-SS anti-tank men survey their handiwork, a brewed up T-34/76, during the summer of 1944. The men are wearing the standard SS camouflage smocks of the period, which were produced in a selection of seasonal colour schemes.

Below: Liberated Soviet POWs were generally pressed into joining the Red Army immediately on release. These men have been judged incapable of bearing arms and are waiting for repatriation to the USSR where life as prisoners and social outcasts was all that awaited many of these unfortunates.

Chapter 3

The Balkan Collapse: September 1944

The End in Warsaw

From 30 August onwards German calls to surrender included the guarantee that members of the AK would be treated as regular soldiers, but few responded. During the first week of September the Polish authorities in London furiously criticised the British government for abandoning the AK. This was followed on 6 September by a message from Komorowski stating that, 'Warsaw has lost all hope of help from Allied air deliveries or from a Soviet advance, which would liberate the city.' Now Stalin began to alter his position and on 10 September he granted permission for British and American aircraft to use Soviet airfields. Three days later the Red Air Force dropped supplies to the insurgents, but by now the pockets were so small that very little reached them and the bulk was captured. To the south Berling, acting on his own initiative, decided to get First Polish Army into Warsaw. The attack would have to be made across the Vistula with the hope of taking the Germans in the rear. The first crossing was to be attempted at a spot some 5km (3 miles) from the main AK position and began on the night of 16 September. Using anything that would float, the Polish infantry pushed off from the eastern bank and were immediately hit by heavy German machine-gun fire. Nevertheless they kept coming and secured a tiny foothold on the opposite side. For the next three days the Poles battled desperately to expand their position but made little headway. On 22 September Rokossovsky ordered them to pull back across the Vistula which they did with losses in excess of 2,000 men

The position of the AK was now hopeless; further supply drops simply fell into German hands and the plight of the civilians was desperate. The whole of the river bank was now under German control and the Red Army had been instructed to assume a defensive posture.

Having been assured good treatment for his men, Komorowski surrendered on 3 October.

The AK laid down its arms and marched into captivity to be saluted by German officers. A grudging respect had developed for the Poles during the weeks that they defied the Wehrmacht, and Hitler was prevailed upon to allow uncharacteristically lenient treatment. Civilian casualties were estimated at 200,000 and the population was deported to the sound of demolition charges that heralded the systematic destruction of Warsaw. German losses were in excess of 27,000. Kaminski was to die, 'accidentally', a short time later and many of his men met a traitor's death at the war's end.

The Warsaw Rising was undoubtedly an heroic episode but one that was marred by inter-Allied disputes and lack of agreement regarding the future government of Poland. The city and its ghosts were now part of the front line and would remain so until early in 1945.

Czechoslovakia and the Slovak Uprising

The division of Czechoslovakia in 1939 resulted in Slovakia becoming a supposedly sovereign state that contributed troops to Operation 'Barbarossa'. The men of the Slovakian Mobile Division had gained a reputation as good soldiers but in early 1944, following a dispute between the German and Slovakian authorities, it was disarmed and converted into construction brigades to be used in Romania, Hungary and Italy.

In common with other eastern European nations Slovakia had a partisan movement that was divided along ideological lines into communist and non-communist groups. In London there was a Czechoslovak government in exile and there were Czechoslovak national formations serving with the British and Soviet armed forces. The Czechoslovak authorities in London had brokered an agreement between partisan groups of all political persuasions to fight the Germans as one and to reunite the country post-war. Against this background the more active Slovak partisans had formed a Slovak National Council that from December 1943 had been planning an uprising against the

Above: From the angle of the camera this is an unposed shot showing a Soviet infantry section going into action. The location is Poland and the men are Guards of an unidentified unit.

Above: Infantry of I Czech Corps proudly display their unit's flag. Similar in design to those used by the Austro-Hungarian Army it shows the lion of Bohemia and the motto *Pravda Vitezi* ('Truth Wins'). Interestingly the men wear a combination of Soviet and British equipment.

Germans and the pro-German government of Monsignor Tiso.

The Slovakian Army consisted of the two divisions of the East Slovak Corps (ESC) assigned to the defence of the Carpathian passes, some 22,000 men, and the Rear Army which garrisoned the towns and cities behind the lines. Plans were laid for the Rear Army to set up clandestine partisan cells which would come into operation should the Germans enter and occupy Slovakia.

On 8 April 1944 the Red Army had reached the former Czechoslovak border and in his May Day speech Stalin gave his word to liberate the Czechs and Slovaks from Nazi domination.

Following this declaration an agreement was reached between the Czechoslovak government in exile and the USSR by which the Soviet Union would take temporary control of liberated areas until replaced by Czechoslovak administrators. However, the Czechoslovak Communist Party appealed directly to the Red Army for help which it promptly gave, parachuting Soviet-trained partisans into Slovakia in July. At roughly the same time 4th Ukrainian Front (General I. E. Petrov) was established to carry out an offensive in the eastern Carpathian Mountains and advance into Hungary. The offensive was to begin during the last week of August but events in Romania moved so rapidly that Petrov's staff were ordered to revise their plans. Furthermore the situation in Slovakia had also changed. The Slovak Army had negotiated with the government in

exile and it had been agreed that the ESC would open the Carpathian passes to the Red Army. This proposal was put to the Soviets who fudged the issue while at the same time negotiating with the communist partisans.

On 24 August reports began to filter out of Slovakia that German and Hungarian forces were gathering, possibly as a reaction to the Romanian situation or as a result of increased partisan activity in Slovakia. The Slovaks now faced a dilemma: should they rise and fight the Germans and Hungarians or should they allow entry to the Soviets? As this debate raged between the representatives of all the Czechoslovak groups plus the Soviets and the government in exile, fate took a hand. A partisan group, led by a Captain Velicheko of the Red Army, assassinated the former German military representative to Romania as he returned home through Turciany St Martin in Slovakia on 27 August. Two days later German troops entered Slovakia at various points and the Slovaks began to fight back. The German forces were a diverse cross-section of what was available: a couple of Panzer units taken from training schools and depots, Ukrainian and Estonian SS men, and a couple of *ad hoc* infantry formations, all entering Slovakia from different directions.

From the outset confusion reigned in Slovakian ranks. The main area of the revolt was central Slovakia but the military muscle was in the east, the ESC. However, the ESC commander issued a set of orders that made no sense with the result that the ESC had been disarmed by the end of 1 September. A similar situation occurred with the 8,000-man garrison in the capital Bratislava. Elsewhere partisan groups took to the countryside and on 5 September British and American officers were flown in to provide advice and support as well as to evacuate Allied POWs from the area.

Above: A Soviet mountain artillery battery moves into the foothills of the Carpathian Mountains. The Red Army had two mountain guns, the more common being the Skoda designed 76.2mm Model 1938. The gun broke down into six horse loads and fired a 21kg (46-lb) shell to a distance of 10,500 metres (11,500 yards). This type of specialist weapon was vital in the rugged mountain terrain of Slovakia.

Meanwhile at 1st Ukrainian Front's HQ the deputy commander of the ESC was cheerfully discussing with Konev how their forces should link up; both were unaware of the problems they would now face. Late on 2 September *Stavka* ordered 1st and 4th Ukrainian Fronts to organise a joint operation into the Carpathian Mountains. I Guards Cavalry Corps was to push through the Dukla Pass and gallop to the support of the partisans followed by a small force of tanks and infantry of I Czechoslovak Corps (General L. Svoboda). Thirty-Eighth Army (General K. Moskalenko) would advance with the aim of cutting First Panzer Army off from AGNU. The Soviet plans were based on the now false premise that the ESC would be fighting to connect up with them. On the same day the Czechoslovak government in London formally requested the Red Army's support for the uprising, which was given. Three days later Soviet transport planes began an airlift of weapons and reinforcements into central Slovakia where the partisans had taken the title of 1st Czechoslovak Insurgent Army. The partisans' area of operations was over 200km (124 miles) behind enemy lines but they did control some ground suitable for aircraft to land. Despite the loss of the ESC the partisans were fighting bravely — amongst their number were many regular soldiers who had brought artillery and machine guns with them. Groups of escaped POWs had formed their own partisan bands, particularly the French and Soviets. Both would render useful service to the uprising.

Facing the Soviet Thirty-Eighth Army in the Dukla and Lupkow Pass region were 20,000 German troops manning a 40km (25-mile) long defensive system which had been constructed during the previous six months. Supported by 200 guns, seeded with minefields and tank traps and with well-prepared fields of fire, it was a formidable position. The Dukla Pass is roughly 17km (10 miles) wide and 20km (12 miles) long. Preceded by a two-hour bombardment, the Soviet attack began on 8 September but made little progress, the hilly, wooded ground proving almost impossible to take without heavier artillery preparation, air and armoured support. Consequently it turned into an infantry slog which involved specialist Soviet mountain troops and I Czechoslovak Corps, both formations suffering heavy casualties. Four days passed until, on 12 September, a narrow corridor was opened in the German lines and through this was inserted I Guards Cavalry Corps. Almost immediately they had passed through, as if by magic, the gap closed behind them. Isolated, the Soviet cavalry would also need to be supplied by air.

In central Slovakia the fighting had become stalemated. The Germans were unable to get to grips with the partisans who

Above: This village in the Dukla Pass region shows the condition of the ground during the autumn. The ubiquitous panji wagon and horses are perfectly at home but off-road to the right the depth of mud increases. The difficulties of attacking across shell-torn and soaking ground are not difficult to imagine and were certainly reminiscent of World War 1.

knew the country well and the Germans were forced to transfer their better units to the Soviet front. The fighting at Dukla ground on with the German defenders exacting a heavy toll for every position the Soviets and Czechoslovaks took.

Although the insurgents had failed to link up with the Red Army they fought on. An administration for 'Free Slovakia' had been established and the 1st Independent Czechoslovak Fighter Regiment, equipped with 22 La-5 aircraft flew in to operate from the main partisan base at Tri Duba (Three Oaks). However, the weather was deteriorating and the number of Soviet supply missions reduced. The Czech parts of the former Czechoslovakia had been incorporated into the Third Reich as the Protectorate of Bohemia-Moravia before the war. However, little or no assistance came from there in part due to the strong German presence and in part due to Czech antipathy to the Slovaks.

Himmler appointed another officer, SS Police General Hermann Höffle, to suppress the uprising in mid-September, as the matter was now becoming more serious by the day. Hitler was concerned at the progress, albeit slow, of the Soviet advance through the Dukla Pass which raised the possibility of an invasion of Hungary. Reinforcements, mainly SS units, were to be assigned to the Slovak 'front' during early October.

Finland

The fighting in Karelia had also quietened down and on 29 August all Soviet operations against Finland were called off. On 4 September an armistice between the USSR and Finland was signed. It now remained for the Red Army to deal with the German troops outside the port of Murmansk, Rendulic's Twentieth Mountain Army. Hitler, not wishing to offend the Swedes and put his iron ore supplies at risk, cancelled Operation 'Pine Tree' (the occupation of various islands in the Baltic) and authorised Operation 'Birch Tree' (the evacuation of Twentieth Army) on 6 September. Rendulic was concerned that the Soviets would attack and that the Finns would join them. When the blow fell it was the Soviets who attacked on 7 September using T-34s in what the Germans regarded as impossible country for tanks.

Twentieth Army began to retreat in good order and recrossed the border into Finland on 24 September where the Soviet pursuit ended. In southern Finland all German forces had been evacuated by 14 September. However, things were proceeding too slowly for Stalin's liking and pressure was put on Mannerheim to speed the Germans' departure. Mannerheim sent one armoured and three infantry divisions to ensure the Germans left on time. The Soviet deadline was 08:00 hours on 1 October; 10 minutes

Above: An Estonian in the Waffen-SS, probably the 20th Division. The armshield in the national colours of blue, black and white is just visible on his left upper arm. The reputation of the Baltic volunteers as brave and doughty fighters was enhanced by their performance in the fighting in the Courland Pocket.

retaining AGN in the area had been to encourage Finland to continue fighting. Although this was no longer a realistic hope, Hitler denied Schörner permission to evacuate his army.

The Soviet Offensive

Soviet strength along the 500km (310 miles) of front had increased dramatically. On the eve of the offensive it included 3,000 tanks, over 1,700 guns and heavy mortars and 2,600 aircraft. However, they faced a series of well-prepared defence lines manned by determined and experienced troops that made use of every stream and grove of trees available. Unfortunately for the Soviets, the Germans were well aware of 2nd and 3rd Baltic Fronts' intentions as they had made little effort to conceal their preparations. This lack of care had not been emulated by Bagramyan's 1st Baltic Front. Equally careless was the reconnaissance undertaken by Maslennikov and Yeremenko and they were woefully ignorant of the strength of the defences opposite them. Consequently 1st Baltic Front made good progress whilst the other two performed badly. Yeremenko's efforts were

before the appointed hour the Finns went into action. Hitler and Rendulic were incensed but at least they had an excuse to carry out a scorched earth retreat. As more Finnish troops arrived in the north the Germans began to pull out here also, destroying everything they could not evacuate.

Baltic States

Across the Baltic Sea the men of AGN were experiencing considerably more problems than their comrades in Finland. All three Baltic Fronts and the Leningrad Front were to concentrate their efforts on the destruction of AGN, the clearing of the Baltic states and the occupation of Riga. *Stavka* allowed some time to reinforce, rest and resupply but it was also necessary to realign the fronts, particularly those units with the job of breaking through the German defences. The offensive was to begin on 14 September with an attack by the Baltic Fronts followed by the Leningrad Front three days later. In line with Soviet practice new recruits had been drafted in from recently liberated areas, increasing the infantry strength to over 900,000 men across the four fronts.

Stavka's plan was simplicity itself. Leningrad Front was to clear Estonia then move south-west and link up with 3rd Baltic

Above: Well-supplied with extra fuel tanks a unit of T-34/85s rumbles into the outskirts of a town in the Baltic states. The 85mm gun was based on the Soviet Model 1939 anti-aircraft gun. This version of the T-34 was considerably more comfortable due to the increased size of the turret.

Front which was to strike from the north-west at Riga. The main thrust towards Riga was to be undertaken by 2nd Baltic Front in co-operation with 1st Baltic Front, which would also press almost directly westwards to cut AGN off from East Prussia. Ships of the Baltic Fleet would guard against the possibility of AGN's evacuation by sea. On the German side the main justification for

further hampered by *Stavka's* insistence that flanking attacks be avoided, head-first being the style of the day.

Schörner's troops fought well, counter-attacking and defending with grim resolution. However, when Leningrad Front came into play on 17 September the northern sector of AGN began to withdraw rapidly. Five days later Tallinn, the Estonian capital, fell to

Above: Introduced in 1942, this 75mm PaK 40 anti-tank gun was the main weapon in the German arsenal that was capable of taking on the well-armoured T-34 series. With a maximum range of 2,900m (3,200 yards) it was a very effective gun. The later models were capable of firing AP, HE and hollow charge munitions. The low profile was a definite asset when fighting on relatively open ground as in this photo.

Estonian units of the Red Army. By 24 September Govorov's men stood on the northern border of Latvia and Riga was within their sights when the order came to halt. Although Schörner had been forbidden to evacuate AGN he did enjoy a degree of tactical flexibility, as Hitler was not involved in the micro-management of the situation. Whenever possible, at the last minute before a Soviet attack, the Germans emptied their front lines but for a skeleton force with the result that the Soviet bombardment fell on almost empty positions. When the guns fell silent the Germans would reoccupy their forward positions and meet the enemy infantry at almost full strength. Later, when the German lines stood inside the Reich itself Hitler's beady eye often forbade this tried and trusted method with the result that his men suffered needless casualties.

Towards the end of September Bagramyan's forces had penetrated as far as the outlying suburbs of Riga and faced the Germans across the broad Dvina River. At this point the Germans launched a strong counter-attack with Third Panzer Army, which had been brought up from AGC with over 400 tanks and assault guns. Although these attacks, which ended on 22 September, did not succeed in breaking through to AGN they did

tie down significant elements of 1st Baltic Front and allowed Schörner time to organise his forces to launch a series of spoiling attacks. With a considerably shorter line to hold, AGN began to dig in around Riga and maintain the tenuous land link with East Prussia. AGN also enjoyed the support of the Kriegsmarine's few remaining big ships which provided much-needed heavy artillery support — the Luftwaffe had been swept from the skies or was occupied elsewhere. The port of Riga itself was capable of handling large merchant vessels which ran the gauntlet of air attack to deliver supplies of ammunition and evacuate casualties. The Soviet fleet confined itself to home waters and the Kriegsmarine had a pretty free run of the southern and central Baltic Sea.

Stavka was now aware that it would be unable to capture Riga 'off the march' or eliminate AGN with the resources to hand. Therefore, on 24 September, a halt was called to all operations in the area and the target was switched to the port of Memel, which lay just inside East Prussia. 1st Baltic Front was to be assigned additional forces to try for Memel but first it had to execute a regrouping on an almost unprecedented scale. For seven days and seven nights, men, tanks and guns were realigned. Fifth Guards Tank Army, three

Above: Marshal I. Kh. Bagramyan, seen here in full dress uniform after the war, commanded 1st Baltic Front from November 1943 until it was absorbed by 3rd Belorussian Front in 1945. An Armenian by birth, Bagramyan planned the final assault on Königsberg, which was carried out in part by his old command, Eleventh Guards Army.

other armoured and two infantry corps, the last from 2nd Baltic Front, moved into their concentration areas north of Shavli (Siauliai) where they waited concealed, with the usual Soviet efficiency in these matters, in the dense forests.

As his men moved carefully into place, Bagramyan co-ordinated his plans with Chernyakhovsky, commander of 3rd Belorussian Front, on his left. Chernyakhovsky was to launch his Thirty-Ninth Army into East Prussia to prevent the movement of reserves to Memel. This operation was to begin in October.

Soviet Planning

Thirty-Ninth Army was to attack in two directions, one south of the Niemen River towards Gumbinnen (Gusev) in East Prussia, the other towards Tauroggen (Taurage). Bagramyan also planned a two-pronged attack with Fifth Guards Tank Army leading the way supported by 29 rifle divisions, roughly half of the front's infantry. This hammer blow was aimed at Memel and the coastline to either side of it. 2nd and 3rd Baltic Fronts would continue to maintain the pressure on AGN, which was falling back into Courland in Lithuania. Schörner had to be kept occupied to prevent his attacking the rear or right of 1st Baltic Front. Leningrad Front was to launch an attack on the islands in the Gulf of Riga from which it could threaten the coast of Courland and to accomplish this its units were issued with American-built landing craft.

Speed was of the essence as the weather was beginning to deteriorate, and although the mud and rain would hamper the Germans' movement it would also add to the Soviets' difficulties in this almost road-less area. As with all Soviet offensives use was made of deception techniques, *maskirovka* being the technical Russian term. With secrecy at a premium, false radio messages were sent between locations regarding real or imaginary units for the benefit of German monitors. Vehicles were driven in all directions and dummy tanks and guns replaced or supplemented the real thing. As the Germans lacked aerial reconnaissance resources, night movement was usually sufficient to disguise redeployments but *maskirovka* was an important aspect of Soviet military doctrine and certainly a tried and trusted one, for the Germans suspected nothing untoward was going on.

Both sides carried out patrolling during this preparatory time, an essential way in which to gather intelligence. The Red Army had specialist scout platoons whose duty it was to undertake intelligence-gathering missions up to 8–10km (5–7 miles) behind enemy lines. The scouts were chosen for their intelligence, initiative, courage, stealth and strength. This last was important, as capturing a German soldier was usually undertaken in the dark and silence was vital. Therefore the captive had to be taken by brute force and recovered to the Soviet lines. Known as 'tongues', for

obvious reasons, such men would be interrogated thoroughly.

Scouts, *razvedchiki*, were generally heavily armed, carrying a sub-machine gun, usually the standard issue PPSh or the German MP 40, which was a favourite because it was light and ammunition easily picked up when on patrol, at least a dozen hand grenades and a knife or sharpened entrenching tool for hand-to-hand combat. In some cases a thin steel breastplate was issued but the protection thus afforded was more illusory than real. The scout platoons were very close-knit units. Teamwork was vital and the bonds of trust and understanding that developed were often difficult for a new man to penetrate. Such was the loyalty to one another that the wounded

and the dead were always recovered. These platoons were the forerunners of the modern Spetsnaz. Before the start of Operation 'Bagration' scout platoons had been inserted behind Axis lines to co-operate with partisan groups.

Prior to an attack scouts would co-operate with the engineers to clear paths through enemy minefields, often wearing items of German issue camouflage kit as Soviet camouflage suits were not always available. Such disguises could lead to friendly-fire casualties on re-entry to their own lines. On rare occasions several scout platoons would be combined to form a combat unit to undertake a particular mission where their specialist skills were at a premium. These assignments

Above: A member of a Red Army scout team dressed in the camouflage suits that were reserved for such specialist units. This man is armed with a PPS-42 or -43, an extemporised weapon developed as an emergency measure during the Leningrad siege. With a 35-round magazine and folding stock it was an ideal close-quarter weapon.

Above: Outside broadcasting of propaganda and patriotic music became a common feature of the Eastern Front. The Soviets, keen to undermine their enemies' morale and encourage desertion, employed units such as this to project a seductive image of life in the USSR to the frozen and hungry Fritzes. The response was often a barrage of small arms fire as the German propaganda machine had cultivated a dread of being captured by the Russians.

Under the terms of the armistice between the USSR and Romania, signed on 12 September, Romania was to declare war on Germany and Hungary and conduct it with no fewer than 12 divisions under Soviet command as part of 2nd Ukrainian Front. The Fourth Romanian Army of 11 divisions was subordinated to the Twenty-Seventh Army. Along with the smaller Romanian First Army (General N. Macic) incorporated into Fifty-Third Army, they would move into Hungary. Equipment for the Romanians was taken from a mixture of captured Romanian and German stock with some Soviet items.

On 10 and 12 September respectively Generals Malinovsky and Tolbukhin were both promoted to the rank of marshal of the Soviet Union as 'front commanders at a time when the national boundaries of the USSR have been restored'.

The 2nd Ukrainian Front was operating in the direction of southern Transylvania, fighting its way along the river valleys and

were infrequent as the value of the scouts when performing their prime task was clearly recognised. Beyond their reconnaissance functions the nocturnal activities of the scouts had an unnerving effect on German sentries and recently recruited troops causing them to lose sleep and undermining their morale by surprise attacks on outposts.

However, another Soviet method of demoralising their enemies was less successful. Propaganda companies equipped with the latest broadcasting equipment would arrive at a sector of the front manned by a unit that someone in the Soviet intelligence community had identified as susceptible to propaganda. Usually it was a newly raised formation or one that had been particularly badly hit by a recent attack. The broadcasters would then set out their stall of offers for German deserters such as increased rations and safe conduct to a POW camp that always sounded more appealing than their current situation. Certainly there were deserters but their numbers were small in comparison with those in the other direction. Having made their 'sales pitch' the propagandists would pack up and leave. Unfortunately their legacy was usually a bombardment of the positions they had occupied and casualties for their own side as a result. The ordinary Soviet front-line soldier did not welcome the arrival of these specialists in psychological warfare for obvious reasons.

Romania

Having declared war on Germany in late August, Romania committed its armed forces to the Allied cause under the operational control of the Red Army. However, the first serious engagement was a joint attack by German and Hungarian formations on

Above: Red Army reserves move from Romania into Hungary. The primitive nature of the roads in this area is self-evident.

Fourth Romanian Army (General G. Avramescu) in Transylvania which forced it to fall back as it was poorly equipped and in a disorganised condition. The Romanians were able to escape their former allies and reformed behind a river line. Soviet support, tank units from the 2nd Ukrainian Front, arrived to restore the situation.

always on the alert for ambushes and counter-attacks from the wooded slopes that surrounded them. Although the Soviet advance in this area was speedy, the Germans and Hungarians were able to establish themselves in good defensive positions inside Romania and block the passes from the southern Carpathian Mountains into Hungary. On 15 September Malinovsky received fresh instructions which ordered him to position his forces for an advance into Hungary. Furthermore 2nd Ukrainian Front was to provide support for 4th Ukrainian Front (Petrov) with the main attack to be in the direction of Cluj–Debrecen. No time was allowed to redeploy carefully despite Malinovsky's pleas that his supply lines were in disarray and stretched back across Romania for hundreds of unsecured kilometres. To *Stavka* the need to push on into Hungary and into the rear of those forces holding Petrov's advance overrode any practical considerations. Although the logic of maintaining the impetus was irrefutable, the rate of vehicle breakdown, shortage of infantry and lack of ammunition were also impossible to deny. The attack was scheduled to begin on 16 September against the Germans in northern Transylvania. Unsurprisingly progress was slow. Here as in the Baltic states, the terrain was in the defenders' favour. The Soviet right flank penetrated a few kilometres but away to the left the penetration achieved was greater although the border defences still held firm.

Malinovsky requested permission to halt. His request was granted with the proviso that the rest and redeployment period was not used as an excuse to relax the pressure on the enemy and allow them to transfer reserves elsewhere. 2nd Ukrainian Front's respite was to last until 6 October.

As 2nd Ukrainian Front marched through Romania, 25 divisions were sent in the direction of Transylvania and others advanced towards Turnu Severin on the Yugoslavian border.

Bulgaria

To the south Tolbukhin's 3rd Ukrainian Front reached the Romanian–Bulgarian border in early September.

Earlier in the war Bulgaria had supported Germany by declaring war on the USA and Britain, allowing Axis forces the right of passage and by providing anti-partisan forces for use in Yugoslavia. Bulgaria's reward was the Yugoslav province of Macedonia.

Bulgarian garrisons were in place in Yugoslavia and Greece where they had replaced the Italians in 1943.

On 2 September 1944 a quasi-democratic government had been formed which announced that it would disarm all German forces entering Bulgaria as well as those already there. The German forces in Bulgaria included submarine and surface naval units at the ports of Varna and Burgas as well as large numbers of training and administrative personnel engaged in instructing Bulgarian armoured troops in the use of 88 Panzer IVs and 50 assault guns just delivered from Germany. Hitler had believed it would be possible to raise two Waffen-SS divisions from amongst the ethnic Germans living in Bulgaria. The German ambassador in Sofia declared that the Germans would not be leaving the country. There was also the possibility that Hitler would order a coup and that Bulgaria would be dragged into the war against the USSR.

Above: Although this image is from an earlier period in the war, it gives a clear picture of the Hungarian Toldi II Model 1942 tank. Named after a Hungarian hero from the 14th century, the Toldi was under-armoured for the late war years however, it remained in service as a reconnaissance vehicle. A 40mm weapon replaced the 20mm gun shown here in 1943. The Hungarian cross was green, edged white within a red circle. Forward of the cross on the turret is the Hungarian coat of arms. The crew wear Italian tank helmets.

Soviet planning had factored in the possibility of German intervention in Bulgarian internal affairs and was prepared for such an event. The main plan was to seize Varna and Burgas from the sea; marines landed by the Black Sea Fleet would hold these ports until Tolbukhin's forces arrived. This seaborne invasion was scheduled to begin on 12 September. However, the Soviets' preferred option was to enter the country on a wave of pro-Soviet feeling in the wake of a popular uprising led by a communist-orchestrated movement. An anti-Nazi organisation, the Fatherland Front, intended to oust the recently formed and Western-inclined cabinet. However, events did not move swiftly enough for Stalin who, by way of encouraging things, declared war on Bulgaria on 5 September.

The following day the cabinet asked for an armistice and on 7 September the communist partisan group known as the National Liberation Army began its march on the capital Sofia. At 11:00 hours on 8 September Soviet troops moved into Bulgaria to be greeted by a barrage of flowers not bullets. The following day the Black Sea Fleet landed marines at Varna while the army continued what amounted to a triumphal march to a pre-determined stop line.

The Fatherland Front took power in Sofia and, during the early hours of 9 September, called for a break with Germany and friendship with the USSR. All across Bulgaria the functionaries of the old regime were gradually replaced by a mainly pro-communist administration. During the course of the next week Tolbukhin advanced to the outskirts of Sofia and on 17 September the Bulgarian Army became operationally subordinate to the Red Army and Bulgaria declared war on Germany. Bulgarian formations in Yugoslavia were ordered to go over to the partisans.

Tolbukhin now received orders from Moscow to prepare for an offensive into Yugoslavia that would involve both the Bulgarian Army and the Yugoslav partisans along with elements of 2nd Ukrainian Front's left wing to form a reasonably continuous line. Some of 3rd Ukrainian Front's units would be sent to the south of Bulgaria to monitor events on the Greek and Turkish borders. The Bulgarians, once their army had been reorganised by the inclusion of Soviet officers, would advance towards Niš and Skopje with the support of the Red Air Force.

This operation was timed to begin in late September and would be supported by gunboats of the Soviet Navy's Danube Flotilla. Some of these vessels had been taken over from the Romanians but the majority were Soviet-made and armed with turrets from T-34 tanks. They were to provide a very useful source of fire support and some were

Above: A Soviet BP-43 armoured train equipped with two standard T-34/76 turrets makes its way west. Just below the tank turrets is a ball mounted DT heavy machine gun for protection against infantry attacks that might come in under the depression capacity of the turret. Turrets from the T-26, T-28 and KV-1 tanks were mounted on similar trucks.

later armed with batteries of rocket launchers. During the next few weeks these ships sailed up the Danube and occupied strategic locations along the river and provided an important means of resupply to advanced Soviet ground troops.

Reconnaissance troops of the Soviet Sixth Tank Army had already reached the Bulgarian–Yugoslav border on the Danube during the first week of September and pushed across the frontier at Turnu Severin, much to the consternation of the German Army Group F which was operating in Yugoslavia.

Bulgaria's defection caused Hitler to order Löhr to withdraw to a line running from Shkodër through Skopje to the Iron Gates Pass on the Danube River. At the Iron Gates Army Group E would link up with Second Panzer Army and form a continuous line from the Adriatic Sea to the Carpathian Mountains with the aim of denying the Red Army access to the Danube Plain.

Albania

With the surrender of Italy, Albania had been taken over by Germany. Albanian nationalists welcomed the arrival of the Germans and the garrison they provided to supplement the local anti-communist forces. However, the communist partisans, led by Enver Hoxha, dominated much of the countryside. During the early summer of 1944 the Germans launched an offensive to destroy the partisans. Fighting alongside the Wehrmacht was the locally-recruited Moslem 21st SS Mountain Division *Skanderbeg* which acquitted itself well fighting its fellow countrymen. Despite some initial success, however, the Germans did not manage to crush Hoxha's forces and by the late summer the partisans, supported by their British advisers, were considering a counter-attack.

With the defection of Romania and Bulgaria's *volte-face* the escape routes from Greece were limited and Hoxha's men found themselves in a powerful position. The Germans, by the end of September, found themselves hard pressed to hold on to Tirana, the capital, and a handful of other vital communications and transport centres.

Hungary

With the Soviets poised along their borders, the Hungarian cabinet and Admiral Horthy felt it was time to take more positive steps towards ending their participation in the war. On 1 September Horthy ordered the arrest of all leaders of the Arrow Cross, the Hungarian fascist party. However, this backfired and they were all given Gestapo protection; furthermore the operation reinforced Hitler's suspicions that Budapest was becoming more unreliable, although Hungary had no anti-German resistance movement to speak of.

Shortly after this Horthy informed the cabinet that he was determined to ask the Allies what terms were available and on 22 September a Hungarian representative was sent to the Allied HQ in Italy. The message Horthy received was simple, repeating the

Above: Hungarian cavalry pause for a smoke. The side cap was an inheritance from the Austro-Hungarian Army. The cockade in the national colours of red, white and green is visible at the front of the cap. The flash on the lapel is in the branch of service colour, which for the cavalry after 1942 was dark blue.

formula of earlier in the year: negotiate with the USSR only. At roughly the same time the Hungarian chief of staff went to Germany to enquire what military assistance Hungary could expect to receive. Earlier in the year the Hungarians had approached Germany to acquire the rights to manufacture Panther tanks but had rejected the terms offered. The discussions reached an impasse. However, late in September Horthy dispatched a secret, high-powered delegation to Moscow to ask for an armistice, a step which Horthy described as 'humiliating'. The delegates were received with courtesy but no progress was made and negotiations dragged on into October.

Yugoslavia

The kingdom of Yugoslavia had been overrun by the Axis in an 11-day campaign during April 1941; it was then partitioned with Hungary and Italy both receiving portions. However, very rapidly a partisan movement developed and by July 1941 Serbia was in revolt. For the next three years the Germans, aided by Italian and later Bulgarian and locally raised anti-

Above: Soviet mounted scouts trot out on patrol on a warm and dusty day. By slinging their firearms over their left shoulders these men differentiate themselves from the Cossacks who traditionally slung theirs over the right shoulder. The central rider is applying his whip.

communist or nationalist formations, waged a mobile war against increasingly successful communist partisan forces led by Josip Broz better known by his nickname 'Tito'. By early 1944 Tito's forces numbered over 20,000 and played host to military missions from the USA, the USSR and Great Britain. Supplies, mainly British, were flown in along with advisors from Italy. Considerable numbers of Axis troops were tied up in Yugoslavia containing Tito's men.

To coincide with Tito's birthday the Germans launched Operation 'Rösselsprung' in an attempt to liquidate the partisan leaders. The headquarters of Tito's AVNOJ (Anti-fascist Council for the National Liberation of Yugoslavia) were in the mountain town of Drvar. Although Waffen-SS glider-borne units and paratroops took the town they were unable to capture Tito. The partisan leadership was evacuated to Bari then relocated first to the

Yugoslav island of Vis and then, in mid-September, to the mainland town of Craiova (in Romania). The partisan movement was reorganised and began to expand as the withdrawal of Axis forces and the advance of the Red Army made it more obvious by the day that the war was drawing towards its conclusion. Partisan brigades operating in various areas of Yugoslavia now began to link up and in early September 1944 moved east to establish contact with the 3rd Ukrainian Front.

3rd Ukrainian Front had reported to Moscow that the partisans were in urgent need of heavy equipment including tanks and anti-tank weapons. Permission was given to Tito to send 500 of his men to the USSR for tank training and supplies were to be provided for the partisans as rapidly as possible. Over the next few weeks munitions were flown in and it was also agreed that Soviet aircraft would be made available for ground-support missions.

Politically Yugoslavia was in a totally different situation to the other Balkan states and when the Red Army appeared on its border Tito decided the moment had arrived to establish the ground rules for Yugoslav–Soviet co-operation. On 21 September Tito flew to Moscow to hold talks personally with Stalin. Between bouts of heavy drinking, an agreement was concluded. The Yugoslavs agreed to 'the temporary entry of Soviet troops into Yugoslav territory' but that they would leave when 'the operational task' was over. Civilian administration would be in Yugoslav hands in all liberated areas including those under Red Army control. Bulgaria and Yugoslavia would conclude an armistice and fight together but the partisans would remain under Tito's control.

When the conference broke up it was clear to Stalin that he was dealing with someone who represented a movement that was not prepared to kow-tow to the USSR and who was recognised by the Western Allies. The post-war dealings of these two men were to underline the independent attitude that Tito struck in Moscow at this time.

Germany

From the perspective of Hitler's HQ the situation on the Eastern Front at the end of September could look nothing but dire. Finland, Bulgaria and Romania were now ranged against the Third Reich and fighting against it, often with German-manufactured weapons. Slovakia was in revolt and Hungary actively negotiating with the enemy. Although the Warsaw Rising had been crushed, the city was now in the front line and the Soviet bridgeheads across the Vistula were growing stronger by the day. To the south partisans occupied vast tracts of Yugoslavia and Albania. The losses sustained during the

months of ceaseless fighting were becoming more and more difficult to replace as Germany was reaching the limit of its manpower reserves. However, AGN was still required to hold its positions in the Baltic states when it would have been of infinitely more value in Poland.

Scraping the Barrel

In late September conscription in Germany was extended even further to include youngsters of 16 and men up to 60, as the last categories of the Volkssturm, Germany's Home Guard, were ordered to make themselves available for active service. Even by 1943 the racial purity rules of the Waffen-SS had become so elastic as to allow the enlistment of formerly unacceptable ethnic groups such as Ukrainians, some Balkan Moslems and categories of supposedly Germanic eastern Europeans; now in late 1944 the floodgates were to open.

The tide of refugees from the liberated areas of the USSR, the Baltic states and the Balkans was sifted through and many were found to be acceptable for Himmler's elite. The SS recruiting sergeants happily enrolled Tartars, Belorussians, Slavs of whatever origin, fascist sympathisers from Greece, Albania, Bulgaria, Romania and Hungary. The simple criteria were the wish to carry a gun for the Führer and eat his rations. This motley crew was

Above: It was men such as this who answered the call to join the Volkssturm in October 1944. Clearly a man fastidious about his appearance, he has well-polished shoes and a starched wing collar. He seems to be lacking the Volkssturm brassard which it was hoped would make up for the men's lack of uniforms and give them rights if taken prisoner.

organised into what were laughingly called divisions, given exotic titles and sent to the front. Amongst this band of 'Aryan warriors' was the British SS unit, named the Legion of St George, raised as a propaganda exercise earlier in the war and now called upon to man the barricades. But for the majority of these men, often accompanied by their families who had nowhere else to go, there was little or no alternative.

Symptomatic of this desperation was the meeting that took place between Himmler and General Andrei Vlasov on 16 September. Vlasov had been a general in the Red Army until he had been taken prisoner in 1942. Having undergone a crisis of faith in communism, the USSR and Stalin's leadership, Vlasov had become the head of a movement to free Russia from its current regime. However, Vlasov did not enjoy the support of other nationalist factions in the German orbit that wished their areas of the USSR to become totally independent of Russia nor did he enjoy great support from the Germans. Himmler was particularly opposed to such schemes. Vlasov hoped to unite all the Soviet citizens in the Wehrmacht and nationalist formations under one banner, the Russian Liberation Army, known by its Russian acronym as ROA. A skeleton for this army existed but Vlasov hoped to put substantial flesh on the bones under his command. A vaguely worded agreement was reached and Vlasov set about organising his force. A similar enterprise was in hand for an exclusively Ukrainian Army but both would have to wait for several weeks before any public announcement was made about these 'new allies'. A Nazi official, displaying a sense of humour, dubbed Vlasov's army 'the V-100' a reference to Hitler's fabled V-weapons, which he had declared would win the war at the last moment.

Another piece of administrative symbolism was the renaming of Army Group South Ukraine as Army Group South, as the Wehrmacht had no men, other than some half-starved fugitives, left in the USSR. Army Group North Ukraine was subsumed into Army Group Centre.

On the central front in Poland both the Soviets and the Germans were gathering breath after the exertions of the summer. September witnessed relatively little fighting other than around the Soviet Vistula bridgeheads and near Modlin, at the confluence of the Vistula and Narev (Narew) Rivers, a vital position still in German hands. Although the Soviets pounded Modlin they were unable to make any real impression on its stout defences which enjoyed a clear view over the Soviet positions.

On the Western Front the Allies had almost reached the borders of Germany despite the failure of Operation 'Market-Garden'.

Above: Vlasov's Russian Liberation Army parades its colours, the pre-Revolutionary Russian tricolour. The ROA armshield can be clearly seen on the men's left arms. The resemblance to the Imperial Army uniform is strongest on the officer in the centre. The others are dressed in more of a Soviet style. The prominent cockades on the caps were another throwback to 1917.

Chapter 4

Belgrade Liberated: October 1944

'My grandma would know how to fight with tanks. It's time you moved.'
Stalin to General Malinovsky

On 29 September Stalin wrote to Roosevelt that, together with liquidating the German forces in the Baltic states, the Red Army had 'two immediate tasks: to take Hungary out of the war and to feel out the German defences on the eastern front by means of attacks by our forces'.

Hungary

Despite the fact that there was a Hungarian delegation in Moscow attempting to negotiate an armistice, Malinovsky's 2nd Ukrainian Front was fighting its way into eastern Hungary. The offensive, which started on 6 October, had breached the line of the Tisza River and was moving towards the city of Debrecen. Further to the left of Malinovsky's line of advance Szeged was captured on 11 October. Taking Szeged cut the line of retreat for the German and Hungarian forces holding the line around Cluj which was itself an important communications centre.

Furthermore, with the loss of Cluj and Szeged, a gap was opened between Friessner's Army Group South (AGS) and the Axis forces in Yugoslavia. Although Friessner had been sent reinforcements the sheer weight of numbers that Malinovsky had at his disposal was irresistible. The Hungarian forces which formed a considerable part of Friessner's order of battle caused him much concern as they were demoralised and poorly equipped. Nevertheless the Hungarian Second Army gave a reasonable account of itself against Romanian Fourth Army in and around Satu Mare on 10 October. The long-standing animosity between the two nations ensured that the fighting was particularly fierce. However, the collapse of Hungarian Third Army opened the way across the flat plains to Debrecen which Zhukov regarded as the main point of 'the Hungarians' entire defensive system'. Hungarian Third Army was composed of raw recruits and elderly reservists who had only recently been called up, therefore, with no experience of modern, mobile warfare, it is little wonder they broke. However, the Germans had not been idle and

were also aware of the importance of Debrecen. Friessner had deployed substantial armoured forces in the area towards which the Soviets were hurrying so precipitately. The concentration of German armour was a result of Hitler's instruction to AGS that it counter-attack in early October to cut Malinovsky's supply lines. The troops released for this mission had been delayed by Allied air strikes and had only recently arrived at the front; their timing could not have been more fortuitous.

Although the 40–50km (25–32 miles) charge of the Soviet tank force had scattered the Hungarians it had led them directly into the sights of 1st and 23rd Panzer Divisions which counter-attacked and slowed them considerably. Fighting centred on Oradea on the Soviet right. Friessner ordered more troops into the area as did Malinovsky, though not at the expense of the push on Debrecen. By 9 October Soviet cavalry and mechanised units were within 20km (12.5 miles) of their goal but were stopped short by units of 23rd Panzer Division.

The Battle for Debrecen

The following day the Axis went over to the attack. The German plan was simply to behead Malinovsky's main thrust by armoured attacks into the Soviet flanks. 1st Panzer Division attacked to the west of the Soviet line and 13th Panzer Division to the east, carving gaps in the front near Debrecen and isolating three Soviet corps. Taken by surprise, Malinovsky's forces struggled to break through the German screen. Inside the pocket the Soviets managed to reach the suburbs of Debrecen while their rearguard desperately fended off attacks from all directions. At Oradea brutal street fighting was in progress but by 12 October the town was firmly in Soviet hands. It was clear to Friessner that his forces were just not strong enough to contain all the Soviet attacks as Malinovsky kept up the pressure on every side. Therefore Friessner requested permission to withdraw but inevitably Hitler prevaricated until the moment had passed and 3rd Ukrainian Front had recovered its equilibrium.

Above: A column of SdKfz 251 half-tracks moves towards the Carpathian foothills in the autumn drizzle. The camouflage pattern is green and rusty brown over dark yellow. The machine gun is the excellent MG42, which was capable of 1,200 rounds per minute. The inevitable barrel change could be accomplished by an experienced gunner in less than eight seconds.

Above: A Soviet KV-1 tank captured by the Germans. Designated a heavy tank, the KV-1 was an effective machine and evolved into the IS series of heavy tanks which were in production from early 1944. Although production ended in 1943, KV-1 tanks and their derivatives the up-gunned KV-85, remained in front-line service until the end of the war.

Above: One of several armoured trains that the Wehrmacht employed on the Eastern Front. The carriage is a captured Soviet one mounting a 76.2mm gun with a quadruple 20mm flak unit at the back.

counterparts in 8th SS Cavalry Division *Florian Geyer.* The worth of horsemen roaming across the huge, empty spaces of the Eastern Front had validated those officers, of all armies, who had argued for their retention as cavalry proved to be a useful asset particularly in the rapid exploitation role or in anti-partisan operations. However, as the fighting moved into more densely populated areas then their value plummeted as their casualties rose. This was not a war of sabres and knee-to-knee charges. The Soviet cavalry suffered heavy losses as they probed for a weak spot in the encirclement.

The Germans were fighting on two fronts, internally and externally. The Soviets battered at them from both directions and the fields were littered with blazing and gutted vehicles as ground was given slowly. On more than one occasion the Germans had to adjust their positions to avoid being surrounded themselves but nonetheless maintained their perimeter. However, the situation inside the Soviet pocket was becoming increasingly difficult as ammunition and supplies were running out. Therefore, on 29 October, Malinovsky issued orders that the encircled corps were to destroy all useful heavy equipment and escape as best they could, a much easier task for the cavalry than the infantry. When 214th Guards Cavalry Regiment returned to Soviet lines it reported the loss of its flag. For that and other reasons the entire regiment was reduced to the status of a penal unit.

As the Soviet stragglers made their way to safety, the Germans and Hungarians counted their trophies which, so they claimed, amounted to 358 tanks and over 1,000 guns and mortars which along with inflicting 25,000 casualties provided Goebbels with a significant victory to trumpet abroad. Axis losses were noted as a little over 100 armoured vehicles and 200 guns. The 3rd Ukrainian Front had been dealt a powerful blow and its offensive held thus enabling Axis forces in Hungary to withdraw in reasonable order and prepare their defences elsewhere along the banks of the Tisza River.

Horthy Deposed

As the fighting around Debrecen ebbed and flowed, events in Budapest ran their tangled course with results that would alter the fate of Hungary and tie it irrevocably to that of the Third Reich. On 11 October the Hungarian negotiators in Moscow were presented with the USSR's terms for an armistice. These were transmitted to Horthy who reluctantly accepted them but, before anything could be done, Hitler struck. A commando-style raiding party kidnapped Horthy's son; German troops and armour took to the streets of Budapest; and on 16 October Horthy resigned, handing

After a period of realignment and regrouping the Soviet advance on Debrecen resumed on 17 October. The Germans pulled back their encircling units and three days later Debrecen fell. Now, in Malinovsky's judgement, was the moment to cut the Germans off. Unfortunately for the leading Soviet units it had been decided that they would push ahead and ignore their flank protection; this lack of caution was to cost them dear. Although they had taken a battering, the Panzer divisions were certainly not out for the count and on 23 October the

Germans counter-attacked again and once more the Soviets were caught wrong-footed. The German operation repeated the earlier tactic of flanking attacks. The leading Soviet infantry units were cut to pieces having had no time to prepare any sort of defences.

On 24 October the Panzers advancing to the east met up with the men of 3rd Mountain Division spearheading the west-bound pincer. Once again three Soviet corps were cut off. As the fighting raged cavalry units of both sides met; troopers of Soviet V Guards Cavalry Corps engaged with their over power to Count Ferenc Szalasi who promptly announced that Hungary would continue to fight alongside the Germans. As rumours of an armistice had already reached some front-line units there were a number of desertions but the opportunity swiftly passed and by 23 October the Germans had taken the Hungarian Army in hand. Guderian noted, somewhat acidly, that a Hungarian general 'assured me of his loyalty to the alliance, and accepted a motor car as a present from me. In this car, my own Mercedes, he drove off a few days later to the Russians.' Such instances were not to be repeated and the attitude of the Soviets can be judged by the order issued to 2nd and 4th Ukrainian Fronts to treat Germans and Hungarians alike as the Hungarians were still fighting.

Despite the defeat at Debrecen the Soviet offensive had, by the end of October, overrun roughly one-third of Hungary. Malinovsky, however, was to be allowed only a brief pause before he received his next orders from *Stavka*.

Slovakia

With Konev's failure to crack the German defences at the Dukla Pass the prospects for the Slovakian uprising at the end of September looked bleak. To bolster the insurgents 700 men of the 2nd Czechoslovak Parachute Brigade were flown in during the first week of October. Further supply drops were also made until deteriorating weather, over the course of the next few weeks, made such operations too hazardous.

However, on 5 October a renewed effort at the Dukla Pass led, appropriately, to I Czechoslovak Corps breaking through the defences. To support the renewal of the attacks the Soviets had deployed over 3,000 guns and heavy mortars. To concentrate this weight of fire the artillery was arranged in ranks with 100 metres (110 yards) between each rank to a depth of 1.5km (1,600 yards). The density of this artillery front was such that there were 140 guns per kilometre (1,100 yards) of front. The effect of such a weight of shell falling on a narrow area can be imagined and was proof positive of the Red Army's doctrine that the artillery was the most effective break-through weapon.

This support notwithstanding, the Czechoslovak infantry suffered heavy casualties, 6,500 men, about 50 per cent of the corps' strength and including their commanding officer General L. Svoboda. At 06:00 hours on 6 October a Czechoslovak patrol crossed the border headed by men whose villages were within sight. There was now a possibility that the Red Army could force its way through to meet up with the insurgents. However, it was not to be.

The weather was deteriorating rapidly and the mud slowed Petrov's advance to a crawl. 4th Ukrainian Front still had to fight elsewhere in the Carpathian range and these battles were as cruel as that at Dukla with the bonus for the Germans of winter setting in. From bitter experience in World War 1 the Soviets were aware of what hostile terrain the Carpathians comprised and in the 30 years since then little had changed to improve the ground. Soviet and German mountain warfare specialists fought where their fathers had battled in similar conditions of mud, slush, snow and ice as thaw and frost alternated. Only in the valleys could much progress be made and then only at a bloody price.

Valley of Death

In one particular area, near the village of Dobroslava, a typical engagement took place, which gained the region the macabre title of the 'Valley of Death'. Petrov's men, seeking a weak spot in the German defences, chose Dobroslava as such a place. Following a heavy bombardment supplemented by ground-attack aircraft strikes, 12th Guards Tank

Above: A close up of the legendary Soviet weapons system, the *tachanka* machine-gun cart invented during the Russian Civil War to provide mobile firepower for cavalry formations. These two vehicles are pictured driving through Szeged in eastern Hungary.

Above: American Lend-Lease M3 half-tracks and a White scout car move carefully along a muddy track in eastern Hungary during the autumn of 1944. The lead vehicle is armed with a 0.50-inch and two 0.30-inch Browning machine guns.

The Soviets did not watch this build-up passively and, when the weather permitted, launched air strikes against the gathering enemy. As a result of several such raids the *Horst Wessel* Division suffered 40 per cent losses en route to its assembly points. Supported by pro-Nazi Slovak troops, the German offensive began in mid-October, but progress was slow as the insurgents were often well dug in and equipped with artillery. With units such as the Dirlewanger Brigade in action, it is difficult to assess the casualty figures for the insurgents accurately given that Dirlewanger's men generally shot anyone in their way. Suffice it to say that the main base of the insurgents, Banska Bystrica, fell on 27 October and with the loss of the Tri Duba landing ground the Czechoslovak planes returned to their Soviet bases. With all hope now gone, the Soviet advisers ordered the remaining men to disperse into the forests and mountains and revert to partisan warfare. The British and American advisers were

Above: The poor bloody infantry of the 4th Ukrainian Front trudge forward into Slovakia. The image of bedraggled, clearly fed-up men was not one the regime looked on with favour therefore this photo is all the more remarkable for its candour.

Brigade with strong infantry support attacked at 11:30 hours on 25/26 October. Driving along the roads and tracks to avoid the glutinous mud, the tanks soon ran into carefully placed minefields. As their losses mounted, the T-34s manoeuvred desperately to find safe ground, only to be hit by a German artillery barrage which forced the supporting infantry to go to ground. Nevertheless the Soviet tanks pushed on penetrating the German lines up to a depth of 1.5km (1,600 yards) until they encountered anti-tank guns and tank-hunting teams armed with the lethal single-shot Panzerfaust. Separated from their infantry, the Soviet tanks were rapidly taken care of and the brigade virtually wiped out.

End of the Slovak Uprising

With the Soviets threatening to break through the Dukla Pass the German operation against the insurgents was stepped up; they intended to crush the Slovaks with all speed. Seven divisions, upwards of 40,000 men, were to converge on the Slovak enclave from all directions including, since the coup, Hungary. Although this was an impressive force on paper, the divisions were often only such in the mind of Himmler and the German element often no more than a stiffening of officers and NCOs. The Waffen-SS was to provide the bulk of this force including units recruited from Ukrainians, Moslem units from the USSR, the Dirlewanger Brigade (fresh from activities in

Above: A very interesting gun and difficult to identify through the heavy foliage. It is a licence built Schneider 107mm Model 1910. Imported as part of the Imperial Army's expansion programme, it was, for its time, an excellent gun. Upgraded by both the Red Army and the French during the 1930s, it went on to give sterling service until replaced by the Soviet M-60 during the war. With an eight round per minute rate of fire, it was deployed at corps level.

Warsaw) and Balkan *Volksdeutsche* of the 18th SS Panzergrenadier Division *Horst Wessel*.

The *Volksdeutsche* were ethnic Germans who had settled all over the Balkans and Russia during the previous two centuries and were now fighting for the fatherland. Many such had few, if any, words of German and were conscripted as fast as they could be processed to provide manpower for the SS before their adopted homes were overrun by the Red Army.

captured along with several Slovak senior officers and, despite their uniforms, were imprisoned and executed before the war ended. As an organised military operation the Slovak uprising was almost over. Its major achievement had been to draw German troops from the front for over a month. The partisans were to be a thorn in the Wehrmacht's side for months more but would not occupy the forces they had in September–October. Interestingly the

Above: Above the snow line in the high Carpathians an anti-aircraft unit deploys for action against ground forces. The concentration of fire from such weapons when directed against soft-skinned vehicles was devastating. They had few aerial targets other than reconnaissance aircraft.

Above: In the mountainous regions of Slovakia small mountain guns such as the one shown here were vital. They provided light, easily manoeuvrable fire support in the heavily wooded countryside. This is a 75mm mountain gun based on a design from 1918 modified with a split trail to allow high-angle fire.

partisan groups, now mainly a communist force, attracted few deserters from the security units opposing them despite several efforts to do so. Probably the SS men were well aware of their ultimate fate should they fall into the clutches of the NKVD. Sadly recriminations between the Czechoslovak government in exile and the partisans were to continue until liberation in 1945 to the detriment of all.

Finland

The Finns' drive to clear their country of Germans proceeded apace. On the shores of the Gulf of Bothnia Finnish units occupied Tornio and pushed northwards. At the same time other Finnish troops liberated the capital of Lappland, Rovaniemi, but the town was a charred ruin leaving the population nowhere to shelter as winter came. It was a grim foretaste of the Germans' increasingly destructive policy in this region. Stalin, dissatisfied with progress, demanded a more aggressive effort from the Finns. Mannerheim increased the pressure on his generals but against a well co-ordinated defence system, manned by reasonably equipped troops, his men could do little but wait and watch as the Germans retired from central and southern Finland. However, the Soviets were preparing their own offensive against the main body of Twentieth Mountain Army further to the north.

The Soviet Offensive

Throughout September and early October *Stavka* had poured men and tanks into the region west of Murmansk. The Soviet Fourteenth Army (General K. Meretskov) had been provided with 75 tanks, a considerable weight of artillery and over 600 aircraft. The Germans had no tanks but they did have substantial defences, a good number of modern anti-tank guns and 160 aircraft with fuel. Furthermore the Soviet armour had almost nowhere to manoeuvre on the hilly, wet tundra other than the roads. Keeping to the few roads only invited an air strike, an ambush or the possibility of running into mines. However, the Soviets had over 100,000 infantry and several units of battle-hardened marines of the Northern Fleet.

Stalin's instructions were clear: Meretskov was to liberate the strip of the USSR lost in 1941, occupy the territory ceded by Finland, and advance to the Norwegian border where he would halt. As the Soviets knew of the German scorched-earth policy they had laid in a considerable amount of bridging equipment and mountains of supplies of all descriptions as winter was approaching fast and no one wished for a repeat of the Winter War debacle.

The Soviet offensive began on 7 October with a two-hour bombardment followed by a probing attack that gained a foothold across

Above: Much of Eastern Europe dissolved into a sodden morass with the coming of the autumn and spring rains as can be clearly seen here. On closer inspection the men's clothing is saturated and caked in mud. The horse drawn *panje* wagon was one of the few vehicles that could negotiate such conditions with relative ease. The men are gathered around such a wagon.

against the town's defences but during the night of 24 October the Germans began to destroy the harbour, the railway and the town itself. The following day the Soviets liberated it and took over responsibility for the homeless population. The remains of Twentieth Army had made good their escape to Norway and at the end of October the Soviets called a halt to their advance.

The thoroughness of the Germans' scorched-earth policy gained for Rendulic the epithet of 'Burner of Finnmark'. The Soviets had their work cut out rebuilding the devastated infrastructure and reopening the mines. There was little or no further fighting in the region as both sides were exhausted and at the end of their supply chains; indeed each had enough to do just dealing with the fearsome Arctic winter. However, the Soviets had achieved their objectives and the northern USSR was now fully back under Moscow's control.

Finland would declare war on Germany on 3 March 1945.

the first of several rivers they would have to negotiate. Hampered by the appalling weather, the Soviet advance was slow allowing the Germans to withdraw in good order. However, a landing on the flank put Rendulic's men in danger of encirclement. Luckily for the Germans the main Soviet force was held up by the exhaustion of the men and congestion on the roads caused by German sabotage and the sheer number of vehicles. A further problem for the Soviets was caused by a German counter-attack along the coast. As his infantry attack seemed to be grinding to a halt, Meretskov's marines pulled off another successful landing behind the Germans on 12 October. This gave the Soviets control of the coast road and prompted the Germans to begin a full-scale retreat to Norway. However, with Soviet marines landing at other points to the west, the Germans would now have a hard fight on their hands to their front as well as their rear. Abandoning Petsamo, the Germans fell back, fighting all the way.

On 15 October the Soviets halted again to rest the men and await orders as Norway was now in sight. Rendulic meanwhile reorganised his forces and determined to leave a strong rearguard in Kirkenes just inside Norway to enable his main forces to escape. Having fought off another marine landing party, the Germans began to fortify Kirkenes

Above: In his role as commander of the Training and Replacement Army Reichsführer Heinrich Himmler (centre in leather coat) was obliged to visit new units. Here he inspects the anti-tank gun element of a newly-raised SS formation. Himmler's use as a military leader was comparable to the value of the gun shown here against an IS-2 heavy tank.

much to the consternation of its 10,000 inhabitants.

With permission to enter Norway granted and the supply lines, including 500 reindeer and thousands of hardy Russian horses, functioning properly, Meretskov began his pursuit. The final river barrier outside Kirkenes was crossed using rafts and Lend-Lease amphibians on 22 October and the next day the route to the west was cut. Despite the Soviets' use of tanks they made little progress

Target Memel

The Soviet offensive to take Memel had been prepared with considerable care. Only on 2 October did the Germans realise the extent of the forces opposite them and the three days left them to prepare were insufficient to achieve much more than the shuffling of reserves.

After a short bombardment, which ended in the middle of the morning of 5 October, the Soviet infantry stormed forward. The German lines were penetrated at some points by up to

Above: Soviet technical troops inspect a pair of abandoned Panzer V Panthers Model D at a former Wehrmacht repair facility. The vehicle nearest the camera has had its side skirt armour removed to facilitate driving through mud, which tended to clog up the tracks.

Above: An unidentified Waffen-SS unit somewhere in Eastern Europe. The open terrain is typical of much of Poland and reinforces the need for natural defensible lines being established along the great rivers of that area.

Above: Soviet infantry advance cautiously through a marshy area of East Prussia. The Red Army's standard rifle, the Mosin Nagant 7.62mm Model 1890/30, is carried by the man at the rear. The bayonet was always fixed in the combat zone in keeping with Russian tradition.

8km (5 miles) but rain and dense fog prevented effective air or artillery support beyond registered targets and therefore a halt was called. Next day, with improved weather, the full magnitude of the Soviet operation became apparent. This was no diversionary attack to draw attention from the plight of Army Group North (AGN) around Riga but an all-out offensive along a 190km (120-mile) front. Soviet Fifth Guards Tank Army, I and XIX Tank and III Mechanised Corps now came into the line and, by pressing their attack through the night, reached the outskirts of Memel on the following morning. By 8 October Forty-Third Army was also facing Memel's defence system. The hole in the tattered German front line was now some 72km (45 miles) wide and many units were losing cohesion. Added to this it began to snow.

On 10 October a small harbour north of Memel was captured at much the same time as the Guards' tanks reached the coast to the south. In less than a week AGN had been cut off and this time such was the weight of men and tanks that it was unlikely that even the organisational ability of Guderian could assemble anything resembling an effective counter-blow. Guy Sajer, a soldier of the *Grossdeutschland* Division who had the

misfortune to be caught up in the battle, wrote a graphic description in his book *The Forgotten Soldier* of the dash into Memel ahead of the Soviet advance:

'We would have to fight our way through, to make passage for ourselves and for the flood of refugees moving with us, constantly slowing us down and often nearly paralysing us — a pitiful, imploring procession, dragging a foot through the bitter cold and the slush of the first snows. In spite of orders, we had to help, reassure, and support this chaotic wash of human beings . . . We passed through towns and villages where the inhabitants had still been living a more or less normal life until four or five days earlier . . . We arrived in Memel with trucks pulled by men and tanks serving as locomotives to trains of incredible length . . . Words cannot describe the end of the war in Prussia.'

But this was not 'the end of the war in Prussia' it was the beginning. The Soviets failed to take Memel off the march and settled in for a siege.

East Prussia

Bagramyan's left flank made slower progress, facing as it did the well-developed and heavily manned defences of East Prussia.

Chernyakhovsky's 3rd Belorussian Front began its offensive into East Prussia on 16 October. The frontier had been crossed briefly in August but this operation aimed at a considerably deeper penetration into the Reich. Spearheaded by Eleventh Guards Army, 3rd Belorussian Front broke through the German lines in roughly the same places as their fathers had done in August 1914. But the defences had been improved since Rennenkampf's march during that fateful summer. The German area commander, General Hossbach, transferred six divisions to contain the Soviet Guardsmen who were advancing rapidly in the hopes of forcing the Insterburg Gap and penetrating the German rear.

German Counter-Attack

On 21–22 October the Germans attacked both flanks of the Soviet penetration and, with the aid of armoured forces rushed into the area, Hossbach inflicted a severe defeat on Chernyakhovsky. The Soviets were thrown back almost to their start line. The Germans had exploited their intimate knowledge of the region and its excellent road and rail networks to the fullest. This first significant breach of the Reich's borders and its bloody rebuff gave Goebbels's Propaganda Ministry a rare opportunity to trumpet a German victory. The retreating Soviet troops were demonised for the atrocities they had allegedly committed in the towns and villages they had briefly occupied, such as: Nemmersdorf and Gumbinnen, providing the Nazis with further tales of Soviet barbarism with which to terrify and galvanise the population into total war. The claim made throughout the war against the USSR, that it was a crusade to rid Europe of Bolshevism and its subhuman, *Untermensch* hordes, suddenly seemed all too real for many German civilians watching the newsreel footage in the cinemas that autumn.

The Germans claimed to have taken or destroyed 1,000 tanks and 300 guns and taken several thousand prisoners as a result of this counter-attack. Chernyakhovsky had received no support from 2nd Belorussian Front on his left as Zakharov's efforts to move out of the bridgeheads across the Narew River had failed. Given that Rokossovsky took over this front in early November and Zakharov was effectively demoted it is likely that his failure was the reason for this change.

The Fall of Riga

Army Group North was now isolated. 2nd and 3rd Baltic Fronts were steadily increasing the pressure around AGN and Schörner's defences, although strong, were beginning to crack. On 8 October Schörner appealed to Hitler for permission to fall back to the west of Riga but was ordered to stand his ground. For the next couple of days a see-saw battle raged around Riga. The Soviets broke through and were driven out several times but finally, on 12 October, AGN was allowed to withdraw. Riga was liberated the next day. In Moscow the event was greeted with the usual artillery salvos and fireworks display and congratulatory messages were sent to the relevant front commanders. As the Soviets celebrated, AGN's 30 or so divisions dug themselves into what became known as the Courland Pocket. The main threat to the battered remains of Sixteenth and Eighteenth Armies was now to come from the south and Bagramyan's right flank.

Above: Guards Sergeant Levchenko displays his captured Panzerfaust 100. Printed near the warhead are the firing instructions complete with a silhouette of the user. Printed towards the end of the tube is the warning 'Beware fire jet' as the back-blast could reach up to 3 or 4 metres. The Soviets made widespread use of these weapons for anti-tank and demolition tasks.

Stavka was determined to prevent any repetition of the German break-through to AGN as had happened several weeks earlier. The four divisions in Memel were to be thoroughly hemmed in, the right bank of the Niemen River was to be cleared of Germans, and Schörner contained by strong infantry units with armoured support.

In fact AGN was in no condition to attempt a break-out from Courland whether the road to East Prussia was firmly held or not. All Schörner could do was sit and wait. With several small harbours behind the German lines the opportunity to mount a seaborne evacuation existed but, failing that,

the Kriegsmarine was perfectly capable of ferrying in supplies. Furthermore, the German pocket battleships *Lützow* and *Admiral Scheer* were patrolling in support of the German garrisons on the islands in the Gulf of Riga and would be available to provide heavy artillery support should it be necessary. As Guy Sajer, a veteran of the Memel siege, was to recall, *Lützow* and its escorting destroyers were able to perform this invaluable service for the garrison. 'Despite zero visibility, the co-ordinates provided by our tanks in forward positions enabled the ships to fire with considerable precision, and the Russian thrust was more or less stopped.'

With the Baltic states virtually free of Germans, *Stavka* decided that it would be sensible to disband Maslennikov's 3rd Baltic Front and redistribute its component parts to 1st and 2nd Baltic Fronts.

Yugoslavia

The Moscow conference had done little to assuage Tito's mistrust of the USSR's intentions towards Yugoslavia, particularly in the light of events in Warsaw and elsewhere. Tito did not intend to begin the final liberation of his country until everything, militarily and politically, was to his satisfaction. The immediate priority was to co-ordinate the plans of the Red Army and the new ally Bulgaria. Bulgaria's participation in the Axis occupation of Yugoslavia was such a recent memory for many of its victims that a very careful public relations exercise would have to be carried out to convince the Yugoslav people that the Bulgars were now truly on their side. On 5 October Tito met with Soviet and Bulgarian representatives to conclude a Yugoslav–Bulgarian armistice and discuss joint operations. It was decided that three Bulgarian armies, First, Second and Fourth, would be employed in Yugoslavia. These included a powerful armoured brigade equipped with German Panzer IVs and assault guns, which had been decorated with the new Bulgarian coat of arms in the national colours and painted overall, when materials were available, in dark green to avoid confusion with similar Wehrmacht vehicles.

With the armistice signed and the plans decided, Tito instructed his First Army Group to move on Belgrade. Ten Bulgarian divisions now became the left wing of Tolbukhin's front and were given the task of interrupting the German retreat from Greece. Units of the Red Army were to cross the Danube River to cut the Belgrade–Salonika railway line and support the Yugoslavian partisans. Soviet liaison officers had contacted other partisan groups, which had agreed to co-operate in blocking the German escape route to the north. At the same time Soviet IV Guards Mechanised Corps was instructed to cross the Morava River and take Belgrade by 14 October.

IV Guards Mechanised Corps faced a march of 190km (120 miles) through very hilly terrain over poor, unmade roads. It had only just arrived in Yugoslavia, the corps having already driven across Bulgaria in record time, which had taken its toll of the vehicles and men. Without lorries, the Guardsmen had to carry everything on their tanks including the infantry. Luckily opposition was negligible and the journey to Belgrade was accomplished without loss. Travelling for the infantry was a hot, uncomfortable experience encumbered as they were with arms and ammunition and perched between jerrycans of diesel fuel. Had there been a Luftwaffe presence worth the name the whole episode could have turned into a bloody shambles.

Second Bulgarian Army had been ordered to take the city of Niš and cut the road and rail links with Belgrade. This was to be a joint operation with the partisans on the left flank of Tolbukhin's 3rd Ukrainian Front. Over on the right elements of 2nd Ukrainian Front were attacking to the north of Belgrade. With Malinovsky's forces in action along the Tisza River and elsewhere in Hungary, there were few if any Axis forces to spare for Yugoslavia. The main task of the Germans in Yugoslavia was to keep open the roads and railways from Greece to allow Army Group E to make its way to safety.

Strung out along several roads, the men of Army Group E formed themselves into self-contained *Kampfgruppen* (battlegroups) often consisting of a battalion of infantry, a platoon of tanks or assault guns and some artillery. Contact with Belgrade was maintained by radio and the call signs were usually the names of the battlegroup commanders, which also identified them on the maps that traced their perilous route to the north. For many of these troops it was their first clash with the Soviets as they had spent a relatively peaceful war in Greece. Indeed Athens had only been evacuated on 11 October. Now, as they attempted to reach Army Group F, these forces were exposed to a somewhat better armed and more experienced force than the Greek partisans. Although the Axis had deployed very few tanks in the Balkans, and those mainly obsolete Italian or French types, the Yugoslav partisans had captured some, which had been organised into battalions and proved quite effective.

The Germans put Belgrade into a state of siege and preparations were made for a prolonged struggle. Incredibly amongst the defenders was the Russian Corps in Serbia also known as the Russian Guard Corps. This remarkable unit was made up of Russians who had fled their homeland following the communist victory in the civil war and settled in Yugoslavia. Having volunteered to fight the communists in the USSR in late 1941, this band of middle-aged former tsarist officers found themselves fighting communist partisans in their adopted country. Now the war had arrived on their doorstep and they realised their ambition of facing the Red Army.

As the Allies prepared to assault Belgrade, Tito reminded the Soviets that it had been agreed that the partisans would be 'first to enter Belgrade'. When the Soviet barrage lifted on the morning of 14 October Yugoslav infantry rode into battle on the backs of Soviet T-34s. For the next six days Yugoslavia's capital suffered the horrors of street fighting as the Germans and their allies contested every house and room. A German counter-attack on 16 October briefly threatened the Allied advance but it was short-lived. From the centre of the Danube Soviet-manned gunboats added their firepower to the almost non-stop barrage. However, the Germans were not about to surrender quietly as many of them dreaded the fate that they believed would befall them at the hands of the partisans. Finally, on 20 October, Belgrade was declared liberated. It only remained for the Soviet engineers to clear the thousands of mines that littered the city. But even these hidden dangers were not enough to stop the population from celebrating.

The fate of Army Group E was all but sealed, as the routes to the north were almost all closed. The Bulgarians had taken Niš and only one road remained open — and that depended on the garrison of Kraljevo holding out. Reinforcements were flown into Kraljevo from Greece, where troops were still arriving from the islands, and they arrived just in time to hold the line. The defence of Kraljevo lasted long enough to allow a considerable number of Axis troops to escape, including a varied collection of units recruited in the USSR and deployed for security duties in the Balkans.

While the Germans scrambled north a parade was held in Belgrade to celebrate the liberation; a more sombre event was the mass interment of dead Yugoslav and Soviet troops in a communal grave. Tito and his partisan army had achieved their long-awaited and hard-fought-for victory and it now remained to clear the northern provinces. It was unfortunate that American aircraft strafed Soviet columns heading in that direction on several occasions. Among the dead was the commander of XIII Rifle Corps.

Yugoslav forces spread out, liberating the towns and villages abandoned by the Axis and installing their own administrators. However, there was still much hard fighting as the Germans had re-established themselves and carried out their usual thorough job of scorching the earth. Alongside them were groups of anti-Tito partisans, some of whom had fought, briefly, alongside the Red Army until the arrival of Soviet commissars who attempted to disarm them at which point they headed for the hills.

Total War

The Soviet invasion of East Prussia, defeated though it had been, prompted the Nazi authorities to take a further step down the road of total war. Although the munitions factories were belatedly producing weapons as fast as they could and men had been combed

Above: A collaborator swings from a lamppost in newly liberated Belgrade. Such summary justice was meted out to such people across the length and breadth of Eastern Europe in the wake of the Soviet advance.

out of every nook and cranny it was still not enough. Therefore it was decided to call out the Volkssturm — the People's Army or Home Guard. Home Guard units had been in existence for some time but this was a more comprehensive measure as every able-bodied man between 16 and 60 not already in the forces and capable of bearing arms would be enlisted.

On 18 October Hitler broadcast a proclamation announcing the mobilisation of the Volkssturm. It was hoped that a wave of patriotism would sweep Germany similar to that of 1813 when, led by Prussia, the German people threw off Napoleon's yoke with an army consisting mainly of volunteers. With Goebbels's usual sense of theatre and timing the broadcast was made on the 131st anniversary of the Battle of Leipzig that had led to the expulsion of the French from Germany. It was a move similar to that undertaken by the Soviets who, in the dark days of 1941, had thrown battalions of hastily mobilised militia, partially trained and armed workers and students in the path of the Wehrmacht in a desperate attempt to slow down the advance on Moscow. Their losses had been enormous but the logic was flawless — if they succeeded in killing one German for two or three militiamen it was a worthwhile sacrifice. Now Hitler and Goebbels, the Reich Plenipotentiary for Total War, intended proving that they were equally ruthless.

From the beginning the Volkssturm was a political body as Hitler's mistrust of the officer corps convinced him that any new military organisations should be subject to the Nazi Party. Therefore Himmler and Martin Bormann were to lead the Volkssturm. Himmler, as commander of the Training and Replacement Army, was responsible for arms and instruction; Bormann, as head of the party organisation, oversaw recruitment and political leadership.

Every party district or *Gau* was to provide lists of men who would be organised into battalions of 1,000 men. The *Gauleiter*, the local party leader, would be responsible for ensuring 'political correctness' and loyalty and the officers and NCOs would be answerable to him. These latter were usually retired soldiers who had last seen service in 1918 and had little idea what a T-34 was.

Hitler's proclamation made all members of the Volkssturm 'Soldiers under the Army code' for the duration of their service, which was to be undertaken when their area was under threat. Uniforms were few and far between so the Volkssturm had to make do with whatever was available. As many German civilian organisations had uniforms these could be worn. Photographs show Volkssturm men in items from the Kaiser's time and the modern

Italian Army but mainly they dressed in civilian clothes. A universal item was an armband showing an eagle and the words 'Deutscher Volkssturm' in an attempt to give them some legal status in the event of capture. Other than for time actually spent in combat, service in the Volkssturm was unpaid which was a source of resentment for many.

Weapons were as much a matter of pot luck as uniforms. If the unit was chosen for a propaganda photo opportunity then modern weapons might be issued only to be taken back at the end of the shoot. The reality was somewhat different and some newsreels reflect this, showing ranks of middle-aged and elderly men marching through the streets carrying all manner of captured weapons often from World War 1. A special weapon production scheme had been introduced, the Primitive Weapons Programme of 1944, to mass-produce simple, cheap arms that could be used by poorly trained troops. One of these weapons, the sub-machine gun MP 3008, a derivative of the Sten gun, went into very limited production as did the Volkssturmgewehr (People's Army rifle). Another was the Volkshandgranate 45, which consisted of an explosive charge encased in concrete with a detonator. With Hitler's Directive 51 still in force the east German Volkssturm were not allocated weapons generously as priority was given to the Anglo-American front; furthermore Himmler was at pains to arm the Waffen-SS before all others. One weapon forever associated with the Volkssturm was the Panzerfaust, the one shot anti-tank missile which was issued in thousands — it was as disposable as its youthful or elderly operators.

Despite its image as a patriotic, historically based organisation, the *levée en masse* that the Volkssturm attempted to be was not popular. Apart from the lack of pay, clothing and weapons, there was a growing undercurrent of antipathy to the Nazi Party and the regime. Pre-war Germany had a long history of socialism and communism which began to re-emerge, albeit in a very low-key manner, towards the end of 1944. Here and there people began to dust off their copies of Marx and Engels just in case. Fighting and dying for Germany was one thing . . . but for the party? That was very questionable. Nevertheless the Gauleiters produced their lists and the men paraded and sometimes even trained. Service in the Volkssturm would prove to be an extremely dangerous duty. Desertion or avoidance of service was punishable by summary execution but if the Red Army suddenly overran the area then a similar fate was possible. The Soviets were well aware of the Volkssturm's existence and were likely to shoot any men as potential stay-behind saboteurs or partisans.

Poland

The central area of the front had been relatively quiet. However, the end of the Warsaw Rising on 3 October was followed by a German attack on the Magnuszew bridgehead the next day. The Germans had chosen their moment well as the Soviets had withdrawn several units back across the river for training. According to Rokossovsky his HQ had notified the area commanders of suspicious activities behind the German lines but the warnings were ignored.

Following a short bombardment, German tanks advanced in such strength that the Soviet line was, at several points, pushed back as far as the Vistula river bank, endangering the bridges. Artillery fire from the eastern bank appears to have gained the defenders sufficient respite to form a line that held long enough to allow Soviet armour to cross and engage the Panzers. Neither side was able to call on air support as the weather was too bad, which made the Germans' situation considerably easier. Although the Germans were finally driven back it took three days of hard fighting.

Even though Rokossovsky made no written criticisms of his subordinates, it had been a salutary lesson for the Soviets. Marshal Timoshenko, *Stavka* co-ordinator for the southern fronts, filed a report shortly after this event in which he pointed out, 'Commanders and their staffs have been somewhat spoiled by the successful actions in Romania and Transylvania and do not properly organise co-operation among types of forces.' Another commentator, General S. M. Shtemenko, noted tactfully in his book *The Last Six Months*, 'After the Romanian operations certain commanders become, so to speak, dizzy with success.'

Considering their achievements it is unsurprising that some Soviet officers were 'dizzy with success'. The Baltic states, Finland, Romania and Bulgaria were no longer any threat to the USSR and the bridgeheads across the Vistula River were now firmly held. Indeed the armistice with Bulgaria was signed in Moscow on 28 October by a new, mainly communist government.

The factories of the Urals and Siberia were turning out tanks, aircraft and weapons in such quantities that the Lend-Lease programme was being scaled down. In Slovakia and Hungary there was hard fighting but the Red Army was firmly established within their borders. In Yugoslavia Tito's partisans were co-operating, although not in a submissive fashion, and progress was being made towards the underbelly of the Reich. It was only in East Prussia that the Soviets had been rebuffed. Therefore it was time to plan the next move into, as so many Red Army traffic signs read, 'the lair of the Fascist Beast', Germany itself. Other roadside graffiti were somewhat earthier.

Chapter 5

Budapest Besieged: November–December 1944

'The army's all loused up, they're scratching at the front. And on our backs a monster louse is creeping.'
J. Hasek, *The Good Soldier Svejk*

Soviet Planning

Now it was beyond the borders of the USSR, the next and final objective for the Red Army was the destruction of Hitler's Reich. The planning for what would be its greatest campaign began in October 1944. Convinced, as its leaders always were, that the Germans deployed their greatest strength on the Eastern Front, this offensive was to be meticulously planned and carried out with overwhelming force as fierce resistance was anticipated. There were two possible routes to Berlin. The first through Hungary, Czechoslovakia and Vienna would involve 2nd, 3rd and 4th Ukrainian Fronts which had been engaged in non-stop fighting for several months. The men and vehicles were reaching the limit of their strength and to maintain an adequate flow of supplies through these areas would be problematic. Therefore logic dictated that the main thrust against Germany would be made straight through Poland to the west. For this operation the 1st, 2nd and 3rd Belorussian Fronts and 1st Ukrainian Front commanded respectively by Rokossovsky, Zhakarov, Chernyakhovsky and Konev would be used. The men were rested, the vehicles in a reasonable state of maintenance, and the supply lines would be simpler to keep on stream.

At the end of October Zhukov and Rokossovsky met with Stalin to discuss the situation. The generals' advice was to attack north of Warsaw while simultaneously delivering a 'powerful splitting blow' towards Lódz and Posen (Poznan). Stalin did not decide immediately but appointed Zhukov to command 1st Belorussian Front, although he was not to take up the post for some weeks.

The planning was not undertaken in detail in Moscow. The situation was considered broadly, taking into account the relative strength of the Germans and the overall strategic position. The fronts were then presented with their objectives. *Stavka*

Above: One of the Wehrmacht's specialist tools of destruction. Denying the Red Army's immense logistical arm the use of the railways was a priority. This hook was lowered into the permanent way and then the double train reversed slowly. The hook ripped the sleepers out of the ground with the effect as shown in the illustration below.

Above: The Soviet advance during the last year of the war was hampered by the poor infrastructure as much as that of the Axis had been during 1941. The comprehensive destruction of roads and more particularly railways had been refined to an art form by the Germans by 1944.

believed that the Germans were presenting their strongest resistance in Poland. Therefore the Wehrmacht's forces would have to be drawn away from this sector by means of flank attacks such as that in progress in Hungary. This pressure would be increased by an offensive against the heavily fortified province of East Prussia. With its resources divided by these attacks, Germany's weakened centre would be hit with the most powerful force that could be assembled under the control of 1st Ukrainian and 1st Belorussian Fronts. East Prussia presented a major problem and a very real threat to the flank of 1st Belorussian Front as it advanced. Any German move from this area was to be contained by 2nd and 3rd Belorussian Fronts. At this stage of the planning it was anticipated that Germany would be finished within 45 days, even taking into account the increasingly fanatical resistance that the Soviet approach to Berlin would generate.

3rd Belorussian Front was to push into East Prussia for a depth of over 160km (100 miles) supported by 2nd Belorussian Front. 1st Belorussian Front would advance on Posen while 1st Ukrainian Front would make for the Oder River above Breslau (Wroclaw). Zhukov was permitted to provide support for 2nd Belorussian Front if required. While heavy fighting in Slovakia and Hungary continued during the first days of November, Stalin was approached to suspend further offensive plans and acceded to Zhukov's wishes. A conference was called in Moscow to discuss the situation. To cover the absence of so many front commanders from their posts the story was given out that they had travelled to Moscow for the celebrations of the 1917 Revolution.

During the second week of November Stalin made a series of announcements to his generals. Firstly, the offensive would start between 15 and 20 January. Secondly, there would be no discussion, as such, of the plan. Front commanders would be given their objectives, make their plans accordingly and put in their requests for men and equipment to carry them out. Thirdly, Stalin himself would be the co-ordinator for the fronts involved, replacing Vasilevsky who would take a back seat. Finally, Zhukov's move to 1st Belorussian Front became official.

As Zhukov's new command was to bear the brunt of the offensive he travelled to Moscow again to discuss his plans. 1st Belorussian Front was to break out of the Magnuszew and Pulawy bridgeheads in the direction of Lódz and follow this move with one in the direction of Posen. With Stalin's agreement an adjustment was made to Konev's 1st Ukrainian Front's line of attack which now was to aim for Breslau. Although this was not 'the shortest route' previously envisaged, it did spare Konev's men the ghastly prospect of

Above: As well as the all-female air force regiments, there were many women ground crew scattered throughout the Red Air Force. Here an armourer prepares to load the 20mm ammunition belts for an La-5 fighter's twin nose cannon.

fighting their way through the industrial cities of Silesia, which had the potential to generate another nightmare epic of street fighting in the manner of Stalingrad. Stalin's reasoning was less altruistic; rather than sparing the men, the Supreme Commander wished to spare the mines and factories, which he wanted as reparation for the destruction of Soviet industry. The factories were to be dismantled wholesale and shipped to the USSR where they would contribute to the rebuilding of the Soviet Union. Quite simply Silesia was, as Stalin described it to Konev, 'gold'.

Although *Stavka* did not confirm the operation until the end of December things were more or less decided by the end of November. It now remained to build up the attack fronts to the strengths required.

Throughout December and early January train loads of ammunition, tanks and guns

Above: Soviet infantry cross a tributary of the Vistula beneath the ruins of a railway bridge. The men's white winter overalls have assumed a rather grubby appearance.

poured west from the factories beyond the Urals and from those already returned to their original locations in Kharkov and elsewhere. '[The] weapons and materiel: 3,240 tanks and self-propelled guns, more than 17,000 guns and mortars, and 2,580 planes' (from a Soviet document) on Konev's front alone would give the Red Army an overwhelming superiority during the next six weeks.

To further his plans for removing Hungary from Germany's side Stalin had established a new Hungarian government behind Soviet lines. Elections were held and a Provisional National Assembly was set up in Debrecen on 21 December with the simple remit of concluding an armistice with the USSR. The Hungarian delegates left for Moscow at the end of the year.

Hungary
Although, following Horthy's removal, Hungary's armed forces had been effectively taken over by the Germans, the Soviet propaganda campaign to undermine their morale continued. Furthermore the Soviets were striving to encourage the Hungarian

population to view the Red Army as liberators not conquerors. Reiterating the words he had used to Roosevelt, Stalin informed Churchill, 'Our chief task is to take Hungary out of the war as quickly as possible, and our main thrust will therefore be in that direction.'

Malinovsky, commanding 2nd Ukrainian Front, reported to Stalin, 'From now on [late October] the front is faced with some very hard fighting. The enemy will not yield Hungary since it is his most vulnerable spot.' To add to Malinovsky's woes the weather was foul with the rain washing away roads and the mud reducing movement almost to a crawl. When one of his subordinates requested additional vehicles Malinovsky told him, 'Get your traction equipment from the enemy.'

While Soviet propaganda leaflets announced that the Red Army was only entering Hungary, 'to defeat the hostile German armies and destroy Nazi Germany's rule in the countries it has enslaved' and assured the people that 'private property was

being respected in Hungary', Stalin ordered Malinovsky to take Budapest.

Already, on 21 October, Tolbukhin had been ordered to move troops from his 3rd Ukrainian Front to cover Malinovsky's left. To the north, Petrov's 4th Ukrainian Front was instructed to push deeper into Czechoslovakia to cover 2nd Ukrainian Front's right. Although the Soviets had suffered a setback at Debrecen they now occupied that city and were well placed to advance on and even take Budapest off the march with, 'relatively light forces'.

In part the optimistic view of the situation taken by Moscow was based on a report from General L. Z. Mekhlis, Political Commissar in the region, who enjoyed a direct line to Stalin. Mekhlis had painted a very rosy picture, implying that Hungarian forces were on the point of collapse:

'Units of Hungarian First Army opposing our front are in the process of breakdown or demoralisation. Every day

Above: Hungarian artillerymen man a 75mm German anti-tank gun. Various German weapons were manufactured under licence in Pest, the industrial quarter of Budapest. These factories continued to produce munitions until overrun by the Soviets. Here the crew has taken advantage of the weapon's low profile in an attempt to blend into its surroundings.

our troops take from 1,000 to 1,500, 2,000 or more prisoners. On 25 October the Eighteenth Army took 2,500 prisoners, with whole units surrendering at a time . . . Owing to the turning movements of our front's forces, many groups of soldiers wander through the woods, some with arms and some without, while some have put on civilian clothes . . .'

To reinforce this cheerful spin, Soviet intelligence reported that German troops were thin on the ground near Budapest. Therefore Malinovsky appeared to be facing an enemy that would fall apart if the slightest pressure were applied. It was decided that Forty-Sixth Army would force the Tisza River line and Sixth Guards Tank Army would then be released to storm Budapest. To the right Fortieth, Twenty-Seventh and Fifty-Seventh Armies, with Romanian First Army's support, would aim to penetrate to the north of Budapest, threatening the rear of the Germans facing 4th Ukrainian Front in Czechoslovakia.

This plan, drawn up by Malinovsky and *Stavka*, anticipated the capture of Budapest by 5 November. Then at 21:00 hours on 28 October the phone at Malinovsky's HQ rang and at the other end was Stalin. In essence the conversation consisted of Stalin telling Malinovsky to capture Budapest in less than five days, 'no matter what it costs you'. Malinovsky tried to discuss the matter but Stalin ended the conversation by saying, 'I categorically order you to go over to the offensive tomorrow.' With Mekhlis at his shoulder Malinovsky had little alternative but to carry out his master's order to attack even though it was too soon and his units would not all be in place.

First Battle for Budapest

Although Soviet preparations were incomplete the first phase of the operation was remarkably successful. Elements of Forty-Sixth Army crossed the Tisza River and established a firm bridgehead from which they were in a position to roll up the Axis defences to the north-east or south-west. But the Germans wasted no time and reinforcements were rushed into place. Although some Hungarian units had broken as predicted, others held their ground. Among them was the 22nd SS Cavalry Division *Maria Theresa*, recruited from Hungarian *Volksdeutsche* only seven months earlier. The Soviet advance to the south-eastern suburbs of Budapest was spearheaded by II and IV Guards Mechanised Corps but the narrow wedge that they had driven towards the city was now exposed. German armoured forces, gathered from four Panzer divisions, struck at the Guards' right flank. As this armoured battle ebbed and flowed across the drenched and muddy ground in what was almost a continual downpour of rain, *Stavka* ordered a revision of the plan.

Above: Hungarian POWs wait for their instructions. Hungary's attitude to the war with the USSR was ambivalent from the outset.

Above: Waffen-SS grenadiers are rushed forward in an attempt to hold a Soviet break-through near Budapest during November 1944. The heavily camouflaged trucks are testament to the Red Air Force's control of the skies. The original caption remarks on the poor condition of Hungarian roads.

Budapest's Jews

With the Red Army approaching swiftly, the authorities in Budapest decided to act rapidly to ensure that the city's Jews did not escape. Before the war a quarter of Budapest's population had been Jewish. This number was increased by waves of refugees to over 250,000 when the Germans occupied Hungary in March 1944. From that time on deportation to the extermination camps began, as did the confinement of Jews in designated buildings marked with the Star of David. However, the process was not as efficient as elsewhere because Hungary was still a sovereign state with a degree of independence and did not subscribe to Hitler's Final Solution. Tragically, when the pro-Nazi Arrow Cross Party came into power following the October coup, a reign of terror was instituted against the capital's Jews and summary executions became commonplace. On 8 November matters took a still more serious turn. 70,000 Jews were rounded up and force-marched towards Austria. Along the way thousands were shot, died of starvation or exposure. The survivors crossed the border in late December and were then distributed to various camps. Many were sent to Dachau but those deemed fit enough were set to work improving the defences of Vienna. In

Budapest the remaining Jews were herded into a closed ghetto in Pest to await their fate. During the early weeks of the siege members of the Arrow Cross took up to 20,000 Jews from the ghetto and murdered them on the banks of the Danube and elsewhere. When the Red Army finally took Budapest over 100,000 Jews were liberated.

Second Battle for Budapest

Stavka's revised plan entailed Malinovsky's right taking Budapest from the north-east and moving into the rear of the German counter-attack. The bulk of the attacking group was the same Mechanised Cavalry Group that had suffered considerable losses only weeks before at Debrecen. To the south-west 3rd Ukrainian Front's Fifty-Seventh Army had crossed the Danube and was steadily expanding its bridgehead but was, as yet, in no position to offer support to Malinovsky.

The second attempt to capture Budapest began on 11 November but it rapidly bogged down in a sea of mud and German counter-attacks. Although a breach was forced between the *Maria Theresa* and Hungarian 1st Cavalry Divisions the Soviets lacked the resources to exploit it to the full. This lack of success resulted in a report being made to Stalin by the local front co-ordinator Marshal Timoshenko in which he noted, 'The 2nd Ukrainian Front is one of the most powerful fronts, with huge forces to crush the opposing enemy, yet recently it has not been successful.' Malinovsky was taken to task for too great a dispersal of his forces and the weakened condition of the Mechanised Cavalry Group. Timoshenko recommended a revision of the present deployment to ensure an 'absolute superiority over the enemy'. Moscow agreed to this and ordered Malinovsky to create this 'absolute superiority' by massing armoured units supported by specialist Breakthrough Artillery Divisions. The Breakthrough Artillery Divisions were created in 1944 but traced their roots back to a similar organisation in World War 1. Their purpose was enshrined in their name, to break through. When the Germans had gone over to a primarily defensive strategy the Soviets retaliated by creating these immensely powerful artillery units. Depending on the type of gun, each division deployed 20–24 battalions with up to 96 in a corps. The calibres ranged from 152mm to 305mm. A sensible precaution was the inclusion of several batteries of the new 100mm anti-tank guns with each division. These remarkably powerful guns could knock out any Axis tank that might slip through to the almost immobile heavy gun lines. Again this concept dated from 1916–17 when several batteries of similar guns had been lost due to the lack of protection from cavalry. Furthermore the concentration of such

Above: Breakthrough Artillery Divisions were equipped with some of the most powerful weapons available to the Soviet forces. This 152mm M 1936 gun is elevated to its maximum of 60 degrees. The flat panels on either side of the barrel are the backs of the gunners' travelling seats.

specialist weapons simplified ammunition and parts replacement. However, movement involved hundreds of vehicles and air cover so committing them to a particular operation was not undertaken lightly and underscored the importance that Stalin attached to the capture of Budapest. Malinovsky was ordered by Stalin to 'concentrate no fewer than two Breakthrough Artillery Divisions in Shumilov's Seventh Guards Army'. Shumilov's army was to be supported by Sixth Guards Tank Army which would be followed by the Mechanised Cavalry Group commanded by General P. A.

Pliev. Tolbukhin's forces would advance from their Danube bridgeheads when he felt the moment to be right. Some support from Petrov in Czechoslovakia was hoped for but, as the fighting there was so bogged down in mud and heavy resistance, little was expected from this quarter.

3rd Ukrainian Front's left flank was now connected to the right of Tito's National Liberation Army which was preparing to break into the former Yugoslavian province of Croatia along the line from Sarajevo to the Adriatic Sea.

Above: A dismounted attack by men of the SS Cavalry Division *Maria Theresa* during operations in and around Budapest. During the siege this formation was all but wiped out. They all appear to be wearing the camouflage suits that were so widespread towards the end of the war. The man nearest the camera is armed with the Austrian made Model 29/40.

Third Battle for Budapest

On 1 December Hitler declared Budapest a fortress and four days later the Soviets launched their third offensive aimed to take the city. A 45-minute barrage hammered at the junction of German Sixth and Eighth Armies to prepare the way for the Soviet infantry attack. *Stavka* often chose army junctions as the point of attack in the hope that a break-through there would maximise disruption and lead to a loss of command and control. However, on this occasion they were unlucky. Although their penetration was successful the German rear did not lend itself to swift mobile operations. The region was a maze of canals and waterways, which had been filled to the brim by the autumn rains. But, with such immense firepower to support them, the Guards infantry pressed forward inclining their line of advance towards the north of Budapest and steadily cutting the city's lines of communication with northern Hungary.

During the night of 4/5 December Forty-Sixth Army had crossed the Danube and gained another bridgehead to the south of Budapest which it exploited with all possible speed. Three days later 3rd Ukrainian Front poured out of its bridgeheads further down the river and drove fast for Lake Balaton. To ensure Tolbukhin did not deviate from the plan, *Stavka* had specifically ordered him not to be drawn towards Vienna. It took 3rd Ukrainian Front only a few days to reach the southern shore of Lake Balaton and to the south-west of it the Soviets pushed straight across the Drava River before the Germans could prepare any solid defences.

While Sixth Guards Tank Army fought its way around the northern outskirts of Budapest, Forty-Sixth Army was paying a high price for every metre of ground it made nor was there much help to be had from 4th Ukrainian Front. The mountainous nature of much of Slovakia had slowed the Soviet advance to little more than a crawl.

So, with casualties mounting to the south, *Stavka* again modified its plans. In view of the decimation of Forty-Sixth Army Tolbukhin's front was to be entirely responsible for the western sector of the planned encirclement. Fortieth, Twenty-Seventh and Romanian Fourth Armies were to move into Czechoslovakia while Fifty-Third and Seventh Guards Armies led by Sixth Guards Tank Army would cut the Danube above Budapest and make contact with Tolbukhin's lead units east of Lake Balaton.

The situation of the Axis forces was now precarious. Sixth Army had been pushed back by Tolbukhin and was just about holding its own along a line from Budapest to Lake Balaton and then down to the Yugoslavian border. In front of Malinovsky the rest of Friessner's AGS, exhausted and losing ground, was unable to prevent Soviet gunners from firing on the transport barges that navigated the Danube and, due to the mud, provided a vital supply system. German Eighth Army was being driven back towards the Carpathian Mountains. But reinforcements were on their way to AGS. Three Panzer divisions and three strong, independent Panther tank battalions were moving into Hungary. As this armour

Above: Soviet engineers watch a ferry cross the Danube with a load of horses and wagons. The locally requisitioned boats have been lashed together and decked with planks. The ferry crew is hauling it across by cable and brute force.

swung into place Friessner requested that it be concentrated to hit Sixth Guards Army which was presenting its flank and practically inviting attack. Hitler had other ideas: two of the divisions were to be used to break up Tolbukhin's attack and drive its battered remnants into the Danube. In common with Stalin Hitler was a big picture strategist who read a map, issued an order and considered that was sufficient to be victorious. The difference was that now Stalin had the resources to achieve his aims whereas Hitler did not. But although the Führer enjoyed unlimited power he did not control the weather. Moreover he resented Friessner pointing out to him that the area earmarked for Tolbukhin's defeat was an impassable morass.

Above: Soviet infantry running for cover in Budapest.

Above: The 4th Ukrainian Front was heavily engaged in the mountains of Czechoslovakia where conditions demanded a less mechanised style of warfare. Here an artillery team drags its weapon up into an ambush position; the barrel has been removed for ease of movement in the trees.

supplement to the rations. The 50,000 Hungarian troops were based around I Army Corps' two infantry divisions (10th and 12th), 1st Armoured Division, 1st Cavalry Division and several assault-gun batteries equipped with a mix of German and Hungarian vehicles. The Hungarian commander was General Ivan Hindy. Several hundred Arrow Cross Party members also volunteered to serve. However, relations between the Germans and the Hungarians deteriorated very swiftly as the latter were viewed as very much a makeweight force unwilling to fight with a great deal of fortitude. A very useful supplement to the garrison's firepower were many heavy anti-aircraft guns, including deadly German 88s, which were capable of stopping most tanks, particularly at short range.

However, there was also the civilian population of 750,000 and for them the Christmas and New Year holiday of 1944–5 was one that they would remember for the rest of their lives.

On 18 December the Panzer divisions were released to Friessner but without their tanks! Naturally the commander of AGS protested vehemently but was told that the tanks would attack where Hitler wanted them to when the frost hardened the ground sufficiently. If this was not to Friessner's liking then he was entitled to resign. In less than a week General Wohler was in command of AGS but during those few days 3rd Ukrainian Front's armour had moved against the German position that gloried in the name of the Margareta Line which was defended by III Panzer and LXXII Corps of Sixth Army. The weak link was the 271st Volksgrenadier Division and it was here that Tolbukhin concentrated his efforts. Under-strength and weak in close support weapons and artillery, the Volksgrenadiers collapsed within a few hours of the attack starting on 20 December. Stalin's order to complete the encirclement of Budapest regardless of the weather or the losses incurred was being obeyed to the letter.

Fortress Budapest

Graced with this title Budapest was almost directly under Hitler's control and beyond the jurisdiction of AGS. Budapest is divided by the Danube, which here runs roughly north to south. On the eastern bank is Pest, then the industrial area, overlooked by Buda on the western bank, which was a predominantly residential area. Pest's factory districts would, so Hitler hoped, bleed the Red Army dry in the same way that Stalingrad had done to the Wehrmacht two years before. Apart from the opportunity to revenge himself for that catastrophe Hitler was desperate to hold on to the tiny Hungarian oilfield to the north-west

of the city which was the Third Reich's last remaining source of fuel.

The city's German garrison of roughly 40,000 men consisted of the IX SS Mountain Corps, a strange title for a formation that mainly consisted of two SS cavalry divisions, 12th Panzer Division with 50 or so Panthers and other tanks, the *Feldherrnhalle* Panzergrenadier Division and several smaller formations. However, the cavalry horses would provide a useful

Soviet Shermans

To the south of Pest the tanks of Sixth Guards Tank Army were under attack by German and Hungarian armoured forces. The two corps of Sixth Guards Tank Army were V Guards Tank 'Stalingrad' Corps equipped with T-34s and V Mechanised Corps using Sherman M4A2s known to their crews affectionately as *Emchas* (M4 being *em chetyrye* in Russian). The M4 was more popular than the British tanks the corps had

Above: A cavalry unit of the 2nd Ukrainian Front marches past Malinovsky, the front commander, in his Lend-Lease jeep. The small flag is the squadron pennant. The bulky black figure in front of the standard bearer is wearing the *burka*, a traditional Caucasian foul weather garment made from camel hair or felt and worn like a small tent.

Above and right: 'Tank desant' men leap into action from a T-34/76 during the early weeks of 1944. Their snowsuits blend well with the background although the tank is beginning to lose its coat of whitewash.

used until early 1944. One reason for the Sherman's popularity was the fact that its shells did not explode as fast as those of the T-34 if the tank was hit in action. Soviet tank crews were forbidden to abandon their vehicles if damaged so they would hide underneath or very close by. If the tank were on fire the Soviet ammunition would begin to explode within a short time with usually fatal consequences for the crew. However, the Sherman's ammunition took considerably longer to do this and therefore the men's chances of survival were greater. The intelligence unit with the formation concerned investigated any cases of tanks being abandoned on the battlefield and, should the explanation not prove satisfactory, the crew would more often than not find themselves in a penal unit for cowardice. However, a disadvantage of the Sherman was its high centre of gravity, which, if the driver was not careful, resulted in it toppling over when negotiating rough terrain. Shermans were also well appointed in terms of the crew's comfort and veterans speak of not being injured by metal shards when a round struck the outside as often happened in a T-34. The Sherman's long 76mm gun was not capable of destroying a Tiger, therefore it was necessary to hunt them in pairs. One Sherman would shoot off the Tiger's track causing it to slew and present its flank so that the other Sherman could fire at the Tiger's side and hopefully set light to the fuel tank. Destruction of an enemy tank was rewarded with a cash bonus of 1,000 roubles. This was a considerable sum and a kitty was sometimes organised so that this bounty money was sent to the families of colleagues killed in action. In cases where it was unclear which tank had

Above: A captured Hungarian-made assault gun, the Zrinyi II, named after a Hungarian hero of the 16th century. Armed with a 105mm howitzer, with a crew of four and carrying 52 rounds of ammunition, this vehicle lacked any real anti-tank capability. The armoured sideskirts were added in late 1944. The track pieces have been welded on to provide additional armour to the basic 75mm frontal plates.

finally killed an opponent the prize was shared. As well as the individual crews keeping scores, the deputy commander of the maintenance company would tour the battlefield to check the tally.

Budapest Encircled

On Christmas Eve Malinovsky ordered the Guards to turn south, leaving their flanks to be covered by the Mechanised Cavalry. The aim was to link up with 3rd Ukrainian Front. Now that the ground had frozen the armoured units around Lake Balaton could move more freely. After stiff fighting, 2nd and 3rd Ukrainian Fronts linked up at Esztergom and by 26 December Budapest was cut off. A further pocket of German troops was isolated

north of the city and Soviet units had reached to within 32km (20 miles) of Komarno, the main German base in western Hungary. Malinovsky detailed two Soviet Guards and one Romanian infantry corps to storm Budapest before the defenders could settle in. This attempt failed and both Soviets and Romanians suffered heavy losses during five days of fierce fighting in the outskirts. The process of solidifying the lines around Budapest now went ahead apace. Attempts were made to induce the garrison to surrender but these came to nothing. The area under siege was roughly 27km (17 miles) in diameter and Soviet estimates of the garrison were roughly double the German figure of 90,000 quoted above .

Above: Men of an *Ostbataillon* prepare to go into action. They are wearing the German helmet dating from 1916. The tunic is cut in the style of the traditional Russian *gymnastiorka* but with a fall collar; the breeches are also Russian. No ROA arm shields are visible nor is it possible to identify the unit further.

Budapest under Siege

The garrison commander was SS Obergruppenführer Pfeffer-Wildenbruch, of whose military abilities the commander of German Sixth Army said, 'At best, one could say that Budapest was being led by a politician.' In part the reason for his appointment was the Hungarian regime's fear that the city's population would stage an uprising so an officer experienced in keeping order was required. But conventional military training, as Stalingrad had shown, was of little or no value in an urban environment. Command and control rapidly became non-existent in a smoke filled warren of ruins and noise. Furthermore, Hitler's orders were simply to hold out and kill Russians which required little imagination, simply courage, determination and ammunition. From his HQ on Castle Hill in Buda Pfeffer-Wildenbruch could do very little.

But Hitler did not intend to abandon the city to its fate. Fourth Air Fleet (General G. Conrad) was to organise an airbridge using Ju-52 transport planes, parachutes and gliders. The Ju-52 had been the workhorse of the Luftwaffe throughout the war and performed many such operations. Known affectionately as 'Tante Ju' by the men of the Wehrmacht it was capable of carrying 5,000kg (11,000lb) of cargo or up to 20 men. During the siege these aircraft were a symbol of hope for all the wounded, who prayed to be evacuated. While this was going on Hitler, without informing any of his senior officers, ordered the transfer of IV SS Panzer Corps from Army Group Centre to Hungary to launch an attack to raise the siege. IV SS Panzer Corps (SS Obergruppenführer H. Gille), constituting almost the entirety of AGC's mobile reserve, left for Hungary on Christmas Day and although Soviet intelligence noted its absence they were unable to track it. The two formations of the corps were 3rd and 5th SS Panzer Divisions *Totenkopf* and *Wiking*, which were well-equipped first-class units. Guderian resignedly noted that, 'In Hitler's opinion the relief of Budapest was more important than the defence of eastern Germany. He advanced reasons of external politics when I asked him to reverse this ill-starred order, and turned down my request.' The SS Panzers detrained at Komarno and went straight into the attack on New Year's Day 1945.

Above: General Andrei Vlasov, leader of the ROA pictured here in his characteristically simple uniform. Vlasov was captured by the Germans in early 1942 and worked tirelessly for a relationship with Germany, which was finally established too late. He was captured by the Soviets and executed in Moscow during August 1946.

Above: Behind the lines the NKVD trawled the towns and villages in search of collaborators and German stragglers. Here refugees are being questioned in the ruins of their home town. The male civilian will probably be sent to the front in line with the regime's policy of conscription.

Slovakia

With the uprising over, the few remaining partisan groups were left to be dealt with by SS units raised in the Soviet Union. Ironically, these troops re-equipped themselves with Czechoslovak or Red Army weapons, supplies and vehicles captured during the uprising. When the Soviet-led partisans realised who they were fighting they began a propaganda campaign to subvert morale and encourage desertion. A German report on this hearts and minds exercise noted that:

'Neither Communism nor the USSR are mentioned . . . instead they write about Russia and the Russian army. Amongst those that [the propaganda] is directed against are the local Slovakian citizens . . . The Bolsheviks portray themselves as liberators of the European people "Russia fights shoulder to shoulder with the people of Europe and America".
We [former citizens of the USSR] will be allowed to return to our home towns without further ado, if we desert. We believe that these leaflets . . . offer us only the signature on our death sentences.'

Although there were some who deserted to the partisans there were very few who trusted Stalin's word.

The main force defending Slovakia was First Panzer Army, ably led by General Gotthard Heinrici, a master of defensive operations. As autumn turned to winter the Germans began to withdraw, gradually moving from defence line to defence line in the face of relentless pressure from Petrov's 4th Ukrainian Front. At times the situation necessitated the formation of *ad hoc* units from the anti-partisan forces so that Russians fought Ukrainians or Caucasians. During these brutal encounters quarter was rarely if ever given and there was a steady flow of deserters from the Red Army, particularly of Ukrainians to join their countrymen in the SS. This was to remain a feature of many similar battles almost until the war's end.

Vlasov and the ROA

Himmler's tenure as commander of the Training and Replacement Army had changed his stance regarding ethnic groups' eligibility to die for the Third Reich. Now there was to be established a fully-fledged Russian Liberation Army (ROA). Himmler only pursued this course of action because Hitler did not intervene to call a halt. Hitler expressed his views in late 1944, 'I was against putting them [former Soviet citizens and soldiers] into our uniforms. And who was for it? Our darling army, which has its own ideas . . . well I can't make them change uniforms now, we don't have any . . . [the Army] puts any tramp into a German uniform.' As well as showing his contempt for the Heer, 'Our darling army', it also displays a certain resignation on Hitler's part as foreign volunteers were now an essential part of the forces on the Eastern Front.

On 14 November the formation of the Committee for the Liberation of the Peoples of Russia was announced with much pomp and ceremony in the Hradcany, the splendid Baroque palace in Prague. Better known by its Cyrillic acronym of KONR, the committee was one of several governments in exile that the Germans were establishing amongst which were Albanian, French and Croatian 'authorities'. Chaired by Vlasov himself, KONR issued a 14-point manifesto which 'welcomed Germany's help under conditions which shall not impair the honour and independence of our country. This help is at this moment the only tangible opportunity for an armed struggle against the Stalinist clique.'

Above: During 1942–3 the Red Army's political officers (*Politruk*) lost much of their previously considerable influence as did the Communist Party itself. To stem this creeping liberalisation the Party began to reassert itself in 1944 and talks by officers such as this became more frequent, particularly aimed at reinforcing the party line with new recruits. Not all of this audience looks suitably captivated, however.

Very few Soviet citizens were prepared to join the ROA despite the fine words regarding the treatment of ethnic groups in any future Russian state. Nor was the KONR popular with Russian monarchists as it supported republicanism. The Wehrmacht was also concerned that the ROA would demand control over the *Ostbataillonen* (East Battalions) which made up a substantial proportion of its manpower (as high as one-third in many units) on the Eastern Front. Consolidating all the East Battalions into one force would give Vlasov powerful leverage to extract further concessions from Germany. Indeed the Gestapo made veiled references to individuals in the ROA and KONR who, so they alleged, were seeking contacts with the Western Allies. Himmler however, was pleased with the situation and wished Vlasov's enterprise 'full success in the interest of the common cause' in a telegram sent on 15 November.

The ROA was to consist of five divisions, not ten as had originally been planned, with a small air force and an armoured unit operating T-34s and captured Soviet aircraft. In the event only two divisions were formed. Although they were initially under the auspices of the SS, a compromise was reached and 600th and 650th Panzergrenadier

Divisions were created from various sources including Kaminski's brigands.

Ukrainian volunteers in both the SS and the Heer had often suggested the creation of a similar Ukrainian force but, lacking a leader with the forceful personality of Vlasov, their appeals fell on deaf ears until January 1945.

Liberated Europe

Although a certain degree of complacency may have set in at the front, behind the Soviet lines the situation was not conducive to such feelings. There were large parts of the Ukraine and Poland that were simply beyond the control of the USSR's security forces which, despite their much-vaunted efficiency and ruthlessness, were too few to control such a huge area effectively. The Axis had not withdrawn quietly and everything that could be of the least possible use to the Russians had been removed or destroyed. Therefore Soviet engineers and labour battalions were working flat out to restore the road and rail systems before the entire supply network ground to a halt. Furthermore, hundreds of thousands of civilians had been forcibly evacuated to deny the Red Army recruits or labourers. Although many escaped and found their way home or were rescued before their trains left for Germany, as was the case at Minsk, there were

those who were unable or unwilling to return.

Stalin was fully informed regarding the anti-Soviet feelings that had pervaded the western USSR during three years of occupation and was determined to stamp them out. In the wake of the combat troops came the men of the NKVD who arrived in the shattered remains of recently liberated towns and villages on the look-out for anti-Soviet elements. Already well-versed in screening techniques from many similar actions, Stalin's political guardsmen spared no effort in weeding out suspected collaborators, fascist sympathisers or nationalists. Those who had not joined the partisans were questioned as to their motives and dealings with the former occupying powers. Ethnic groups such as German colonists, Chechens and Crimean Tartars were deported wholesale beyond the Urals for collaborating. In the Ukraine nationalist partisan groups who had fought the Axis now turned their guns on the Red Army. Indeed in February 1944 Marshal N. F. Vatutin, commander of the 1st Ukrainian Front, was ambushed and killed by Ukrainians. Nor was the situation much better five months later. During the early part of Operation 'Bagration' Rokossovsky remembered, 'We made the journey [through the Western Ukraine] in an armoured train, as the forests were still infested with Bendera men and other fascist hangers-on.' 'Bendera men' were Ukrainian nationalist partisans named for their leader Stepan Bandera, who was at that time in prison in Germany; they and other nationalist groups were to fight on against Soviet rule into the 1950s.

Stalin was also keenly aware how many Soviet POWs had been captured as one of his sons was amongst them. As these men were liberated by the advancing Red Army the vast majority were immediately re-enlisted, given a gun and sent off to fight. But many former POWs, brutalised by years of barbaric treatment, physically and often mentally scarred, did not want to fight for anyone let alone the system that had outlawed them. Consequently they deserted in their hundreds, forming gangs that were often larger than the forces sent to contain them. A senior member of *Stavka* and close associate of Stalin, wrote in 1978, 'Taking advantage of the wartime situation, certain groups of shady characters (including Ukrainian nationalists) bestirred themselves. They murdered officials, stole public property and destroyed stores of foodstuffs and fodder . . .' Although he was referring specifically to Poland his comments applied equally to a much wider area.

Indeed a Red Army veteran recalled the fear he felt on the streets of Minsk in 1945 when passing through on his way home to Moscow:

'It was unsafe to be alone as criminal elements roamed the ruins in search of extra rations or black market goods to trade for that universal currency, cigarettes. They were usually armed with a discarded weapon picked up during the Fritzes' retreat the previous year. It was not uncommon for careless Soviet soldiers to be murdered for the clothes on their back and their bodies dumped in a ditch.'

Civilians reduced to living in mud and rubble shanties were a common sight and, as in Romania, venereal diseases spread like wildfire as women resorted to the oldest profession to supplement their meagre rations.

To add to the security and rear services' problems, groups of German stragglers emerged from hiding when the fighting had moved to the west and tried to make their way home. There are some references to such groups existing as late as early 1945. Occasionally the Luftwaffe risked a supply flight to drop weapons and medicines but few, if any, men returned.

The populations of eastern Poland and the Baltic states, who had experienced 20 years of non-Russian rule before the war, did not look forward to the return of their former masters, whatever their politics. Consequently thousands of men had enlisted in the ranks of the Wehrmacht or the Waffen-SS during 1943–4 not so much out of sympathy with Nazi ideals but simply in an attempt to prevent Soviet reoccupation.

The Reassertion of Communist Party Power

Soviet troops were now fighting abroad in countries where their political masters believed they would be in danger from 'bourgeois-nationalist' propaganda and similar possibly subversive influences. This was not merely an example of Stalinist paranoia but a fear that had existed in the minds of Russia's rulers since the early 19th century. In 1825 Tsar Nicholas I had exiled a group of officers who espoused 'revolutionary' beliefs picked up in the west at the end of the Napoleonic Wars. Stalin had no intention of letting history repeat itself.

As the Red Army had rolled across western Belorussia and the western Ukraine men were conscripted to replace the heavy casualties suffered. It was essential that such recruits were 're-educated' in Soviet ways. As early as March 1944 the Main Political Administration of the Red Army had issued a directive that gave the highest priority to ensuring that new conscripts underwent political as well as military training.

The influence of the Communist Party and the political commissars attached to military formations had been curbed in late 1942 when patriotism rather than party was the call used to motivate the people and soldiers of the USSR to fight. However, by late 1944, with the crisis past, it was felt necessary to rein in some of the more 'liberal' tendencies that the regime had encouraged.

Courland Pocket

In late October the first Soviet offensive to liquidate the Courland Pocket began. Schörner had established the Sixteenth and Eighteenth Armies which constituted Army Group North in strong defensive positions, the key to which was the port of Libau (Liepaja) on the western coast of Courland. Holding Libau was vital to the existence of AGN, as it was the main point of entry for supplies and evacuation.

The Soviets opened their offensive with a heavy artillery bombardment, which ended on 26 October. Infantry and armour then moved off and rapidly penetrated the German first line of defence. Their objective was to split AGN, push on to the coast and then destroy each army individually as the opportunity arose. However, the Germans were well prepared and their defensive tactics, unencumbered by Hitler's 'hold everything' orders, allowed for the thinly held front line to be penetrated. When the Soviet infantry and armour were beyond artillery support the Germans would counter-attack, using the carefully husbanded tanks of 4th, 12th and 14th Panzer Divisions to slice through the base of the Soviet salient and mop up the remains. With offshore artillery support from the Kriegsmarine, this tactic worked and the

line held. For the next two weeks the Soviets attacked furiously but achieved nothing more than increasingly heavy casualties. The offensive was called off on 7 November. The Red Army repeated this exercise almost to the letter for the last 10 days of November with an equal lack of success.

Whether the Soviet commanders in the area were subject to a complete lack of tactical imagination or had some remarkably devious plan in mind, the same operation was undertaken at the end of December and in January. The attacks all took place near the town of Frauenberg where the German armies met and every time they were driven back, having suffered substantial losses.

The so-called Fifth Battle began on 20 February and this time the Soviets almost succeeded in splitting Army Group Courland, as AGN had been redesignated on 25 January, in two. Only the efforts of two infantry divisions saved the day and the offensive was called off on 15 March. However, it had been close and this prompted Admiral Dönitz, commander of the Kriegsmarine, to draw up plans for the evacuation of Army Group Courland. Under the code name Operation 'Laura', the navy's plan would take nine days to execute. The Kriegsmarine knew the waters off Courland well as it had been evacuating refugees and ferrying in supplies for several months nor did the Germans fear the Soviet Baltic Fleet which interfered very little. Hitler rejected Operation 'Laura' on 18 March 1945, the day on which the sixth attack began.

The latest Soviet effort was noticeably less vigorous than the others had been. Although *Stavka* had rotated troops through the Baltic Fronts, by now the men were all aware that the war was nearing its end and few if any wanted to die for a soggy field. But Stalin had other ideas and the fighting continued in the same old way until 31 March.

With the weary patience bred of familiarity, the Germans spent April preparing for the seventh attack. However, it never came and the month ended on a relatively peaceful note. Since Schörner's departure in January two more commanders had been and gone and on 6 April a third, General Carl Hilpert, arrived.

Ardennes Offensive

From September 1944 Hitler had it in his mind to launch an offensive in the west that would cripple the Allied advance into Germany from that direction. He hoped that the offensive would do so much damage that 'this artificially bolstered common front may collapse with a mighty clap of thunder'. Orders were issued from Hitler's HQ at Rastenburg in East Prussia for the attack to begin in November but bad weather forced its postponement.

Above: A Latvian volunteer police unit. The German officers are members of the Ordnungspolizei as can be seen from their armshields and the brown cuffs on their tunics. Although uniform detail dates this image before 1944 it was men such as these who transferred to the Baltic Waffen-SS divisions later in the war.

Finally, on 16 December, Operation 'Autumn Fog', better known to history as the Battle of the Bulge, began. In order to oversee matters more thoroughly Hitler moved his HQ to the west, forgetting that three months earlier he had predicted that, 'If I leave East Prussia then East Prussia will fall. As long as I am here, it will be held.' The target of 'Autumn Fog' was the port of Antwerp. Antwerp was beyond the reach of the Wehrmacht's Western Front despite it having received the lion's share of the Reich's faltering munitions output including 640 Panther tanks and jet aircraft to reach this objective.

Despite its initial successes 'Autumn Fog' failed to achieve even its immediate goals in the field, let alone its long-term political ambitions of shattering the East–West alliance. By the end of the year, 120,000 men, 600 tanks and guns and some 1,600 aircraft had been lost — the last reserve of the Third Reich was spent.

The Chief of the General Staff, General Heinz Guderian, drove from his HQ at Zossen, south of Berlin, to see Hitler in person to plead for the offensive to be called off. When presented with figures on the Soviet build-up Hitler's response was typically histrionic, 'It's the greatest imposture since Ghengis Khan . . . who's responsible for producing this rubbish?' Amongst the 'rubbish' was the date, 12 January, on which German intelligence believed the Soviet offensive would begin. Himmler dutifully supported his master with the words to Guderian, 'You know my dear colonel-general, I don't believe the Russians will attack at all. It's all an enormous bluff.' Guderian had suggested on 24 December, 'It was necessary to change direction and face east once again before it was too late.' But this was not to be.

A week later, when the western offensive had clearly failed, Guderian visited Hitler once more to argue the case for reinforcing the Eastern Front. In discussions with Jodl, Hitler's sycophantic chief of operations, Guderian was reminded of the Führer's words, 'We can always give ground in the East, but never in the West.' Guderian returned to Zossen from where he would set out in early January to 'talk to the various commanders in chief on the spot, to see if they could give me any assistance, and form a clear opinion of our future prospects'.

Over on the Soviet side of the front the prospects were daily becoming cheerier as men and supplies arrived in ever-increasing numbers. To quote Stalin, 'If we judge not by the boastful utterances of the German propagandists, but by the actual position of Germany . . . the fascist invaders are now on the brink of disaster.'

And so they were. Only 12 months before, in late December 1943, Guderian could have travelled from Berlin to view the spires of Leningrad from the German siege lines. Now, following what Soviet historians later dubbed 'The Year of 10 Victories', the rubble of Warsaw was about as far to the east as any German observer could safely go.

Chapter 6

On to the Oder: January 1945

'It's the greatest imposture since Ghengis Khan . . .'
Hitler on the possibility of a Soviet offensive

Hungary

As the IV SS Panzer Corps (Gille) travelled towards Hungary consideration was given to the direction from which the relief operation should come. The Germans had two options. Attacking Budapest from the north meant a shorter route but through wooded, hilly country not well suited for armoured operations. The southern axis, from Lake Balaton, was longer but the ground was better for open warfare and success offered the chance to split Tolbukhin's 3rd Ukrainian Front in two. Hitler decided on the northern route as he favoured a speedy victory. As the city had been designated a fortress the garrison was not allowed to attempt a break-out and had to wait patiently until help arrived.

IV SS Panzer Corps began its first attempt to relieve the garrison of Budapest at 22:30 hours on New Year's Day 1945 under the code name of Operation 'Konrad'. For three days Gille's armour pushed ahead, covering some 40–48km (25–30 miles) and taking its first objective, the road and rail junction at Biscke halfway to Budapest.

Tolbukhin, commanding the external ring around Budapest, moved four corps to bolster the units being pushed back by the SS. Malinovsky was ordered to counter-attack with Sixth Guards Tank Army leading off in the direction of the main German base at Komarno. As the relief force battered its way along the southern bank of the Danube, the Soviets advanced along the opposite shore. Sixth Guards Tank Army launched a fierce attack supported by the infantry of Seventh Guards Army with the intention of crossing the Danube and working its way into the rear of the SS units. Tolbukhin was to push armour towards Komarno to complete the encirclement.

On 6 January Malinovsky's Guardsmen forced a crossing of the Danube tributary the Hron and gained a bridgehead, which they attempted to expand during the course of the morning. Blocked by German reserves, the Guards now found they were in danger of encirclement and the counter-attack bogged down. At the same time three armoured divisions of III Panzer Corps began an attack to join up with the SS at Biscke. However, in four days of desperate fighting the Soviets stopped this German thrust and inflicted heavy casualties, forcing III Panzer Corps back to its start line. With the northern route blocked, Gille was ordered to alter his axis of attack and, disengaging the *Wiking* division, withdrew to begin again. The move caught the Soviets off balance and by 12 January the division was within 23km (14 miles) of Budapest. At that point the Germans were held and Gille ordered his men to pull back as their position was under threat and the moment when a break-out attack by the garrison might have succeeded had passed. IV SS Panzer Corps was completely disengaged and entrained to attempt the relief operation from the south. Inside the city the armoured formations were to waste away, condemned by Hitler's stand-fast order, fighting in the ruined streets until their fuel ran out.

Under Siege

By the end of December the city's defenders had fallen back to a line that ran for about 8km (5 miles) from the Danube on the Pest side and to one of similar length in Buda. The key points in the latter were the Rose, Eagle and Schwabian hills and the Farkasret cemetery.

The first Soviet attacks were concentrated in Buda where the semicircle of defences roughly followed a railway embankment. Luckily for the defenders the early attacks were held by reserves rushed across from Pest. While the Soviets paused to reorganise themselves, civilians were mobilised to dig trenches and strongpoints on the hills. As rapidly as possible the large houses and government buildings that dotted the area were fortified and garrisoned with artillery and machine-gun groups. Behind such points mobile groups of assault guns and infantry waited to seal off any Soviet break-throughs. As far as possible foodstuffs were removed from the buildings but it became policy to leave alcohol in the hopes that the Soviet infantry would drink themselves into a stupor thus creating a favourable opportunity for counter-attacks after a suitable time had elapsed. Buda's population took to their cellars or sought refuge in the warren of caves and tunnels that ran through the limestone beneath Castle Hill

Above: A river gunboat of one of the Soviet Navy's inland waterways flotillas covers the landing stage at one of the crossing points on the Vistula River. These flotillas provided invaluable support on the great rivers of Eastern Europe during the last year of the war and operated a wide variety of craft as well as providing naval units for land operations.

Above: The destruction of bridges and drainage systems coupled with the underdeveloped infrastructure in eastern and central Europe generally led to the Red Army improvising crossing points such as the one shown here. A pair of jeeps make their way slowly across a waterway in Hungary. The variety of clothing worn by the men near the camera is of interest for its lack of uniformity.

infiltrated the Soviet lines to eliminate one broadcasting unit manned by collaborators.

As the airport had been captured in late December the racecourse in Pest had been commandeered as an airstrip and provided with a heavy ring of defences including an artillery brigade. However, the racecourse was overrun on 12 January. The only suitable place for aircraft was now the park below Castle Hill. The engineers cleared trees and bushes to create a 750-metre (820-yard) landing strip, which rapidly gained the nickname 'Bloody Meadow' for obvious reasons. It was soon littered with the remains of gliders as the Soviet artillery designated it a priority target. Many of the gliders, which operated at night, were piloted by members of the Hitler Youth's air section, most of whom accomplished no more than one flight. Covering fire for these in-bound flights was provided by anti-aircraft guns on Castle Hill and Margit Island as Soviet fighters were wont to strafe the airfield whenever the opportunity presented itself.

The garrison alone required 80 tons of supplies per day, a target beyond the Luftwaffe's capabilities, so efforts were made to ship munitions in along the Danube on barges. This method was relatively successful until the river froze.

Early in the siege Malinovsky had given several Romanian and Soviet infantry units the task of taking Budapest. When it became clear that the garrison was not going to surrender or the city be taken swiftly off the march this group was reorganised under the command of General I. M. Afonin and titled the Budapest Battle Group. Buda was a difficult area in which to fight therefore Pest was to be the first objective. Regiments were allotted zones of attack often no wider than 200 metres (220 yards) and heavy artillery was to be held in close proximity simply to smash anything in the way. If necessary Pest would be taken house by house even if this meant demolishing them all.

Afonin was given two days to break through the defences and reach the Danube by means of a two-pronged attack that would split the enemy. Soviet and Romanian infantry moved up both sides of the streets by blowing holes in the buildings and thus avoiding the German and Hungarian fields of fire in the open. The larger buildings were to be heavily bombed and shelled prior to the attack. The operation began on 12 January and very quickly the racecourse was taken; elsewhere the Soviets also advanced with German and Hungarian armour being destroyed where it stood, having run out of fuel and ammunition. On the flanks, fighting revolved around the Eastern and Western railway stations. Underground in the sewers a *Rattenkrieg*, 'rat's war', was waged by groups

which dominated the city. Here they huddled side by side with the wounded who were brought to the hospitals that had been established underground. Conditions for both civilians and soldiers deteriorated rapidly as the winter was bitter and water pipes froze if they still operated at all.

Across the river in Pest the front line followed another elevated railway embankment but was generally flatter, with factories dominating the landscape. Amongst them were munitions plants that continued to turn out weapons until they were flattened by Soviet artillery or ran out of raw materials. It was also the location of the Jewish ghetto.

As well as maintaining an almost continual artillery and aerial bombardment of the city, the Soviets waged a propaganda campaign to undermine the civilians' and soldiers' morale. Thousands of leaflets were dropped and loudspeakers trumpeted messages of hope if they gave up and despair if they refused. Radio links with the relief force were monitored and commented upon by the Soviets who countered every positive announcement with one that contradicted it. Parallels with Stalingrad were drawn, one declaring that, 'The black ravens are flying from Stalingrad . . .' obviously in search of a good meal. Hungarian paramilitaries

Above: A good frost has solidified the ground enabling the use of a Finnish *akjas*, a boat shaped sledge, by this German infantry section. Equally useful over mud or snow, the *akjas* was typical of the simple technology that the Wehrmacht lacked during the first winter of the war in the east.

and aircraft mowed down hundreds in the traffic jams. Soviet machine-gun teams at the mouths of the sewers added to the carnage as did infantry who found good cover on the roofs of shattered buildings. Leaderless groups of Hungarian and German soldiers wandered around in a daze and were rounded up to be marched to the rear while only metres away their former comrades battled to gain time for others to cross to the apparent safety of Buda. Finally the order to blow the bridges was given. However, the Hungarian officer on the spot refused permission for this, declaring the bridges to be of historical significance and claiming that the ice on the river was thick enough for tanks to cross in any case. Responding that this was no time for history, the Germans destroyed the bridges during the night of 17/18 January. The remaining

of Hungarian municipal workers and Soviet infantry including marines of the Danube Flotilla. In this surreal, foetid atmosphere, where every bend or shadow could mean ambush, small units of men battled to gain or deny access to the river bank. To the sound of gunfire and the explosions of grenades and with the occasional searing blast of a flame-thrower to light their way the Soviets pushed inexorably forward. At times these men would emerge simply to breathe fresh air or to take a prisoner for interrogation. If the Soviets captured Panzerfaust anti-tank weapons they were used to blast through walls or take out machine-gun nests. Throughout 14 January the Hungarians and Romanians fought their own battle for the Eastern Railway station. When it fell on 16 January Malinovsky withdrew the Romanians as their presence had motivated the Hungarians to fight harder than they would have, such was the hatred between the two nationalities. On the same day the Western Station was captured and the Soviets were within 1,000 metres (1,100 yards) of the Danube where fanatical members of the Arrow Cross were murdering Jews as fast as possible.

On 15 January *Stavka*, reacting to the renewed German offensive, made Malinovsky solely responsible for the reduction of Budapest. Simultaneously Hitler agreed to allow the garrison of Pest to retire across the Danube. Now soldiers, civilians and paramilitaries poured into the tiny enclave around the bridges into Buda. A frantic stream of humanity tried to cross; vehicles drawn by terrified horses got caught up with the few vehicles with fuel; and Soviet mortars

Above: A snow covered KV-1 heavy tank taken by the Germans in Hungary. This is an early model with a welded turret, many continued to serve until the end of the war as the type was well armoured and armed.

defenders of Pest, isolated and with no hope of rescue, surrendered that night and Afonin announced that the fighting there was over.

The next task was to clear Margit Island. Formerly a fashionable resort of cafes and baths, this 250-metre (270-yard) wide, 1,000-metre (1,100-yard) long, strip of land was heavily fortified and provided one of the few spots where air drops of supplies could fall as well as providing anti-aircraft covering fire for 'Bloody Meadow'. The mixed garrison held out for a short time, blowing the remaining half of its bridge before it too surrendered. Buda now stood alone.

To the south of Budapest the relief column had made remarkable progress. On the same day that Pest surrendered, Gille's IV SS Panzer Corps had begun its third attack. Carving its way through a Soviet infantry corps, it covered 32km (20 miles) on the first day. This success was followed by the destruction of VII Mechanised Corps; two other units were pushed into the gap but failed to make progress and, on 19 January, Tolbukhin discussed the possibility of withdrawing to the

Above: Soviet infantry advancing past an abandoned tram in Budapest. The public transport system continued operating under increasingly difficult conditions during the siege.

Above: The original caption reads, 'Sergeant Manakov of the 145th Infantry Regiment in Budapest. The sergeant killed 50 Germans and destroyed seven gun emplacements.' Manakov is armed with a ROKS 2 flame-thrower which had a range of more than 50 metres (55 yards) and was an important weapon in street fighting.

Danube as his front was now split and in danger of collapse. Ironically, at roughly the same time, the Hungarian delegation in Moscow was signing the armistice.

Tolbukhin was instructed to remain on the defensive, orders transferring units from 3rd Ukrainian Front to Malinovsky's were cancelled and Tolbukhin concentrated his forces on staving off the threat to the Danube crossing points and supply line posed by the German advance which had now been joined by III Panzer Corps. By 23 January the reconnaissance battalion of 1st Panzer Division had reached the Danube and the main body of the relief force was within 24km (15 miles) of the city. However, not all the German tank formations were experiencing such rapid progress. Heavy Tank Battalion 509, operating Tiger IIs, was finding almost any movement difficult due to the unsuitable conditions. Virtually every bridge had to be reinforced to take the Tigers' 70-ton bulk, and

the snow-covered ground forced them to stick to the roads necessitating the establishment of 'Tiger routes'.

With the sound of battle clearly audible on Castle Hill, Pfeffer-Wildenbruch radioed a message encouraging the Panzer troops to make one last effort and ending with the words, '10,000 of our wounded are waiting'. This was followed by a request to Hitler for permission to break out but again this was denied. Morale in the city was raised, but it was momentary. Already Soviet troops were moving into position; V Guards Cavalry Corps rode for 24 hours covering 105km (65 miles) and, along with other formations, stopped the German armour. With the lead units of the relief force now dangerously exposed to a counter-attack, Operation 'Konrad' was called off on 28 January. The reports submitted by Balck at the end of January noted the strength of IV SS Panzer Corps' two armoured divisions as 23 operational tanks. Wohler, AGS commander, reported that Gille was 'not corps commander materiel . . . staff work at the corps HQ is poor . . . command and control is insufficient . . . he is very brave . . .' Bravery was simply not enough.

Morale in Budapest plummeted to rock bottom, as rumour became fact and Malinovsky organised his forces to administer the *coup de grâce*. With his 2nd Ukrainian Front facing three ways, into Buda, towards the north-west and into Slovakia this was not a simple matter.

Above: This Tiger II (Royal or King Tiger) shown here on a misty street in Budapest has the later Henschel turret and a liberal coating of Zimmerit. The front glacis armour plate was 150mm (6 inches) thick and set at 40 degrees to the vertical, a feature derived from the Panther. The crewman is removing the gun's dust cover from the muzzle brake.

Hitler's Plans

Competence or the lack of it was not something that Hitler recognised in himself. Convinced of his own military genius, despite the evidence of the maps that he studied daily, the Führer now proceeded to rake over the ashes of his shrinking empire for the resources to launch yet another offensive in Hungary. The near splitting of 3rd Ukrainian Front achieved by III Panzer Corps and the SS had inspired Hitler to try again in the same location but this time on a more grandiose scale. This time not only would the Hungarian oil fields and refineries be secured and Budapest relieved almost *en passant* but also the southern flank of the Red Army would be scattered and pushed back to the Danube and beyond. This would involve a far greater force than before. And which formation was better to lead it than Sixth SS Panzer Army under Hitler's former bodyguard commander Oberstgruppenführer Josef 'Sepp' Dietrich?

Slovakia

In Slovakia Petrov's 4th Ukrainian Front continued its slogging. It had been anticipated that support from Malinovsky to the south would have broken what almost amounted to an impasse in this region but the German offensive towards Budapest had diverted Sixth Guards Tank Army from this task. Furthermore, the cavalry group sent by Malinovsky had to be withdrawn after it suffered heavy casualties. Thick snow now added to the problems of the Red Army as it followed the Wehrmacht's line of retreat along roads that had been mined or purposely torn up by heavy vehicles. As the Germans fell back into the Little Carpathian Mountains their rearguards were able to stand for longer and the fighting soon lapsed into stalemate. The Soviet supply lines in Slovakia were in desperate need of improvement and the men and animals were crying out for a rest. Furthermore, Petrov was instructed to prepare his Thirty-Eighth Army for a supporting role in Konev's attack on Cracow (Krakow). Indeed Petrov's apparently lacklustre performance in Slovakia had not gone unnoticed in Moscow. *Stavka* was only prepared to tolerate a certain degree of sluggishness before it intervened. As 4th Ukrainian Front approached the border with Germany's Czech protectorate, Bohemia-Moravia, Petrov would be given one more chance to prove his competence.

Above: Josef 'Sepp' Dietrich in conversation with two senior officers during 1944. As commander of Sixth SS Panzer Army in Hungary Dietrich was unable to hold the Red Army's advance. On the sleeve of his camouflage jacket is the rank badge that shows him to be an Obergruppenführer (SS general). After the war Dietrich was arrested and imprisoned for a time for war crimes. He died in 1966.

Dietrich was summoned to a meeting with Hitler and informed of his part in the upcoming operation in mid-January. At that time Sixth SS Panzer Army was resting and refitting in Germany after taking part in the Battle of the Bulge and was expected to take delivery of a large share of what was almost the last production run of tanks and armoured vehicles. When Sixth SS Panzer Army was combined with units from Army Group South (Wohler), Army Group E (Löhr) in northern Yugoslavia, Sixth Army (Balck), and various Hungarian units the striking force would number ten armoured and five infantry divisions. The offensive's code name was Operation 'Spring Awakening'. 'Spring Awakening' would be preceded, in mid-February, by Operation 'South Wind', which was to clear the Soviet bridgeheads over the Hron River near Komarno. But, as Hitler dreamed of glory and oil wells, other more lucid minds attempted to drag him back to the realities of East Prussia and Poland where the front was collapsing, as Guderian had predicted, 'like a house of cards'.

Above: By the early months of 1944 the Panzer III had become ineffective in combat. Those that remained in service were converted to less dangerous roles, such as this command version. Equipped with a dummy gun and a powerful communications system, they remained in service with the Panzer divisions until the end of the war. The usual side armour for the turret can be seen here.

East Prussia and Poland

Following his tour of the front commanders in early January Guderian travelled once more to see Hitler and plead his case that more troops be sent to the Eastern Front. It was a futile exercise, and, with arguments and protestations dismissed out of hand, Guderian returned to Zossen. On 11 January the Germans intercepted an ominous message declaring, 'Everything ready . . .' Truly the Soviets were ready and on an awesome scale.

To facilitate the reinforcement of Zhukov's and Konev's fronts over 20,000 lorries had operated day and night catching in their headlights labour battalions working to clear the snow from the roads or camouflage the mountains of munitions that were pouring into the assembly areas. To add to this Herculean labour 2,000 trains delivered ammunition, tanks, and food by the wagonload along tracks that had only recently been rebuilt. By the middle of January over 2,000,000 tons of supplies had been deposited to ensure that all was in place. Such movements can hardly have gone unnoticed by the German intelligence services but there was little that they could do beyond reporting their sightings with a mounting sense of impending doom. Even had the weather been more clement the Luftwaffe was now so short of aviation fuel that mounting a bombing mission was almost beyond it. Fending off the bombing raids over the Reich and supplying Budapest were adjudged higher priorities.

But fine targets there were. 1st Belorussian Front's bridgehead at Magnuszew only measured 169 square kilometres (105 sq miles) and into this Zhukov had packed 400,000 men and 1,700 tanks and self-propelled guns along with hundreds of pieces of artillery and other vehicles. The bridgehead of Konev's 1st Ukrainian Front at 4,650sq km (1,800sq miles) was relatively spacious and was serviced by 30 bridges and three ferries. To add to the Germans' worries a grand *maskirovka* of 400 dummy tanks and 1,000 fake guns 'advertised', as Konev said, a false line of attack from his left flank towards Cracow. While the Soviet troops enjoyed a relatively peaceful winter in their trenches their German opposite numbers must have passed a less than carefree holiday season. A Soviet infantry veteran remembered this as a very quiet time spent in the warmth of his dugout, 'making up for lost sleep, examining the weapons for any possible faults . . . there was no training of any kind . . .'

Between them Zhukov and Konev controlled 2,000,000 men, 32,000 guns and heavy mortars, almost 6,500 armoured fighting vehicles and 4,800 aircraft spread along a front of little more than 500km (310 miles).

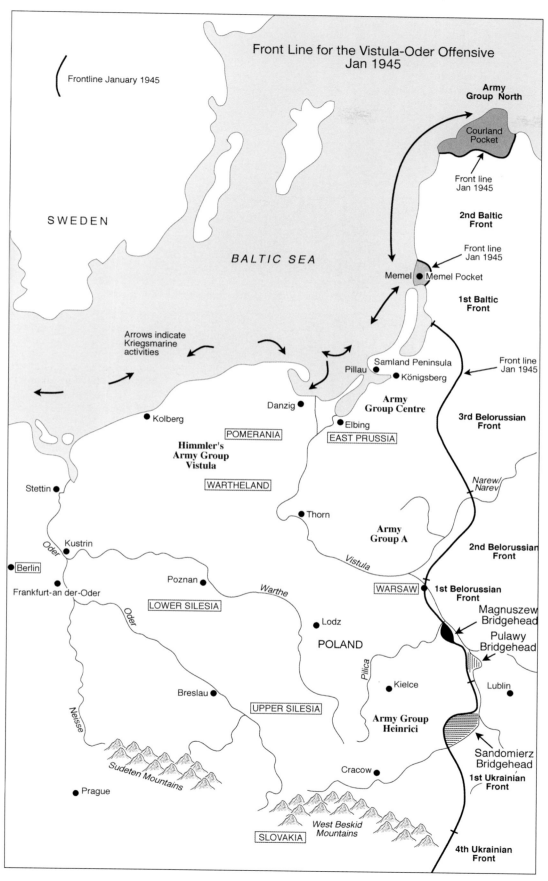

Front Line for the Vistula-Oder Offensive
Jan 1945

Frontline January 1945

SWEDEN

BALTIC SEA

Army Group North

Courland Pocket

Front line Jan 1945

2nd Baltic Front

Front line Jan 1945

Memel ● Memel Pocket

1st Baltic Front

Arrows indicate Kriegsmarine activities

Samland Peninsula

Pillau ●
● Königsberg

Front line Jan 1945

3rd Belorussian Front

Army Group Centre

Danzig ●

● Kolberg

● Elbing

EAST PRUSSIA

POMERANIA

Himmler's Army Group Vistula

WARTHELAND

Narew/ Narev

Stettin ●

● Thorn

Army Group A

2nd Belorussian Front

Oder

Kustrin ●

Vistula

● Berlin

WARSAW ● 1st Belorussian Front

Frankfurt-an der-Oder ●

Poznan ●

Warthe

Magnuszew Bridgehead

LOWER SILESIA

● Lodz

Oder

Pulawy Bridgehead

POLAND

Pilica

Lublin ●

Neisse

Breslau ●

UPPER SILESIA

● Kielce

Army Group Heinrici

Sandomierz Bridgehead

1st Ukrainian Front

Sudeten Mountains

● Cracow

● Prague

West Beskid Mountains

SLOVAKIA

4th Ukrainian Front

Above: Soviet T-34/85 tanks and infantry go into the attack in Poland in January 1945. The tank to the left has been disabled.

Above: East Prussia was the scene of heavy fighting in early 1945. The dense woods provided the defenders with excellent cover and plentiful scope for ambushes. Here a pair of T-34s move forward closely supported by the infantry.

Facing them to the south of Warsaw was Army Group A (General J. Harpe) with roughly 1,000 tanks and assault guns, 400,000 infantry, 240 aircraft and 2,500 guns and behind this meagre force were few reserves. Holding the line from north of Warsaw to the Baltic coast was Army Group Centre (General Reinhardt) with over 500,000 men, 700 armoured vehicles and 500 aircraft. The disparity in armour reflected the heavily fortified nature of East Prussia, which with its forests and lakes was poor tank country.

On 9 January Konev was given warning that his attack would begin three days later. His major concern was that the weather would improve and allow the good air support that was no longer the luxury it had once been for the Red Army.

1st Ukrainian Front

At 05:00 hours on 12 January Konev's artillery opened fire. The first step on the road to Breslau was about to be taken. The frontage of the attack was narrow at 32km (20 miles) but into this lane would be packed Thirteenth, Fifty-Second and Fifth Guards Armies, followed by three tank corps. Fourth Tank Army would head north-westwards to co-operate with Zhukov's thrust and Third Guards Tank Army would break through to prevent the Germans consolidating any defences along the various rivers in the region. Battered by over 250 guns per kilometre, the German defences were subjected to a terrible pounding, which then stopped. As the German infantry peered into no-man's-land they were greeted not with the usual Soviet reconnaissance attack but a full-scale infantry assault with the punishment battalions taking heavy casualties as they were sacrificed in the minefields. Within a few minutes the first German line had fallen as wave upon wave of

Soviet infantry flowed over their shell-shocked opponents who barely had time to clean the dust from their weapons before they were shot down or had the presence of mind to surrender. Orders were issued not to touch anything or hunt for souvenirs as the Germans had a nasty habit of booby-trapping items that might be worthwhile trophies.

Once more the Soviet artillery opened fire and amongst the victims of this second barrage was the command post of the Fourth Panzer Army along with many of the reserves that Hitler had insisted be kept close to the front line. As the morning drew on and the snow fell steadily Konev ordered his tanks into action. Whitewashed with Ukrainian chalk, the Soviet tanks moved off. By the end of the first day Konev's troops had broken into the German lines to a depth of 19km (12 miles) along a 40km (25-mile) front and the T-34s were moving deeper into the German rear. However, a counter-attack was already in preparation that aimed to cut off the head of

Above: Killed in action. Two of the three-man team that served the 81mm mortar lie beside their weapon. Given the amount of ammunition available, the mortar was probably pressed into service with the Red Army.

the Soviet advance. The stage was being set for one of the biggest tank engagements since the Battle of Kursk, but this time the setting was the snowy forests of Poland.

The Battle of Kielce

The German formation given this onerous task was XXIV Panzer Corps (General W. Nehring) which was composed of 16th and 17th Panzer Divisions and 20th Panzergrenadier Division; together these had over 250 tanks and assault guns including a battalion of 60 Panther tanks. Attached to this force was Heavy Tank Battalion 424 which was equipped with 45 Tiger II tanks and a number of Tiger Is. These units were ordered to assemble around the town of Kielce.

Lelyushenko, commanding Fourth Guards Tank Army, was informed that two German tank columns were converging on Kielce. An attack was planned in co-ordination with Third Guards Tank Army that would hit the Germans before they had mustered their entire force. As the Germans moved towards their jump-off positions they found some to be occupied by Soviet units. Advanced companies of two Soviet tank formations, which had dealt with the artillery of 17th Panzer Division in the process, had captured the village of Lissow. The Soviet commander decided to hold the position and await further orders, digging in his T-34/85s and anti-tank guns as a precaution. While this was going on 16th and 17th Panzer Divisions came under flank attack. As the Germans attempted to create some sort of order out of the chaos that was fast engulfing them Heavy Battalion 424 was ordered to recapture Lissow. After a short

bombardment the Tigers advanced. Very quickly they were in trouble when a bridge collapsed and several of these immense vehicles attempting to cross the part-frozen stream wallowed and stuck fast in the mud that they churned up. Now under fire from the concealed anti-tank guns and T-34s, the Germans realised that Lissow was not an easy target. Nevertheless their battalion commander pressed on with his attacks despite the solidity of the defence and the

limited space in which his tanks could manoeuvre. The buildings of the village and the shell holes caused the Tiger drivers to move in low gear so presenting the concealed Soviet gunners with excellent targets. And although the Tiger II was armed with an excellent gun the vehicle itself was 6 metres (7 yards) long and therefore hardly an asset in a built-up area. It is possible that the Soviets deployed a company of five IS-2 heavy tanks and some of the recently introduced SU-100 tank destroyers. These latter were similar to German assault guns but more heavily armed, in this case with a 100mm gun and designed specifically for tank hunting.

During the course of the next few hours the fighting swirled around the village, with both sides losing their commanding officers. The Soviet right flank was breached but a timely counter-attack restored the situation. Late in the evening Soviet reinforcements arrived and the Germans withdrew leaving 35 wrecked tanks on the battlefield.

By 16 January, after three days of confused fighting, the German mobile reserve had been shattered and Kielce taken. Forced into action prematurely by the Soviet attacks and let down by poor reconnaissance at Lissow, XXIV Panzer Corps had almost ceased to exist as a cohesive force. Even if the Soviet armoured losses were greater, they were in possession of the battlefield and able to recover their damaged vehicles; the Germans simply had to write theirs off.

During the night of 13 January Hitler had issued orders for the *Grossdeutschland* Panzer Corps in East Prussia to move to Kielce in

Above: Heavily laden men of the Belgian 28th Waffen-SS Division *Wallonie* arrive at the Oder front. Under their camouflage smocks they appear to be wearing their greatcoats for extra warmth.

support of the counter-offensive there. Guderian protested, logically, that to weaken Army Group Centre at this point would be foolish and that by the time *Grossdeutschland* arrived in Poland it would be too late to affect the issue. While the decision hung in the air *Grossdeutschland*'s men and machines waited in their railway trains. Inevitably Hitler got his own way and part of the corps moved south, arriving to join up with XXIV Panzer Corps almost a week later, by which time the situation had changed out of all recognition. But by that time Hitler had returned to Berlin and was already immersed in his plans for the Hungarian operations.

The remnants of XXIV Panzer Corps had made a last attempt to recapture Kielce but this came to nothing. With his right flank now secure, Konev could unleash his armoured units out into open country. Rybalko's Third Guards Tank Army was supported by Fifth Guards Army. Driving hard and brushing aside anything that got in their way, they reached Cracow just as the German evacuation was almost complete. To the south of Cracow other formations of Army Group A were also pulling back to avoid envelopment as 4th Ukrainian Front's contribution to the offensive began to advance into their rear. By 20 January, with Cracow in Soviet hands, the way was now open for 1st Ukrainian Front to press on to the Oder River. Several infantry corps would be used to surround the Upper Silesian industrial region, Stalin's 'gold', while the tanks and mechanised forces would keep the Germans on the move. Speed was now of the essence as *Stavka* had ordered Konev to aim his main thrust towards Breslau and reach the Oder by no later than 30 January. As the Soviet ring around Silesia tightened, German industrialists appealed to the Wehrmacht to supply them with security troops as they were concerned that the foreign workers in the factories would stage an uprising.

On 20 January the first of Konev's men crossed the frontier into the Third Reich to be rapidly followed by others across a wide front. Two days later units of Fifth Guards Army reached the banks of the Oder, crossed and established a bridgehead. During the course of the next few days other units reached the eastern bank of the river but were unable to cross it. With the Soviets pouring into Germany itself, Guderian implored Hitler to allow him to use the forces released from the Ardennes and was informed that the Hungarian offensive was to get them. Guderian wrote that, 'On hearing this I lost my self-control and expressed my disgust to Jodl in very plain terms, but could get no response from him whatever, beyond a shrug of the shoulders.' The discussions of the merits or otherwise of the Hungarian

Above: The *Grossdeutschland* Panzergrenadier Division was the elite formation of the Heer. It was upgraded to a Panzer Corps in November 1944 but was nowhere near the strength implied by this title. The photo shows the reconnaissance battalion. Note the white helmet divisional sign and the heavy camouflage on the vehicles towards the rear.

offensive continued for several days but for Hitler there was no alternative. With the synthetic fuel plants reduced to ruins, his argument was straightforward and he couched it to Guderian in the following terms, 'If you don't get any more fuel your tanks won't be able to move . . . you must see that.' Black gold acted as as much of a lure for a fascist dictator as industrial gold did for a communist one.

Nor did Guderian's requests for the transfer of Army Group North from Courland prove any more fruitful. The bulk of those men would remain where they were, although some of 4th Panzer Division was evacuated during the following weeks. As if to compensate for the collapse of the Polish front Hitler decided that now would be a good time to rename the army groups in the east. Army Group North became Army Group Courland,

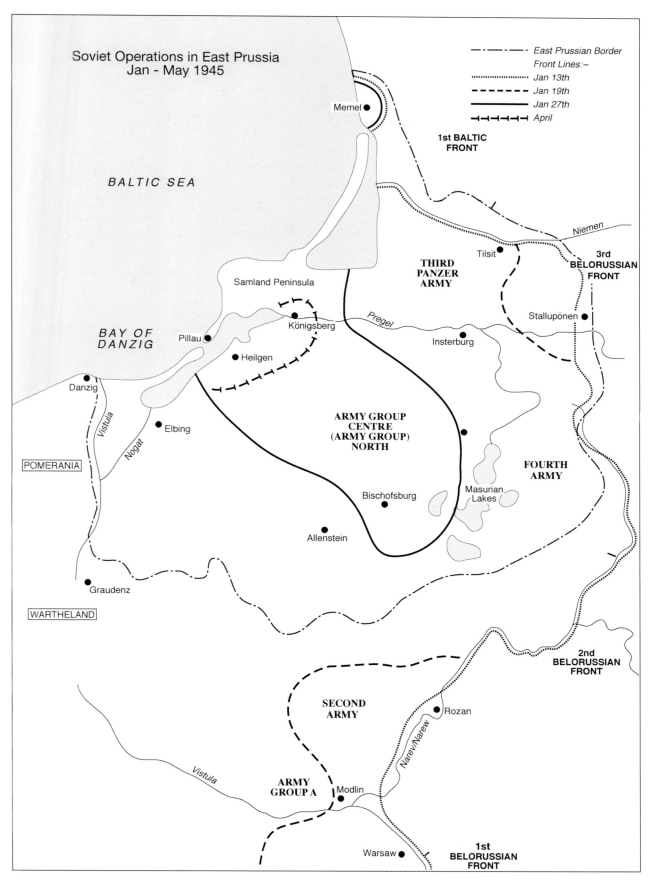

Soviet Operations in East Prussia
Jan - May 1945

	East Prussian Border
	Front Lines:—
	Jan 13th
	Jan 19th
	Jan 27th
	April

BALTIC SEA

Memel

1st BALTIC
FRONT

THIRD
PANZER
ARMY

Niemen

Tilsit

3rd
BELORUSSIAN
FRONT

Samland Peninsula

Stallupönen

Königsberg

Pregel

BAY OF
DANZIG

Pillau

Insterburg

Heilgen

Danzig

Vistula

ARMY GROUP
CENTRE
(ARMY GROUP)
NORTH

FOURTH
ARMY

Elbing

Nogat

Masurian
Lakes

POMERANIA

Bischofsburg

Allenstein

Graudenz

WARTHELAND

2nd
BELORUSSIAN
FRONT

SECOND
ARMY

Rozan

Narev/Narew

Vistula

ARMY
GROUP A

Modlin

1st
BELORUSSIAN
FRONT

Warsaw

Army Group Centre became Army Group North and Army Group A became Army Group Centre. With the change of names came a change of commanders. And now came Himmler's chance to prove his military prowess as he was given command of a brand new formation, Army Group Vistula, consisting of the remains of Second and Ninth Armies. For a man who had hardly ever fired a shot in anger it was quite a moment. Within hours of Himmler's elevation the Red Army discovered evidence of the Reichsführer's other talent, mass murder, when they liberated Auschwitz extermination camp.

3rd Belorussian Front

In common with all Soviet offensives from Stalingrad onwards, front attacks were staggered to create a ripple effect, generating uncertainty in their enemies regarding the commitment of reserves, Hitler's orders to the *Grossdeutschland* Panzer Corps being a case in point. Chernyakhovsky's mission in East Prussia was to push directly to the west smashing through the Tilsit–Insterburg (Sovetsk–Chernyakhovsk) defensive system and take Königsberg (Kaliningrad), the main port and capital of the province.

The defences were extensive and based on those constructed before and during World War 1 when the German Army intended to hold the Russians in this very area until victory in the west was achieved. Indeed the village of Tannenberg (Stebark) had lent its name to a crushing victory over the Russians in August 1914 inflicted by Hindenburg whose body was interred in a colossal monument nearby. Königsberg was well fortified as were several of the other towns and the 13 German infantry divisions with their Volkssturm auxiliaries were prepared to fight for every inch of their homeland. There were probably some amongst them who believed another Tannenberg was possible.

3rd Belorussian Front began its attack on 13 January leading off with a mighty barrage. But the rapid penetration enjoyed by Konev's forces was not to be repeated in East Prussia and an infantry slogging match ensued with heavy casualties on both sides. After three days' fighting the Soviet tanks were brought into action with air support previously unavailable due to the weather. Now reinforced with Forty-Third Army from 1st Baltic Front, the advance began in earnest and, on 18 January Pilkallen fell, followed 24 hours later by Tilsit, opening the way to Königsberg and outflanking the main German defence line to Insterburg. Nevertheless this was no race to the sea and 3rd Belorussian Front had to fight its way through line after line of German defences and the tangle of the Masurian Lakes and forests which were proving every bit as troublesome as they had in 1914. However, Chernyakhovsky did have the satisfaction of capturing the ruins of Hitler's eastern HQ at Rastenburg, the infamous 'Wolf's Lair'. But it was to be almost a month before Soviet troops ventured into the former heart of Hitler's war machine as the site was riddled with mines and booby traps. Slowly but surely the Germans were driven back on Königsberg and by late January 3rd Baltic Front was taking up positions around the city. This pocket measured 64km (40 miles) wide by 17km (12 miles) deep and contained the majority of Army Group Centre alongside hundreds of thousands of refugees. Having been prevented from taking the city by a spoiling attack from the west, Chernyakhovsky accepted the necessity of a longer campaign. Although their progress had been steady rather than spectacular, these troops had fulfilled their role during January's operations.

Other fronts would have to provide the headline advances.

2nd Belorussian Front

Rokossovsky's front was to break out from the Rozan and Serock bridgeheads and accomplish two tasks. The first was to co-operate with Chernyakhovsky in the conquest of East Prussia; the second was to cover the northern flank of Zhukov's 1st Belorussian Front as it advanced to the west.

Launching his offensive on the same day as Zhukov, Rokossovsky's main attack was to head to the north-west with one tank and four infantry armies. The usual barrage lasted for most of the day, possibly because of the quality of the Soviet infantry formations which had been filled up with former POWs, recent conscripts and men combed out from the rear services who were not as experienced or fit as those on other fronts. As Rokossovsky commented, 'When the artillery preparation ended, the brunt of the battle fell on the infantry.' Relatively little progress was made on the first day and when the Germans counter-attacked the next day they threatened to recapture what had been lost. Gorbatov's Third Army was the particular target for counter-attacks by elements of the *Grossdeutschland* Panzer Corps. Gorbatov himself recalled:

'We had decided to attack again at 09:00 hours, but the enemy prevented us. At 08:20 hours he laid down an artillery barrage . . . At 08:30 hours he then counter-attacked the troops which had got through his defences. In two hours seven counter-attacks were driven off. At mid-day the German Panzer divisions came into action. By evening we had had 37 counter-attacks. Fighting died down only at nightfall.'

An irony of combat in this area was that many of the defensive works through which the Soviet infantry were trying to advance were based around old tsarist fortifications

Above: A group of German refugees drag their few possessions through the snow in early 1945. The film recently shown at the Capitol cinema is the 1943 production *A Colleague Comes* and the Nazi sign indicates a building that was a meeting point for the wounded. Such groups were a common sight towards the war's end and facilities for them were often sadly lacking.

requesting permission to shorten his line to compensate for the loss of the majority of the *Grossdeutschland* Panzer Corps:

> 'Mein Führer, in my anxiety for the safety of East Prussia, I venture again to turn to you . . . Examination of a captured map reveals the Fifth Guards Tank Army, with four tank corps, is to make for Danzig . . . if the Guards Tank Army is able to force its way through we shall be caught in the rear: here we have no resources at all.'

He also requested permission to withdraw Fourth Army from its 'present exposed position' at Lötzen (Gizycko) in the Masurian Lakes. Hitler's response was a curt order to Reinhardt to make further use of the Volkssturm and hold his current position as the 4th Panzer Division was on its way by sea from Courland as were 20 infantry battalions from Denmark. These reinforcements would not arrive in time to salvage the immediate situation, as Reinhardt's information about the threat to his rear was all too accurate. Indeed Rokossovsky had only been informed of this move a day or so before.

Stavka had altered the line of advance for 2nd Belorussian Front to compensate for the lack of progress being made by Chernyakhovsky to the north-east. Fifth Guards Tank Army was now to head for Elbing (Elblag) roughly mid-way between Danzig (Gdansk) and Königsberg on the Baltic coast at the mouth of the Vistula River. The aim of this move was simply to cut AGC off from the rest of Germany. One of its consequences would be a reduction in the flank guards available to cover Zhukov's northern wing, forcing him to employ his own men for this vital task.

On 20 January Soviet Third Army crossed into East Prussia, storming the defences in front of Allenstein (Olsztyn) and opening the way for Fifth Guards Tanks to push ahead into relatively open country with a good road network. Piling their tanks high with fuel and other supplies and attendant infantry, the Guards, with a considerable number of Kursk veterans amongst them, prepared to advance towards the sea. Taking the war into Germany itself was the goal for which so many of these men had fought for years and that ambition was about to be realised. Their march to the sea began on 23 January.

Such an operation, surprise though it was to Rokossovsky and angering as it did Zhukov, was a product of Soviet pre-war military thinking which emphasised exploitation in depth of a break-through in an enemy's defences. The relevant wording in the regulations read:

Above: The forward guns of an unidentified German warship fire on targets around Königsberg. The Kriegsmarine's work evacuating troops and civilians and as floating artillery has received scant attention. How long the pockets in East Prussia and Courland would have survived without naval support is debatable.

designed to keep the Germans out of Russian Poland before 1914, doubtless a point not lost on Rokossovsky, himself a former soldier in the Imperial Russian Army and half-Polish.

Furious German counter-attacks did not prevent the Soviets from resuming their offensive on 16 January and this time, with the benefit of air support, a major break-through took place. By the end of that day Ciechanow, an important transport centre,

was in Soviet hands. Other breaches of the German lines followed swiftly and by 19 January 2nd Belorussian Front had broken through along a stretch measuring 97km (60 miles) to a depth of 56–64km (35–40 miles) and was almost in sight of the East Prussian border.

Caught between two fronts, Reinhardt, commanding Army Group Centre, contacted Hitler for the second time in three days

Above: One of the most common Soviet howitzers, the 122mm Model 1938 M-30, pictured here in its winter camouflage scheme. Note that the inside of the gun shield is painted as well. Although most of the Red Army's artillery was motorised by this stage of the war, the specification for this weapon still notes that it required a team of six horses. The gunners are all wearing gloves to protect their hands from exposure to the cold metal.

'. . . a bold pursuit. This is undertaken independently by tank and infantry units . . . The pursuit is pressed home with all possible vigour, all commanders exercising their initiative to the utmost. In the pursuit any waiting for flanking units to catch up is out of the question. By boldness of action the very smallest of infantry or tank elements may inflict a decisive defeat on the enemy.'

As Rokossovsky shifted his axis of attack, the Guards, commanded by General V. T. Volsky, raced off, as their special oath declared, 'to conquer'.

Spearheaded by a *perdovoi otriad* (forward detachment) of XXIX Tank Corps, a mixed force of tanks, infantry and self-propelled guns, the Guards carried all before them, allowing very few of the Volkssturm units time to muster let alone put up any sort of effective defence. In towns and villages Nazi officials were often discovered before they had time to destroy the evidence of past doings and were frequently shot out of hand. There is little doubt that many of the men of 2nd Belorussian Front committed atrocities as they sliced their way through the rear of AGC, details of which are documented elsewhere (see Introduction). In its wake the

Soviet advance had left a trail of German units that now had to choose between surrender, flight to the west or making their way into one of the fortified areas that Hitler was calling into being all over the region. Also to the Soviet rear was the forlorn monument to the Battle of Tannenberg, now reduced to a pile of shattered masonry by German engineers. Hindenburg's corpse had been shipped to safety, which was more than could be said for AGC which became Army Group North under the command of General L. Rendulic on 26 January. Rendulic had been ordered to hold Königsberg whatever the cost as Hitler dreaded the prospect of an alternative Soviet-sponsored government being established there.

During the early hours of 24 January the advanced guard of the Soviet attack burst into Elbing and drove through with headlights blazing to the coast at Frisches Haff (Zalew Vislany). By early the next day AGC had been isolated from the rest of the Wehrmacht. However, before Rokossovsky could consolidate the gossamer-thin strand of armour that ran to the seashore, the Germans

launched a counter-attack. In a move conceived before Reinhardt's tenure at AGC ended, one Panzer and seven infantry divisions struck at Forty-Eighth Army. During the last week of January the Germans made some progress in their battle to reach a bridgehead on the Vistula at Graudenz (Grudziadz). However, as more and more Soviet divisions moved into line their enemy's attacks petered out.

The refugee columns that had attached themselves to the German forces were now left to their own devices, to fend for themselves in the bitter winter with temperatures consistently below zero. Driven to despair by Goebbels's propaganda of the previous autumn and the evidence of their own eyes, they expected no mercy from the Red Army. Very few East Prussians stayed at home that winter. Scattering to the north and to the west they now underwent for the first time the effects of total war. It was not a pleasant experience. Until now, for most German civilians in this area, the war had been viewed from a comfortable seat in the local cinema.

But reality was not newsreel footage of a

smiling *Landser* (ordinary soldier) driving across the fields of a faraway country towards some smoking hovel or a town where dazed people stared in blank incomprehension at the Panzers in their streets. This was the Reich and the tanks were Soviet. Following the T-34s were infantrymen, a large number of whom had been brutalised by three years or more in POW camps where the guards placed bets on who would survive the scramble for food or be reduced to cannibalism. There were few, if any, glamorous Luftwaffe pilots flying overhead to combat the dreaded *Shturmovik* ground-attack aircraft that shot up anything that moved. Life did not mirror art in early 1945.

1st Belorussian Front

The targets for 1st Belorussian Front were Lódz then Posen, to which were allotted four infantry and two tank armies that would break out from the Magnuszew bridgehead. Included amongst these was the veteran Eighth Guards Army (General Chuikov) of Stalingrad fame. The operation would be launched across a narrow front of 17km (10 miles) into which three infantry armies, Fifth, Eighth Guards and Sixty-First would be poured to rupture the German defences. When this was accomplished First and Second Guards Tank Armies would be inserted to exploit the gap, push towards Lódz and cut off the German retreat from Warsaw.

From the Pulawy bridgehead two armies, Thirty-Third and Sixty-Ninth, supported by two armoured corps, would cover the southern flank and co-operate with Konev while moving on Lódz. The ruins of Warsaw were to be liberated by First Polish Army.

The barrage from the Magnuszew positions lasted a mere 25 minutes and was followed by such a powerful infantry attack that the German first line collapsed in a remarkably short time. By the middle of the day Zhukov's tanks were in action and very soon Second Guards Tank Army captured a bridge capable of taking the heaviest of vehicles. As night fell at about 18:00 hours the Soviets were 32–48km (20–30 miles) inside the German lines.

The attack from Pulawy began the next day and was preceded by a longer bombardment. In a matter of hours the German defences around Warsaw were in danger of collapse. Despite its fortress designation Warsaw had a garrison of less than an infantry division which began to withdraw on 17 January. Simultaneously Polish infantry crossed the Vistula River from Praga.

Naturally Hitler was beside himself with rage and two days later arrested several members of Guderian's staff in an effort to find a scapegoat. Kaltenbrunner, head of the Reich's Central Security Office, intensively

Above: To provide the Panzer divisions with self-propelled heavy artillery the chassis of a Panzer IV was coupled with a 150mm howitzer to produce the Hummel (Bumble Bee). The official designation was SdKfz 165 and 666 were built in 1943–4. The bipod at the front supports the gun barrel when travelling.

questioned Guderian at his insistence, which ended the matter. The fall of Warsaw was recorded at OKH in Zossen by the turning off of the exchange's switchboard light for the Polish capital. Earlier in the war the huge communications centre at Zossen had lights for every major city from the Channel to the Volga River. By this stage of the war the few remaining lights indicated German cities.

Stalin received the news of Warsaw's liberation by ordering Zhukov to reach the Oder River by no later than 4 February. This was a reasonable instruction under the circumstances as there was virtually nothing in the way of 2nd Belorussian Front other than a mass of fleeing disorganised troops. Lódz had just fallen to Eighth Guards Army whose greatest danger seems to have been the Soviet bombers who mistook the advancing Guardsmen for Germans. Taking full advantage of the good road network of

western Poland and using frozen rivers where the Germans had demolished the bridges, Zhukov's armour pushed rapidly westwards. Defensive positions that showed fight were by-passed for the supporting infantry to deal with. Late in the month Posen was cut off and by 29 January much of Zhukov's command was within sight of Germany itself; the first bridgehead over the Oder River was gained the same day. Second Guards Tank Army reached the Oder on 31 January followed by other units the next day.

Memel Falls

The siege of Memel had dragged on through the winter. Thousands of civilians and soldiers, minus their heavy equipment, had been evacuated. Indeed, as one survivor, Guy Sajer, noted, 'The navy was performing a prodigious task. We would have been lost without it.' With the need to supply Army

Group Courland, Memel, and now the East Prussian pocket, the Kriegsmarine's resources were stretched to their utmost. The Soviets nibbled away at Memel's shrinking perimeter but did not seem in a hurry to take it. Virtually all the buildings had been destroyed so the civilians and soldiers were driven into the cellars or whatever cover remained overground. Shelled, bombed, sniped at, permanently hungry and cut through by the icy Baltic winds, evacuation was the dream of everyone that January. Inevitably the Volkssturm had been called out and the same veteran described them in the following terms:

'The oldest boys were about 16, but there were others who could not have been more than 13 . . . carrying guns which were often as big as they were . . . their eyes were filled with unease, like the eyes of children at the reopening of school . . . Several were carrying school satchels . . . The old men . . . stared at them with incomprehension.'

Finally, on 27 January, the agony of Memel came to an end.

The date 30 January 1945 marked 12 years of Nazi government in Germany and traditionally on that day Hitler broadcast to the Reich. 1945 was to be no exception but it was notable as the last occasion on which the Führer spoke to his people. Calling for fanatical resistance from both soldiers and civilians he predicted, 'In this struggle it will not be inner Asia that will conquer, but the people that has defended Europe for centuries against the onslaughts from the East, the German nation.' With refugees pouring into Berlin and points west, spreading tales of horror that were echoed and embellished by the Propaganda Ministry, there were few amongst Hitler's audience that took his speech seriously. Nor was it easy to believe Goebbels's outpourings as, until very recently, the fighting was supposedly still going on around Warsaw.

A monitored conversation between two senior officers, captured in the USSR two years before, encapsulated the truth of Germany's position. 'All Hitler thinks about is how to force the German people into new sacrifices. Never before in history has lying been such a powerful weapon in diplomacy and policy.' Speaking again he said, 'It is two years since the Stalingrad catastrophe, and now the whole of Germany is becoming a gigantic Stalingrad.' If any man could recognise the truth of the matter it was the last speaker, Field Marshal Paulus, the man that Hitler denied the opportunity to surrender and who had lost at Stalingrad.

Above: One of the workhorses of the Wehrmacht's armoured forces, a Panzer IV, burning and abandoned. The various upgrades of the Panzer IV ensured that it remained in service throughout 1939–45. This is a Mark H by the appearance of the drive wheel. The additional armour around the turret was a standard production feature after March 1943.

Above: An armoured column made up of Panzer IVs and headed by a Panzer V Panther makes its way along a wooded track in early 1945. The markings indicate that the SS Panzer Division *Das Reich* used the rearmost vehicle. However, when divisions were transferred from front to front during the latter war years, vehicles and tanks were sometimes left for replacement units to take over.

Chapter 7

The Fall of Budapest: February 1945

'Losses due to enemy action are enormous.'
German commandant of Budapest

'The appalling month of January', as Guderian so aptly described it, had ended with the Soviets having reached and crossed the Oder River and Army Group North cut off and requiring supplies to be shipped in. The creation of Himmler's Army Group Vistula (AGV) to fill the gap from AGN to the Warthe (Warta) River where it connected with Army Group Centre (AGC) was under way.

AGV reflected Hitler's lack of faith in the German Army and its leaders and therefore it was to be an almost exclusively SS force, staffed by SS officers, often cronies of Himmler who lacked any outstanding ability other than that of sycophancy. Units from all over Germany and from the less-endangered fronts were drafted in. Amongst them were one French and two Belgian SS infantry divisions. However, division was now a term rather than a reality as most of these units numbered fewer than 5,000 combat troops. Although they included a solid cadre of Eastern Front veterans, as often as not the ranks were padded with conscripted factory workers and refugees, usually from the appropriate ethnic background. With such troops being sent to the front line where their commitment would, it was hoped, stem the Soviet advance, the reserve formations were not of such high calibre. Included amongst them were a Dutch SS division recently shipped out of Courland, the remains of a Latvian division, a regiment of Russians, Romanian fascists and an Arab security company that had arrived from Greece. Officer and NCO training schools were turned out to fight in units that were divisions in name only. One such, composed of wounded and invalid SS men, was 32nd SS Grenadier Division *30 Januar*, named to commemorate the date on which Hitler came to power. Luftwaffe ground crew, sailors and others were all drafted in regardless of their specialisms, which were fast becoming worthless. Many of these new soldiers were told to get their weapons from the Volkssturm,

Above: German and Hungarian POWs are marched out of Budapest at the end of the siege in mid-February 1945. In the background are the remains of the Franz Josef Bridge (now the Liberty Bridge).

Above: The supply column of a Luftwaffe field division pause to inspect the road conditions. The majority of the men are wearing the M1942 white/field grey reversible winter tunic with trousers in the same style. They all appear to be well fed and have the air of men recently 'combed out'.

as shortages were now so acute. Second and Ninth Armies were also included in AGV's order of battle. Even Hitler's bodyguard regiment was committed to the front along with that of General Vlasov. Although the ROA men failed in their mission they acquitted themselves well, several earning Iron Crosses, no longer the exclusive preserve of Aryan troops, and a congratulatory telegram from Himmler to Vlasov noting that his guard had 'fought quite outstandingly well'.

The southern flank of AGV lay on the Warthe River line, which was held by a dozen Volkssturm battalions reinforced at the end of January by 21st SS Mountain Division *Skanderbeg* composed of Moslem Albanians. When 1st Ukrainian Front gained its first bridgeheads across the Oder it was decided to press on to the Warthe. The defences in this area had been built during the 1920s against the possibility of a Polish attack and were solidly constructed of concrete with good, clear fields of fire. Unfortunately the guns had all been transferred to the Atlantic Wall in 1943 and not replaced. When the Soviet attack began on 29 January it took two days to overrun these positions and reach the Warthe. Amongst the trophies gathered up by Konev's men were over 100 four-engined Fw 200 Kondor bombers which had been waiting for fuel before operating as a part of the U-boat support group. However, more importantly, the link between AGV and AGC was broken.

One of the units brought into being at this

Above: T-34/76s carry their infantry supports forward. The T-34 did not give a smooth ride for crew or passengers as it had a tendency to bounce violently when travelling over rough ground at anything more than a crawl.

time was the *Panzerjagd* (Tank Hunter) Division, which consisted of Hitler Youths and others who were to cycle around the countryside hunting Soviet tanks which they would destroy with the Panzerfausts each carried strapped to his front forks. The 'manpower' would be found as, on 5 February, Hitler had ordered that every German male over 16 was liable to conscription, as were all policemen under 50. The effect of this latter change was to increase the amount of looting, rape and black market activities. Ordinary people complained that

foreign workers, 'were becoming more abusive and lazy every day and that the streets were becoming unsafe'.

While his troops fought and died, the commander of AGV sat in his personal train composing orders of the day to encourage and enlighten them. In the manner of his Führer, Himmler was not given to encouraging his men by anything other than fear of retribution. In a document with the inspirational title of, 'Death and punishment for failure to carry out one's duty' the Reichsführer, clearly not a man imbued with 'personnel skills', threatened all and sundry with summary execution for not reporting for duty, withdrawal without permission and unaccounted loss of equipment. German women were forbidden to give food to retreating soldiers. Blocking detachments with almost God-like powers of life and death roamed the rear looking for stragglers to execute and soon the trees and lampposts within AGV's zone of command were decorated with the corpses of those who had not fulfilled their duty. However, to combat rumours about the uncontrolled migration of party officials (nicknamed 'Golden Pheasants' on account of their uniforms) who had ordered the citizens in their areas to remain behind, often under threat of death, a Burgomeister was executed for leaving his town 'without giving an evacuation order'.

Although Himmler had served in World War 1 he had been a clerk in the rear. His lunatic writings, his strutting and posturing and the executions in his name must have caused more than a few men in the sodden trenches to curse his name quietly under their breath that month. A more patriotic line was taken by men of the *30 Januar* Division when Soviet deserters presented them with a copy of *Pravda* outlining the arrangements for a conquered Germany: 'We simply have to win' was their response.

Counter-Attack: Operation 'Solstice'

During the first week of February there had been heavy fighting as the Soviets attempted to expand their Oder bridgeheads and the Germans tried to hold theirs on the opposite bank. Guderian, believing the time to be ripe for a counter-offensive, travelled to Berlin to broach the matter with Hitler. As a result of what he perceived as defeatist, traitorous, incompetent Wehrmacht generals, Hitler had issued a directive on the question of command in an attempt to clarify matters. The Supreme Commander of Germany's Armed Forces now made his senior officers from divisional commanders upwards:

'. . . personally responsible to me for reporting in good time:
Every decision to carry out an operational movement.
Every attack planned in divisional strength and upwards which does not conform with the general directives laid down by the high command.
Every offensive action in quiet areas of the front, over and above normal shock-troop activities, which is calculated to draw the enemy's attention to the sector.
Every plan for disengaging or withdrawing forces.

Every plan for surrendering a position, a local strongpoint, or a fortress.'

The instructions went on to stress that such requests had to allow for decision making and reply time. Furthermore Hitler emphasised that: 'Every report made to me either directly, or through the normal channels, should contain nothing but the unvarnished truth.' Failure to provide the latter would incur 'draconian punishment'.

On arrival at Hitler's bunker under the Reich Chancellery, Guderian and other visitors were subjected to a security check to prevent any assassination attempts. It was against this background of paranoia and mistrust that Guderian made his presentation to Hitler, Himmler and members of the staff.

Guderian outlined the situation in West Prussia and Pomerania drawing his audience's attention to the facts, the 'unvarnished' truths that Second Army had been forced back to the Vistula estuary as well as protecting Danzig and Gdynia and that overland communications with AGN were virtually impossible. Compliments were paid to the Kriegsmarine for the artillery support it was giving to AGN from its ships and the work of supply and evacuation that was continuing apace. However, Guderian explained, there

Above: Taking up a firing position in such an exposed location during the winter of 1944–5 must have been as a result of imminent danger. The weapon is a 210mm mortar, which is in the position for loading before elevating the barrel anywhere up to 70 degrees. This operation involved most of the 15-man crew. The wheels were raised to allow the mortar to rest on its firing platform.

could be carried in its 70-ton, heavily armoured body. If carelessly driven off-road the likelihood of the Jagdtiger being recovered from bogging down was marginal. This pill-box on tracks was purely a defensive weapon, reflecting the nature of German armoured vehicle design that had switched to this philosophy during the months following the defeat at Kursk.

On the other hand the attack force had considerable weaknesses. One of the divisions earmarked for 'Solstice' was 111th Panzer Division which at the end of January had consisted of only two weak tank battalions. The tanks included a company of Panthers but the rest were the tried and trusted Panzer IVs plus various tank destroyers and assault guns. Fuel was in very short supply. Panzer crews were ordered to drain the fuel from any disabled vehicles 'as soon as enemy fire slackens'. There would be no air cover as the Luftwaffe was so short of fuel that offensive missions had all but stopped, the planes being

Above: A Nebelwerfer battery lets loose a volley. The Wehrmacht first used this highly manoeuvrable six-barrelled rocket launcher in 1941. Nicknamed 'Moaning Minnie' due to the noise made by its projectiles, it was fired by remote control and took 10 seconds to reload. It was an inaccurate weapon but when fired *en masse* the effects were impressive.

was a golden opportunity to restore the situation if a counter-attack was launched, as rapidly as possible, into the gap that existed between Rokossovsky's and Zhukov's fronts. Once again Guderian asked for troops to be shipped from Courland but in such terms that Hitler's temper tantrum surpassed his previous outbursts and Guderian had to leave the room. When the atmosphere became calmer the discussion continued with Guderian requesting that his nominee, General Walther Wenck, be given operational control of the counter-offensive not Himmler. Himmler was not in favour of the operation and argued against it; possibly his prevarication and lack of martial ardour tipped the balance as Hitler suddenly seemed to cave in and permission was given to launch Operation 'Solstice' in two days' time on 15 February.

The speed with which the forces for Operation 'Solstice' were assembled hints that Guderian had possibly already issued surreptitious orders to that effect. Despite the fact that the major SS Panzer units, equipped with what amounted to the final issue of tanks, were already lining up in Hungary a substantial force of up to six Panzer divisions moved into Third Army's rear area. Re-designated Third Panzer Army and commanded by the experienced armour leader General Erich Raus, this was a remarkable concentration of force for the time. It was also one of the few operations

Above: A flight of Il-2 *Shturmovik* ground-attack aircraft pulls out from an attack on German supply lines. The *Shturmovik* was a versatile weapons platform capable of carrying rockets, bombs and anti-tank guns. The pilot was well-protected by the armoured cockpit, the rear gunner not so. The simplicity of design and robust undercarriage made it possible for the Il-2 to operate from what were virtually open fields.

that included the use of the most powerfully armed German tank destroyer, the Jagdtiger (Hunting Tiger). Armed with the fearsome 128mm gun, the Jagdtiger was capable of destroying any Allied tank that came within range. However, the gun was in a fixed mounting not a turret so it could only fire forwards and with fuel consumption of just under 4 litres per road km (1.4 gals/mile) it was not the most useful machine available. The size of the shells was such that only 32

reserved to fly defensive operations such as bombing raids against Soviet bridges or supply and tank columns. Allied air supremacy was such that Soviet tanks now carried markings to protect them against British and American ground-attack aircraft.

Operation 'Solstice' began on schedule and very quickly German tanks burst through the thin Soviet defences and relieved the garrison at Arnswalde (Choszczno). Other small towns and villages were recaptured and during the course of the next 48 hours a salient some 17–19km (10–12 miles) deep was pushed into the Soviet line. However, little further progress was made and with the Soviets deploying increasingly larger numbers of IS-2 and T-34/85 tanks this became an almost exclusively armoured operation. Several of the German Panzer units had been transferred from the Western Front and it was noticed that their men showed 'a marked aversion to operating in the daylight hours'. Experience of Allied air power in the west had taught them some bitter lessons that they did not intend to relearn at the hands of the Il-2 *Shturmoviks* that enjoyed a fine reputation as tank-busters. Nor were all these tank crews veterans; many of them were recent recruits from training depots or bombed-out factories and slowly the experience of the Soviet tankers began to tell. To complete Guderian's circle of woe, Wenck was involved in an accident and had to be replaced by General Krebs who presided over the final hours of 'Solstice' which was grinding to a halt in the face of increasingly solid defences.

Raus, commanding Third Panzer Army, recalled:

'Even before I took command [effective from 21 February] I had issued orders for the construction of a dense network of tank obstacles in the army's rear. Stout-hearted members of the Volkssturm, who had been trained in the use of the Panzerfaust, guarded these barriers. Moreover, men equipped with anti-tank weapons were held in readiness with bicycles and motorcycles for mobile employment and the rapid establishment of strongpoints. Never before had an area been transformed into such a tightly meshed anti-tank obstacle within so short a period of time as we had accomplished in Pomerania. The aim of this measure was to prevent Russian tanks that had broken through the front from carrying out a surprise advance, or at least to delay such an advance.'

Now was the moment for the Soviets to counter-attack as the Germans began to pull back to their start line.

The Soviet Riposte

Stavka instructed Zhukov and Rokossovsky to mount a joint operation to eliminate Third Panzer Army by deploying the right of 1st Belorussian Front and the left of 2nd Belorussian Front. The target was to be Kolberg (Kolobrzeg) on the Baltic coast and the aim was to split the German forces in two. When their troops reached the coast, Zhukov's men would head west while those of Rokossovsky would go east. 2nd Belorussian Front would lead off on 24 February, followed by Zhukov on 1 March. By a remarkable coincidence an epic feature film of the Prussian defence of Kolberg during the Napoleonic Wars was being shown in Berlin at the time and a French POW remembered seeing it and watching the audience's almost hysterical joy at this reminder of Germany's heroic military past.

Above: A Soviet infantry combat team fighting from house to house.

Above: The crew of an IS-2 tank fraternise with civilians on the outskirts of Posen during the early days of the siege. The majority of the whitewash used for snow camouflage has worn away to reveal the original green factory finish.

However, as the Soviet assault formations negotiated the mud and slush to their start lines, the Germans launched a spoiling attack that prompted Rokossovsky to increase his front's retaliation before the offensive proper began. On 22 February Raus received information that Soviet tanks were 35km (20 miles) in the rear of Third Panzer Army. Furthermore:

'The Russian spearhead had forced the remnants of Second Army's crumpled left wing into Third Panzer Army's sector. There they caused unrest among my improvised units, especially in the Pomeranian Reserve Division, which already suffered from low morale. My own flank thus became enveloped and was pushed towards Neustettin.'

Although the main Soviet barrage was short it was effective and the German line was soon breached. The Dutch, Belgian and French SS infantry were unable to stop the advancing Soviets for more than a few hours and took heavy casualties from air strikes as they fell back over the almost featureless ground. By 26 February the breach was 56km (35 miles) wide and 48km (30 miles) deep. As the troops pulled out so did the civilians. Their straggling columns soon covered the roads as they struggled to find somewhere peaceful to rest.

The Fall of Posen

No real support for Rokossovsky was forthcoming from Zhukov during this period but behind his lines units from Eighth Guards and Second Guards Tank Armies were mustering for the final assault on Fortress Posen which had been isolated since late January. The Guards had been given until 20 February to take the city. The designation of fortress had been made to ensure that Posen, positioned as it was on important communications lines on the route to the Oder, would not be given up without a struggle. Zhukov recalled that the initial intelligence reports gave a garrison of 20,000 men, and that this figure was later revised to 60,000. Forbidden to leave the city by Gauleiter Greiser, the civilian population was caught up in the struggle. Greiser left to resurface at Himmler's HQ in search of a job.

This was to be the first serious street fighting that Chuikov's Guardsmen had been involved in since Stalingrad and the veterans of that nightmare soon found their experience and advice in demand from the new men. Moving from house to house and room to room, the Soviet advance was slow but inexorable. Zhukov, desperate for the return to the front of these units, was critical of Chuikov's performance but little could be done to speed the process. As Chuikov himself wrote:

'It really is amazing when you consider our battle experience and our wonderful intelligence that we failed to notice one little detail. We didn't know that there was a first class fortress at Posen, one of the strongest in Europe.'

Above: With his back to the camera a Soviet flame-thrower operator waits his turn before moving up the line. The rifle-like stock of the ROKS-2 is visible to the man's right. Such men in all armies were a priority target for anyone within range of their lethal equipment.

The final objective was the old fortress itself. Following a lengthy bombardment including volleys from the dreaded *Katyushas*, the truck-mounted rocket launchers of the Guards mortar detachments, which saturated the confined defences with explosives and screamed during their brief flights, the infantry attack went in. After crossing the moat with the help of fascines, groups of engineers and machine gunners overcame the last defenders. In the early hours of 23 February the garrison surrendered following the suicide of its commander.

With Posen's fall the flow of supplies could move with increased efficiency. Equally valuable, the troops released could rejoin their parent units.

If Hitler was satisfied with Fortress Posen's resistance then he would be even happier with that of Fortress Breslau. Breslau, the capital of

The city had not been heavily bombed but the Soviets brought in heavy self propelled guns and tank destroyers and the streets were soon barely recognisable. As the casualties on both sides rose, the conditions for the wounded, both troops and civilians, deteriorated as the hospitals filled to overflowing and medicines ran out. Experience taught the Soviets that small assault groups should be provided with 'grenades, sub-machine guns, daggers and sharpened spades to be used as axes in hand to hand fighting'. The Soviet PPSh sub-machine gun proved highly effective in this role with its simplicity of maintenance and high rate of fire. Armoured vehicles were particularly at risk from groups of Volkssturm or Hitler Youth armed with Panzerfausts, which were lethal if the operator had the nerve to wait until point-blank range before firing. Squads of infantry escorted the armour, spraying any suspicious target with flame-throwers or machine-gun fire to flush out tank stalkers. It was essential to keep up the offensive's momentum and Chuikov recommended, 'You need speed and a sense of direction, great initiative and stamina because the unexpected will happen . . . Chuck a grenade at every corner. Go forward.' For the few surviving Stalingrad men these reactions were once again becoming second nature; for the new troops it proved to be a steep learning curve.

Above: When Posen fell to the Red Army one of the more grisly trophies was this execution block.

Silesia, was the fiefdom of Gauleiter Hanke who, in late January, had caused a mass panic by ordering the civilian population to leave. Those that did heed the warning but were unable to pack foodstuffs soon found themselves hungry and at the mercy of others in the same condition as no organisation had been set up to care for them. Only days before, the establishment of such an organisation would have been condemned out of hand as defeatist. Unlike many of his kind however, Hanke did remain in the city. During the course of the Soviet advance almost the entire German population of Silesia had in fact decamped to the west, leaving their homes to shelter the Soviet troops from the bitter weather.

In the event, 1st Ukrainian Front bypassed the city although it did seize the airport to prevent supplies being airlifted to the garrison and to secure a good quality runway for the Red Air Force. Breslau fell into the zone of Army Group Centre, commanded since late January by a fervent Nazi, General Ferdinand Schörner. Schörner ordered 169th Infantry Division into the city to prop up the Volkssturm and Fortress Battalions that formed its garrison. Every male left in Breslau was conscripted to man the defences as its position straddling the Oder River and its bridges made it a desperately important place.

A little over a week later, at 06:00 hours on 8 February, Konev's forces began the operation that would bring them to the banks of the Neisse River. But the few days prior to the attack had given the garrison and the remaining population time to connect up the old fortifications with trenches and dig new gun positions. The city held out, causing 1st Ukrainian Front to dig in around it. The main attack was launched from the Steinau (Scinawa) bridgehead north of Breslau, with a secondary one from the south. Within a week Breslau, with a garrison of 40,000 men and possibly as many as 80,000 civilians, had been cut off from the rest of Germany and Konev's bridgehead had expanded to over 930 square kilometres (360 square miles), more than enough room to house a force aiming for Berlin if such was the decision. Also cut off was another so-called fortress, Glogau (Glogow). But this effort had cost the Soviets their last front-line reserves. As Konev pointed out to Stalin and *Stavka* on 16 February, nothing more could be expected of his men or their machines until reinforcements and supplies arrived. Still unsure of the whereabouts of Sixth SS Panzer Army, Stalin cautioned Konev to be careful of his left flank. Indeed Fourth Guards Tank Army had been caught by a surprise counter-attack by the *Grossdeutschland* and XXIV Panzer Corps which was finally defeated after two days of savage fighting but not before the

Above: Pretty as it must have looked to the untutored eye, such a barrage of *Katyusha* rockets usually presaged an attack with the attendant horrors of night fighting.

Guards' rear echelons had taken a considerable hammering.

Konev now held roughly 100km (60 miles) of the Neisse river bank. It remained for his troops to close up with Zhukov's 1st Belorussian Front to their right, an operation that Konev prepared from his HQ near Breslau. Inside the city there was plenty of food but a shortage of ammunition. The loss of the airfield precluded air supply other than by parachute. Two attempts to fly in paratrooper reinforcements failed in late February. The men of Army Group Centre held the Soviet advance along the Neisse and waited for the thaw to increase their security. However, as Schörner's troops dug in, away to the south-west the SS were about to launch the first phase of their offensive in Hungary.

Operation 'South Wind'

When Sixth SS Panzer Army (Oberstgruppenführer Sepp Dietrich) began to arrive in Hungary its appearance lifted the spirits of the men who saw the hundreds of new vehicles, armour and infantry. Such a sight had been denied Army Group South for some time. However, its arrival was not widely trumpeted; having evaded Allied intelligence thus far it would have been foolish to lose the element of surprise at the eleventh hour. The 1st SS Panzer Division *Leibstandarte* travelled under the name of SS Ersatzstaffel (replacement squadron) *Totenkopf* and 12th SS Panzer Division *Hitler Jugend* as SS Ersatzstaffel *Wiking*. Both the *Totenkopf* and *Wiking* Panzer Divisions were still in the area refitting therefore the cover made sense to a casual monitor. The *Leibstandarte* and *Hitler Jugend* Divisions

constituted Sixth SS Panzer Army's I SS Panzer Corps.

Units of Seventh Guards Army (General M. S. Shumilov) occupied the 400 square kilometre (154 square miles) Hron bridgehead. Shumilov had made what he felt to be adequate defensive preparations but he had not anticipated the storm that was to break over the area. Furthermore, all Soviet attention had been focused on events in Budapest and the relief attempts. Now, with the city in their hands, Malinovsky and Tolbukhin were to receive further instructions from *Stavka*. On 17 February both front commanders were ordered to plan for the destruction of AGS, the liberation of Hungary and the occupation of Vienna to be followed by the development of a threatening position towards southern Germany. By carrying out these operations the German position in Italy would be put under pressure and Axis forces in Yugoslavia isolated. The first phase of this offensive was to be conducted from the Hron bridgehead beginning on 15 March. As they were given less than four weeks to prepare for these new operations both front commanders set about issuing redeployment instructions that day and were caught completely off balance by the SS offensive.

To preserve the integrity of the other formations earmarked for the main part of Operation 'Spring Awakening', Operation 'South Wind' was to involve only I SS Panzer Corps to exploit an infantry break-through. The German attack was preceded by a two-hour bombardment that ended at 04:00 hours on 17 February. The 46th Infantry Division went into action against Soviet 6th

Above: The Red Air Force gave permission for the formation of all-female squadrons in October 1941. Two members of the 588th Regiment stand in front of a U-2/Po-2 bomber. It was designated the Po-2 after the death of the designer (Polikarpov) in 1944. The Po-2 was a modified trainer that could carry a payload of almost 360kg (800lb) at a maximum speed of 177km/h (110mph). Nicknamed the 'Night Witches' by the Germans, the members received 23 Hero of the Soviet Union awards.

Above: One of the immediate effects of the Buda garrison's attempted break-out was the littering of the streets with wrecked and abandoned vehicles such as this Panzer IV which appears to have taken a round directly through its front armour. Some vehicles were later found to have been sabotaged with sugar in their fuel tanks.

Guards Airborne Brigade which inflicted heavy casualties on the Germans before withdrawing. Around daybreak the *Leibstandarte* mounted a two-pronged attack, one with infantry, the other with tanks including support from 501st Heavy Tank Battalion's 19 Tiger IIs. At first things went well and this powerful armoured force linked up with the men of 46th Infantry Division but then drove straight into a Soviet ambush, incurring heavy losses from well-emplaced anti-tank guns. During the course of the day the SS picked off the anti-tank guns but their advance had been slowed considerably. This resistance enabled Soviet engineers to destroy the bridges over the Paris Channel, a waterway before the river, the crossing of which was an important first-day objective.

During the afternoon the *Hitler Jugend* Division began to move towards the Paris Channel but found it to be impassable. The banks were saturated and turning to mud so that the heavy armoured vehicles were in danger of bogging down. It was not until late in the day that a ford was found and bridgeheads established that allowed German engineers to create a solid crossing point. The next day the *Feldherrnhalle* Battlegroup, supported by heavy tanks, fought its way through elements of XXV Guards Rifle Corps only to be held up by dense minefields. Elsewhere the *Hitler Jugend* and other units had to face fierce but poorly co-ordinated counter-attacks but *Leibstandarte* made reasonable progress.

By 19 February the Soviet command had realised that the situation was becoming critical and began to move troops in to maintain the bridgehead. For the next two days heavy fighting took place around a group of important villages. With losses rising, the staff of Sixth SS Panzer Army requested the withdrawal of the *Leibstandarte*. The infantry and *Hitler Jugend* Divisions carried out the final operations. In the early hours of 24 February, as the smoke of the barrage cleared,

the tanks of the *Hitler Jugend* rolled forward yet again into the narrow sliver of Soviet territory near the banks of the Hron River. Supported from the opposite bank by artillery fire, the Soviet Guardsmen fought tenaciously for every inch of ground until they were finally overrun and the last bridge blown.

During the week it had lasted Operation 'South Wind' had cleared the bridgehead and inflicted considerable losses. One of the *Leibstandarte*'s tank commanders was awarded the Knight's Cross for destroying 11 tanks in one day. Amongst the trophies I SS Panzer Corps claimed to have captured were 30 Hungarian, Italian, British and German-built tanks. The Soviet paratroopers used American White scout cars and British Universal carriers and Sixth Guards Tank Army, units of which were involved in the fighting, had had Matildas, Churchills and Valentines on its roster in 1944.

The first phase of Operation 'Spring Awakening' had achieved its goal and more troops were moving into the area for phase two. However, the SS armoured divisions had not escaped unscathed and were in need of replacement tanks, their losses being almost

Above: As well as camouflage suits the Wehrmacht also provided the troops with the Zeltbahn, which doubled as a quarter section of a bivouac. Issued in two styles, watery and splinter, the main colours were brown and green. It could be worn either tucked up or loose as shown. Both men have coloured their faces and added foliage to break up their outlines.

Above: A very dejected group of Soviet POWs files past a BMW R-75 motorcycle combination. The StuG III assault gun has a 75mm gun and additional armour on the front. The mudguard has been damaged which has possibly necessitated the removal of the 5mm armour side skirts.

50 per cent. Although many damaged vehicles were repairable, spare parts were in increasingly short supply even for elite units such as these. The front commanders and Shumilov were censured by higher authority for poor reconnaissance, neglect of the defences and ignoring the German build-up.

With the loss of the Hron bridgehead it was clear that the Germans meant to attack again in this area but the question remained where? At the end of February the Soviets decided that Tolbukhin's 3rd Ukrainian Front would be the target and that the operation would take place in the region between the 500 square kilometre (190 square miles) Lake Balaton and the smaller Lake Velencze. The interrogation of Hungarian deserters during late February indicated that the Soviet analysis of the situation was not far from the truth but that the time for preparations was limited.

Yugoslavia

Since the fall of Belgrade there had been little activity to the left of Tolbukhin's front. As the winter had been severe and the mountains did not lend themselves to large scale operations the war had become one of fairly static lines. Tito's People's Liberation Army, while dealing with the Germans fleeing north from Greece and Albania, fought what amounted to a civil war with a variety of groups both behind and beyond the front. Partisan bands from Tito's forces had infiltrated the enemy lines into Croatia and Slovenia where there were now very few German units. A quite remarkable variety of troops was now in position replacing German formations which had been transferred to other fronts. By early 1945 six corps, under German command, were deployed in Croatia and Slovenia including XV SS Cossack Corps, German XXI Mountain Corps and the I, II and III Corps

of the Croatian Army. Alongside them were a rag-tag collection of security and other units including the Serbian Volunteer Corps and Chetnik royalist partisans. Held in reserve was 7th SS Mountain Division *Prinz Eugen*, itself locally recruited from Yugoslav *Volksdeutsche* who had been fighting Tito's partisans since 1942. As it included tank and cavalry battalions it was one of the strongest units in the region.

The Bulgarian First Army fighting alongside Tito was preparing for an offensive during the early part of January. However, on 3 January the Cossack Corps and *Prinz Eugen* Division launched a spoiling attack north of the Sava River. Although it did not prevent the Bulgarian operation it did cause its postponement and when it finally began very little was achieved. This increase in activity caused the Germans to move the numerically strong infantry division, the 14th SS Waffen Grenadier Division *Galizien*, into the region. Raised in the western Ukraine in 1943, this division had been all but destroyed at the battle of Brody in July 1944 and since that

Above: An artillery piece of the 7th SS Mountain Division *Prinz Eugen* in action in Yugoslavia in 1945. The bulk of its personnel were locally recruited *Volksdeutsche*. During its three-year existence the division operated almost exclusively in Yugoslavia fighting the partisans. Towards the end of the war it absorbed many members of local fascist organisations and disbanded security units.

Above: Cossacks of the 1st Cossack Division (later XV SS Cossack Cavalry Corps) on the march late in 1944. This machine-gun team has an MG 42 on the pack horse nearest the camera. The only distinguishing feature visible on their German field dress to identify them as Cossacks are the collar tabs, which show crossed lances in the colour of the appropriate Host.

time it had been engaged in anti-partisan operations in Slovakia. On 21 January the Ukrainians were ordered to move to Slovenia, a journey of roughly 1,000km (621 miles) through Austria without the benefit of rail or other transport. The division marched off on 28 January with a few horses and carts and some lorries that the men had confiscated. While they were making their way through the snow and slush the fantasy politics of the Third Reich were conspiring against them.

Vlasov

For some time nationalists had been pressing for the creation of a Ukrainian version of Vlasov's ROA but there had been little support from the German authorities. However, as the disasters of 1944 unfolded, and the need for manpower increased, German enthusiasm grew, aided by such reports as, 'The nationalist Ukrainians are waging an extraordinarily successful partisan struggle against the Soviets in the form of a general popular revolt.'

Written in December 1944 by the head of the Eastern Section of the Propaganda Ministry, and somewhat exaggerated, it did provoke a positive response and a committee representing a broad spectrum of Ukrainian politicians from socialists to monarchists was formed. However, no agreement among such a diverse group was possible and it was not until late January that General Pavlo Shandruk was found to head the UVV, the Ukrainian Liberation Army, and the movement began to take shape. The UVV had existed mainly as a propaganda tool since 1943 but was now renamed the Ukrainian National Army and serious thought was given to where the manpower would come from. To avoid dissension in the ranks of what he viewed as his eastern army, Himmler wrote that he did not 'desire the formation of a Ukrainian Committee independent of General Vlasov, as it would make our policy towards General Vlasov appear in a double-dealing light.' Such scruples from the man responsible for the deaths of innocent millions in the death camps of the Final Solution seem truly remarkable.

To give further weight to Vlasov's endeavours a remarkable piece of symbolism was enacted on 28 January. Hitler formally transferred command of the ROA from himself as Commander-in-Chief of the Wehrmacht to the KONR with Vlasov as commander. This recognition of an army of men so long described as *Untermenschen* was in line with Hitler's thinking at this time. As he said, 'One does not win a war with political parlour tricks.' Recruiting anyone capable of bearing arms was vital but the disillusioned Führer also commented at roughly the same time, 'Every wretch is put in German uniform. I was always against it.'

However, Göring had changed his attitude to Vlasov's Russians but little and when they met, on 2 February, the Reichsmarshall spent the time discussing Soviet uniforms. Appearance was always a matter close to the Luftwaffe chief's heart. Furthermore a credit agreement was reached between the German Foreign Ministry and KONR that funds would be made available to pay for KONR. Incredibly Vlasov received representatives of the Spanish Government and the Papacy plus several of the fascist governments in exile during early 1945. Such 'international acceptance', limited though it was, did not prevent Henlein, the Gauleiter of the Sudetenland, from insisting that the hotel to which Vlasov's staff transferred was 'much too good' for Russians and that he would have the Volkssturm chase them out. Although the order was speedily countermanded it left a bitter taste in the mouths of the Russians.

When Turkey declared war on Germany on 22 February concern was expressed in the Wehrmacht as:

Above: A very young Yugoslav partisan smiles proudly as he shows off his badge. He is a member of the Boy's Battalion, Victor Javavonok.

'A certain tension has developed in the ranks of the Turkic and Caucasian volunteers, who undoubtedly have sympathy for Turkey . . . this question must be handled so as to say henceforth that Turkey had always been sympathetic to the Reich . . . and declared war only under Allied pressure.'

Hungary

The fall of Pest in mid-January led to a reorganisation of Malinovsky's Budapest Battlegroup, which was now led by General I. M. Mangarov. Criticisms had been made of the way that operations in Pest had been conducted and these had reached *Stavka*. The areas of concern included a lack of close-support artillery, the dispersal of men and equipment and generally poor organisation. In future Soviet tactics would be different.

The position in Buda had altered little during January. The area was less densely populated than Pest, more heavily wooded and somewhat hillier. In some parts there were gaps of more than 50 metres (55 yards) between buildings. The strategically important Farkasret cemetery had been converted into a

strong defensive position, with its mausoleums acting as bunkers and being connected by a trench system. What semblance there was of a front line enclosed hundreds of thousands of troops and civilians. Almost everyone was suffering from diarrhoea and malnutrition and was infested with lice. Water had to be fetched from the Danube, an exercise that cost dozens of lives. But there was still plenty of horsemeat as thousands of redundant cavalry horses had been rounded up and shot. Amongst the supplies parachuted in was a container of medals. In an effort to keep up morale these awards were to be made as if the situation was normal. What the thoughts were of those who risked life and limb to bring this container to safety can be imagined. The situation for the wounded was dreadful. Conditions in the cellar hospitals were described by one survivor, 'In every hall, corridor, there were wounded, operations were in progress on ordinary tables, we heard cries and wailing everywhere . . . Hell itself.' On the streets conditions were little better, 'The Foreign Ministry was in flames . . . the Ministry of Defence . . . was aflame too . . . there were bomb craters, trenches, wreckage . . .'

Above Farkasret cemetery and dominating the defences was Eagle Hill which was held by Battlegroup *Portugall*, commanded by SS Hauptsturmführer Karl Portugall, a mixed formation of infantry, artillery and engineers,

well-provided with 88mm guns. The 88 was a dual purpose weapon equally effective against tanks and aircraft. From their position on Eagle Hill these guns could pick off advancing Soviet tanks as they made their way slowly through the wide streets and open spaces of Buda. But, as ammunition ran short, the gunners had to be sure of a kill before loosing off a precious round. In their snow-shrouded positions among the government buildings and opulent villas of the city's rich, the German and Hungarian garrison waited for the inevitable. Pfeffer-Wildenbruch acknowledged the position and feelings of his command when on 30 January a message was sent to Hitler stating, 'The people have lost hope.'

The Soviet reorganisation and modification of tactical methods lasted until 3 February when Malinovsky ordered a fresh effort to conquer Buda that was to start no later than 7 February. Over the course of the intervening days the pressure of Soviet attacks increased, particularly around the cemetery and Schwabian Hill. The defenders were forced to concede ground. On 6 February Battlegroup *Portugall* pulled its 88s into the last positions on Castle Hill. By capturing Eagle Hill Soviet forward observation officers could now look down on the pocket and call in artillery fire with deadly precision.

Above: A T-34/85 emerges from a river in Hungary in almost pristine condition. This tank was officially capable of fording up to a depth of 1.3m (4.3 feet) though this was often exceeded. The gun is at maximum elevation for obvious reasons. The cylindrical fuel tank to the rear had a capacity of either 90 litres (20 gallons) or 110 litres (24 gallons).

With the end so clearly in sight some Hungarian troops began to desert. Those their captors felt to be sufficiently reliable were placed in the ranks of the 1st Magyar Volunteer Detachment, fighting under their own officers as a part of the Soviet 320th Rifle Division. Others were subordinated to 83rd Marine Brigade and other Soviet units. These Hungarians were recognisable by the red silk strips taken from German parachutes that were attached to their uniforms.

With the defensive area now reduced to less than a couple of square kilometres, there was little choice for the others in the garrison but to fight on. The members of German security, police and SS units knew they would receive no quarter from their opponents. Soviet heavy artillery was brought up to demolish any building that held troops and tank destroyers roamed almost at will blowing holes from building to building. A running battle amidst the tracks and wagons

of the Southern Railway Station resulted in a victory for the Soviet marines who then pushed on to overrun the positions on Gellert Hill. By 10 February the defenders had been virtually split into two groups. A Hungarian civilian remembered new arrivals in his family's cellar:

'Mongol-looking Soviets, Siberians probably, padded down our stairs with tommy guns raised . . . Later I was rounded up by a Soviet work crew and rolled barrels down to the Danube to build pontoons in place of the wrecked bridges.'

From another cellar several hundred metres away under the Royal Palace Pfeffer-Wildenbruch gave permission for his remaining men to attempt a break-out. The last statistics for the garrison, dated 11 February, gave a total of just under 24,000 German troops of whom 9,600 were wounded and 20,000 Hungarian troops including 2,000 wounded. Roughly 30,000 attempted to escape and three groups were organised to head in different directions. The Hungarian commander was not informed of the break-out attempt until 16:00 hours on 11 February, the day it was to be made. This lack of communication

was symptomatic of the poor relations between the Germans and Hungarians that had prevailed throughout the siege. The first wave was to consist of the *Florian Geyer* and 13th Panzer Divisions with the remaining armoured vehicles, the second of *Feldherrnhalle* and *Maria Theresa* Divisions along with those Hungarian units who chose to join them. The third wave consisted of the walking wounded and baggage train crews. Heavy equipment was to be abandoned and ladders carried to cross anti-tank ditches. It was assumed that thousands of civilians would join in. Assembly points were designated beyond the city. The first move was timed to begin at 20:00 hours.

It is unclear whether the Soviets had forewarning of the break-out attempt but in the event it made little difference. The whole affair rapidly degenerated into chaos as orders were misinterpreted, units became confused and panic set in. Although such a mass attack was difficult to contain, particularly as it had the benefit of cover from fog, thousands of the escapees were mown down as they charged. Whether from the effects of mob psychology or desperation, they kept going despite the mounds of dead and dying all around them. One survivor described how the scene:

Above: Inside the face of a clock in Budapest. Such positions were ideal for snipers who were celebrated by the Red Army in much the same way as Luftwaffe pilots were in Germany.

'. . . went beyond the wildest flights of the imagination . . . today Moskva Square was almost as bright as day with the many tracer bullets, flare rockets and searchlights. The tracer bullets drew horizontal streaks of light behind them. Shell after shell exploded. I am not exaggerating if I write that there were mountains of dead bodies everywhere.'

Incredibly thousands made it through the hail of bullets and sought refuge in the woods and parks that covered the area. However, with patrols of Soviet infantry scouring the suburbs of Buda, few of the fugitives got away from the city limits and here they ran into a Soviet cordon that was thickening by the hour. As a ruthless manhunt developed, the Soviets also moved into the remains of the Royal Palace. Captured SS men were usually executed on the spot but not so Pfeffer-Wildenbruch who was escorted to Malinovsky's HQ. Apparently under orders from Stalin to spare Pfeffer-Wildenbruch's life, Malinovsky expressed his frustration by telling the German that he would have

hanged him 'in the main square of Buda Castle for all the trouble' he caused by such a stubborn defence. Fewer than 1,000 Germans and Hungarians made good their escape to the west where they were sent to join the cadres of their units which had not been involved in the siege. There is no information available on the fate of the 6,532 POWs listed in the garrison's last returns for 11 February.

The Hungarian capital could at last be marked on *Stavka*'s map with a Red Flag. The city was officially Soviet-held from 14 February. Prisoner and casualty statistics have proved somewhat controversial since that time.

Debate and Indecision

The Soviet advance to the Oder had taken *Stavka* by surprise because virtually all of the forces engaged had reached their objectives ahead of schedule. The original plan to take Berlin within 50 days now looked perfectly achievable. Therefore it would have been surprising if all concerned were not tempted

simply to push on, especially since good bridgeheads over the last major barrier, the Oder River, had been established. With the Reich's capital less than 100km (60 miles) away (less at some points) it seemed too good an opportunity to be true. After the war Marshal Chuikov claimed that it would have been possible to keep going in early February:

'The situation favoured us . . . Of course, this would have been fraught with great risk. But what military operation is without risk? I think it would have been more correct to throw five armies from the 1st Belorussian Army Group against Berlin instead of sending them to the north . . . in the beginning of February Hitler had neither sufficient forces and materiel to defend the capital of Germany nor prepared fortified lines of defence. Consequently the road to Berlin was open.'

Above: A Waffen-SS anti-tank gun crew loads its heavily camouflaged 75mm PaK 40 with an armour-piercing round. Theoretically a gun of this type was served by a team of eight. At 1,520kg (3,350lb) it was relatively heavy due to the wartime shortage of light alloys.

Chuikov criticised *Stavka* for not having reacted promptly to the rapidity of the advance and for not overcoming logistical problems sooner. He also criticised Zhukov for agreeing to support 2nd Belorussian Front's operation to the north:

'I do not understand why Marshal Zhukov . . . did not attempt to convince Stalin of the necessity of waging the offensive against Berlin instead of Pomerania . . . Why did he agree with Stalin without a murmur?'

Written 20 years after the event and more than a decade after Stalin's death, Chuikov's words would appear to make good sense. He also included references to the problems of logistics and stated that the supplies earmarked for the Pomeranian operation would have sufficed for an attack on Berlin.

However, Chuikov was looking at the situation from a purely military point of view. Stalin was obviously aware of the political ramifications surrounding the capture of Berlin, and so to a lesser extent was Zhukov. Stalin strongly suspected that the Germans were trying to cut some sort of deal with the British and Americans that would involve sparing German forces in the west for possible combined operations against the Soviets when their forces were stretched to the maximum. Churchill, a firm opponent of the Soviet Union from 1918, was viewed as particularly likely to favour any scheme that would bring the USSR crashing down. This was not a paranoid fantasy but one based on bitter experience, as Churchill had been the prime mover behind intervention during the Russian Civil War when the communists had been fighting for their very existence. Stalin had been heavily involved in this matter and was not someone who forgave or forgot. Furthermore, Churchill and his military advisers were pushing Eisenhower, the Supreme Commander of the forces in the west, to drive on Berlin without delay which was not a course of action he favoured.

And there were other factors to be considered.

Soviet intelligence knew that Sixth SS Panzer Army was heading east but was unaware of its destination. The likelihood was that it would join AGV for a counter-attack in Pomerania. The condition of the SS force was open to speculation but that of the Soviet tank forces was plain. Whereas the SS tanks were being transported by rail, Soviet armour had driven hundreds of kilometres which obviously affected the machines' performance. The vehicles, particularly their engines and tracks, were in need of thorough maintenance and overhaul. Nor, for many weeks, had the Soviet tank crews enjoyed more than a few hours' rest at a time and they too were reaching the point of exhaustion.

For days unit returns had been arriving at higher commands requesting spares, ammunition and fuel which were almost non-existent or held up in eastern Poland. As the weather alternated between rain, snow and frost, columns of lorries often bogged down and then froze in place during the night. Inevitably such convoys came under attack from German stragglers and, so Stalin claimed to Churchill at the Yalta conference that month, 212 Soviet troops had been killed by partisans of the Polish Home Army which was opposed to the Soviet puppet regime. However, until the railways had been converted to broad gauge there was little alternative to road transport.

Above: The spoils of war. In the remains of a town in eastern Poland, a pair of German guns. Nearest the camera is an 88mm FlaK 36 anti-aircraft gun; to the rear a 150mm FH 18. By this stage of the war the Red Army's superiority in artillery was well established.

Regarding assessments of enemy strength *Stavka* was wary. It believed that the threat to Berlin would trigger a wave of withdrawals from Norway, Italy and elsewhere to defend the capital. The Western Allies were asked to maintain the pressure in Italy to prevent this happening. Equally worrying was the stout defence of the Königsberg region where virtually no progress had been made during February. In the middle of the month Chernyakhovsky had died of wounds and been replaced as front commander by Vasilevsky. Additionally, the Luftwaffe had increased its presence over the Eastern Front and, although its activities were severely curtailed by the fuel crisis, its aircraft enjoyed the benefit of concrete, all-weather runways. The Red Air Force controlled virtually no airfields of that quality so could only fly from well behind its own lines, limiting operational effectiveness. *Stavka* did not believe that the highway to Berlin was as open as it appeared to be to Chuikov and had absolutely no intention of allowing anything to go wrong at the eleventh hour. The attack on Berlin would take place when the front line was 'tidied up' along the entire length of the Oder River, supply lines fully operative, the attack units brought up to strength and most importantly when Stalin said it would. The Red Army was the physical expression of Soviet policy and would do as it was told.

Of course Zhukov was not privy to all this information in late January when he had proposed that his front continue on the way to Berlin. However, the plan was shelved and the order went out to army commanders to 'consolidate gains and move supplies from the rear'.

Silesian Gold

The golden prize that was the Silesian area was the most important mining and industrial region in Germany after the Ruhr. As noted earlier, Stalin wanted as much of the plant and equipment in this 6,000 square kilometre zone (2,300 square miles) captured intact to compensate the USSR for its own industrial losses. To achieve this Konev had worked out an interesting plan. As he recalled, 'We decided to use tank forces for a wide envelopment of the area and then, in co-operation with the (infantry) armies advancing into Silesia from the east, north and south, to force the Germans out into the open under threat of encirclement, and to rout them there.' The forces at his disposal included the Thirty-Eighth, Fifty-Ninth and Sixtieth Armies (infantry) and the Third Guards Tank Army. Facing them, according to Soviet intelligence reports, were the nine infantry and two Panzer divisions of Seventeenth Army plus a collection of units that had ended up there following the retreat from Poland. German reinforcements were on the way as this maze of steelworks, mines and factories was of vital importance to what was left of the Third Reich's armaments industry.

To make the Germans' situation plain Konev ordered Third Guards Tank Army to alter the line of its envelopment to allow them an obvious escape route. Infantry would be then be pushed towards the pocket and the Germans would, hopefully, leave as a result of this pressure. Konev wrote, 'I can still visualise the picture with all its contrasts: Silesia's smoking chimneys, the artillery shelling, the clang of the tank tracks, the curtain lace (for camouflage) on the tanks and the accordion-playing tank-borne infantry, whose melodies did not reach us . . .' The plan worked like clockwork and by 27 January Eighteenth Army was, with Hitler's approval, retreating towards the Oder. Hitler had authorised the retreat because he anticipated the entire region would be German again within a matter of weeks. Two days later 1st Ukrainian Front was able to report that the factories and mines were, with few exceptions, in full production again. It was a remarkable achievement and, although casualties were taken during the pursuit of Eighteenth Army, they were nowhere near as high as they would have been if a protracted battle for the factories had taken place.

Chapter 8

The Reich's Last Offensive: March 1945

'We retreat but we will win.'
German Nazi graffiti

1st Belorussian Front

Zhukov's front began its offensive against Army Group Vistula on 1 March. Senior German officers had generally believed that this attack would be directed towards Berlin and therefore it was a pleasant surprise to them when it was not. As they were already engaged heavily with Rokossovsky's troops, the Germans had little to spare to plug the gaps torn in their line by 1st Belorussian Front. Therefore three days later units of First Guards Tank Army reached the Baltic at Kolberg deep in the German rear. Behind the tanks came First Polish and Third Shock Armies, moving more slowly, consolidating ground and clearing points of resistance. In reality there was no longer a front line as such.

This was in accord with Soviet doctrine, which taught that pressure should be maintained on the enemy by pursuit across a wide front. The advance of First Guards Tank Army spread out and aimed for a selection of objectives, confusing the defenders thoroughly. The Soviet attack had resulted in the envelopment of X SS and another corps inland from Kolberg. Raus, commanding Third Panzer Army, had requested permission from Himmler to order this corps to retreat. The request had been turned down, Himmler emphasising the point by threatening courts martial for senior officers. There was now no alternative but to fight on. By 6 March the SS were surrounded. The following day, as a Soviet veteran recalled, 'Over 8,000 German POWs were captured including the commanding general of the X SS Corps, Lt General Krappe, with his staff.'

On 7 March Raus was summoned to a conference with Himmler to discuss the situation. The meeting took place in the Hohenlychen Sanatorium where the Reichsführer, suffering from angina, was under the care of his personal physician. Raus recalled:

'Himmler began by congratulating me, saying, "You have passed through some very difficult days, but in spite of all the obstacles you have once again stabilised the front." I told the Reichsführer, "During the enemy offensive you repeatedly issued orders that prevented me from acting along lines demanded by the tactical situation . . . Had I been allowed to do so, unnecessary losses would have been avoided, and forces released for the creation of reserves."'

Above: Infantrymen jog to keep pace with their tanks. Although they are unencumbered with much personal equipment the standard issue greatcoat was not exactly designed for cross-country running and increased markedly in weight when wet.

All this stream of criticism was nothing but the 'unvarnished truth' that Hitler himself had demanded some days earlier. Raus continued:

"'Even after the two corps had been encircled, impossible orders from your headquarters did not stop. The 10th SS Panzer Division *Frundsberg*, ordered back to us from Silesia, abruptly received orders to re-establish contact with Second Army by attacking across Pomerania through the territory already occupied by several Russian armies. This altogether impossible mission seemed to demonstrate the extent to which you and the Supreme Command had misjudged the situation." Himmler listened to these remarks in a serious and attentive manner and then replied, "I know you understand the situation on the Pomeranian Front and predicted these events in advance . . . Calm down. There will be a turning point soon. We shall win this war.'"

Within two weeks Raus was to pay for this outburst of honesty. However, 10th SS Panzer Division *Frundsberg* was desperately trying to

Above: With the turret their only protection, a unit of 'tank desant' men move forward on the back of a T-34/85. The Maxim gun in the foreground is a pre-1943 model that lacks the filling port on the water jacket. It used the same bullet as the infantry rifle and was typical of the Soviet armament industry's policy of producing simple to maintain, reliable, easily manufactured weapons.

Above: Classified as a medium self-propelled gun the SU-100 mounted a modified 100mm anti-tank gun on the robust chassis of a T-34. This factory-fresh machine is finished in the standard Red Army green. The external fuel tanks were essential, as these vehicles were only capable of 0.4km/litre (1.1 miles per gallon). The gun was capable of firing both high explosive and armour-piercing shot and was manned by a crew of four.

Above: The Wehrmacht's equivalent of the bazooka, the Panzerschreck.

extract itself from the position it found itself in having embarked upon its 'impossible mission'. *Frundsberg* had been recalled to Pomerania at the end of February. The first unit arrived on 2 March and immediately went into action. The following day more of the division arrived and also went directly from the trains into combat. By 4/5 March most of the division had assembled and a reconnaissance team was sent out in the direction of Second Army. The division found strong Soviet tank forces to the north so headed to the south-east. For the next few days *Frundsberg* was engaged in a series of running battles as it struggled to fulfil its orders. The division was, for the time, a remarkably well-equipped formation, with over 100 tanks and tank destroyers, almost half of which were Panthers. But conditions were such that the division seems to have been unable to mount any sort of concentrated attack and it was driven back piecemeal to the various bridgeheads over the Oder River. Eventually part of the division crossed the river on barges while another section, along with the rearguard of 28th SS Panzergrenadier Division *Wallonie*, crossed a railway bridge elsewhere on 17 March. At roughly this point General Hasso von Manteuffel took command of Third Panzer Army.

By 9 March Zhukov's forces had reached the lower Oder to the north and south of Stettin (Szczecin). Various units had begun to break out to the west from Pomerania, one of

the largest being a battlegroup from the French SS Division *Charlemagne*. Second Army's commander General Weiss, who was soon replaced by General Saucken, sanctioned their escape. Before Saucken flew to Danzig to take up his new command on 13 March he extracted from Hitler the assurance that he would not be subject to the orders of the local Gauleiter.

2nd Belorussian Front

The HQ of AGV had, by 8 March, lost contact with its left flank, Second Army and parts of Third Panzer Army. And now Rokossovsky prepared to move in for the kill. Rokossovsky was loaned 1st Guards Tank Army, which would enable his offensive to maintain its momentum towards the east while Second Shock Army advanced on Danzig from the south. On 8 March Marienburg (Malbork), another of Hitler's so-called fortresses, fell followed two days later by Elbing. Keeping in contact with the retreating Germans every inch of the way Rokossovsky's tanks managed to prevent them from forming any substantial defensive systems along the waterways that criss-crossed the area. Very soon the Soviets were positioned around Gdynia and Danzig where a substantial German force was squeezed into a pocket including the two ports. The reduction of frontage from 240km (150 miles) to 60km (37 miles) benefited both the Germans and the Soviets. Conditions inside the pocket were grim as thousands of refugees jostled with the soldiers for food and accommodation. Saucken was determined to

hold out for as long as he could to allow the Kriegsmarine time to evacuate as many of the civilians as it could. Estimates for the middle of March run as high as one million. However, such is the confused nature of the records, that their accuracy is difficult to verify. Guy Sajer, who survived, described the situation:

'Everything was calm in the city, despite the tragic spectacle of hundreds and thousands of refugees. The war was to the south of us, so that we escaped its noise, although frequent air raids struck at the heart of the crowded city. Danzig had become the terminal point of the Prussian exodus, and, although huge crowds were living day and night without shelter, there was nonetheless a substantial and organised effort to help them . . . A large ship had come into Neufahrwasser, and the crowd had flowed towards the pier. The ship had not yet cast off its mooring lines, and everyone would have to wait for several hours before they were loosed again, but in Danzig then time counted for nothing . . . As always there were the children, with their small faces twisted by emotion, staring and hating without comprehension, and without looking for explanations.'

Rokossovsky described the defences in the region as having been 'facilitated by the terrain and the spring flooding. In retreating the Nazis demolished and mined roads and

Above: General Hasso von Manteuffel views the battlefield. Manteuffel took command of the Third Panzer Army, part of Army Group Vistula, in March 1945. He had fought both in North Africa and on the Eastern Front as well as commanding the *Grossdeutschland* Division during early 1944. His forces surrendered to the Western Allies on 3 May 1945.

opened dams flooding whole areas.' From offshore, as at Memel and Courland, the heavy guns of the cruisers *Leipzig* and *Prinz Eugen* provided as much covering fire as they could.

The Soviet assault on the ports began on 14 March with an attack that aimed to split the pocket in two. However, the German troops were well motivated and in strong positions so that, although inexorable, the Soviet advance cost them dearly. Supported by the concentrated firepower of four Breakthrough Artillery Corps and round the clock bombing, the Soviet infantry pushed on and finally, on 26 March, Gdynia and its port fell. On the same day Rokossovsky called upon the defenders of Danzig to surrender but to no avail.

At 10:00 hours Moscow time the next day the Soviet bombardment began and when it lifted specialist assault teams went forward. A typical unit consisted of three flame-thrower tanks, two self-propelled guns, four pieces of light artillery, an infantry company, 10 engineers and half a dozen men armed with as many Panzerfausts as they could carry. These were to be fired in volleys to destroy strongpoints, barricades or walls. One Soviet veteran recalled:

'At the city limit the advance was delayed. Each house was a fortress and could only be taken after a fight. Flame-throwers proved to be indispensable. The flame suppressed the defence in the cellars and fortified machine-gun positions. Infantry moved forward to pave the way for tanks, which supported them by fire . . . My tank took out the gate easily. The infantry poured onto the territory of the port . . . A slogan in black letters on the side of a warehouse read *'Danzig bleibt Deutsch'* [Danzig remains German]. Five shots took care of the warehouse . . . and the slogan of Doctor Goebbels.'

One of the armoured formations that took part in the final assault was composed of Poles who were allowed to raise their flag over the city when it was finally declared clear of Germans on 30 March. The remains of the

garrison sought refuge to the east in the marshes at the mouth of the Vistula River. From there they managed to reach the small port of Pillau (Baltiysk) at the tip of the Samland Peninsula. Now all that remained of Germany's forces in East Prussia were the divisions in and around Königsberg.

3rd Belorussian Front

The 1st Baltic and 3rd Belorussian Fronts were, in mid-March, preparing for what Vasilevsky (now commanding 1st Baltic Front) hoped would be the final assault on Königsberg. It was to be a three-stage operation. The first stage would be the destruction of the Heiligenbeil (Mamonovo) position, the second the attack on Königsberg itself and the third the liquidation of German forces in the Samland Peninsula to the west of Königsberg. Forty-Third Army would attack from the north-east, Eleventh Guards

Above: Yet another river crossing during the last year of the war. The rounded rear hatch between the exhaust pipes identifies this as the 1942 model of T-34. Thin armoured casings protected the exhausts.

Army from the south. Gunboats of the Baltic Fleet would support marine landings on the Samland Peninsula. The code name for the whole offensive was Operation 'Samland'. Soviet intelligence indicated the presence of 19 divisions in the pocket. Furthermore, Königsberg was a real fortress district, not merely the product of Hitler's feverish imagination. Indeed it was, and had been since the 19th century, Germany's premier fortification in the east. The defences had been upgraded regularly from before World War 1 and continually improved since that time. However, although reinforced-concrete bunkers and pill-boxes were scattered liberally across the spaces between the forts themselves, in common with other defence systems in the east, the guns had been removed for use elsewhere over a year before. Writing after the war, General Raus commented that some positions had been neglected to the extent that the keys were missing! In March 1945 three defence lines protected the city, one along the outskirts covering the approaches, one following the line of the suburbs and one guarding the port and city centre.

General von Lasch, the garrison commander but subordinate to Muller's Fourth Army, wrote, 'As for the numerical strength of Königsberg's garrison before the commencement of the Russian assault, one can give only an approximate figure, because precise data are not available.' His rough estimate was 30,000–35,000 men, excluding the Volkssturm. He also said, 'The number of civilians varied from 90,000–130,000.' Raus described the local Volkssturm in the following manner, 'In East Prussia the Volkssturm did a better job than anywhere else', and claimed that the organisation had 'made the greatest progress as 32 battalions were raised' giving roughly 20,000 men. What the real figures were is again difficult to establish, as the East Prussian Gauleiter, the repulsive Erich Koch, was hell-bent on currying Hitler's favour. Having refused permission for an evacuation of the region in January, Koch had probably terrorised the population into adopting some form of martial stance with his lunatic utterings. Doubtless he reported to his master that everyone was prepared to go down fighting for National Socialism to the accompaniment of some Wagnerian crescendo.

Stavka had agreed Vasilevsky's plans but Moscow was not prepared to provide any reinforcements nor would any allowance be made for the foul weather, which Vasilevsky cited, when asking for a postponement. Furthermore the Heiligenbeil position had to be taken by 22 March and the attack on Königsberg was to begin no later than 28 March. Vasilevsky then used his direct line to Stalin who not only granted the postponement but also ordered reinforcements to be sent. These additional forces included large numbers of heavy guns and aircraft.

1st Baltic Front took less than 10 days to accomplish phase one of the plan. Vasilevsky described the fighting thus:

'In the second part of March 1945, acting under severe weather conditions, our forces managed to fulfil their plans to break down and defeat the German grouping stationed in the Heiligenbeil Fortified District . . . I will never forget the fighting on the southern bank of the Frisches Haff bay. The spring high water resulting from the melting snow flooded the ground transforming the battlefield into a swamp. Our soldiers were driving through deep mud under fire . . . In a desperate attempt to escape the Germans were running to the boats, barges and other ships . . .'

Above: By early 1945 Germany was pressing men into service who were considerably older than the usual recruit. Not all waited to join the Volkssturm but opted to volunteer for better-equipped and experienced units such as the Volksgrenadier divisions. These recruits doubtless had much experience from the Kaiser's army. Just visible to the right is the legend '40 hommes 8 chevaux' (40 men or 8 horses) the loading capacity of transport wagons in French service.

Apparently thousands were drowned when a dyke burst. These scenes of carnage on the Baltic beaches were made even more ghastly taking place as they did amongst the beach huts and paraphernalia of happier days. On 26 March Hitler finally saw fit to order the evacuation of troops but only when their heavy equipment had been rendered useless. In the event both were lost. Königsberg was next on the Soviet list.

The Fall of Königsberg

At the cost of much sweat and to the sound of the wonderfully varied Russian vocabulary of mother curses, the heavy artillery was hauled into position. Lucky the gun crews responsible for the super-heavy artillery weapons that could be moved on their own caterpillar tracks, even luckier the crews manning the specialist batteries of naval railway artillery. These mobile batteries had been designed for coastal defence and their guns were long-range pieces that could engage the vessels of the Kriegsmarine on reasonably equal terms. While the infantry shivered in their bunkers the naval gunners enjoyed a warm, comfortable life on their trains. They were part of Stalin's grant of reinforcements and had travelled down the coast from carrying out a similar task at Memel. Correcting long-range fire was the job of the 3rd Airship Battalion whose observers worked from captive balloons covered by batteries of anti-aircraft guns. In all something approaching 5,000 guns and heavy mortars

were brought to bear including dozens of *Katyusha* rocket launchers. Other resources included aircraft of the First and Fifteenth Air Armies, the Baltic Sea Fleet and bombers of the Long Range Air Arm (ADD), a total of 2,400 machines, all under the personal direction of Air Marshal A. A. Novikov, the commander of the Red Air Force. The ADD was led in person by its commander General

A. Ye. Golovanov. Both men were waiting for an improvement in the weather and paying close attention to the work of the labour battalions that worked to improve and maintain the airstrips. The Luftwaffe had about 100 aircraft with which to attempt to stem this tide.

The Soviet build-up was carried forward with none of the usual *maskirovka*

Above: Loading the ordnance for heavy bombers on improvised airfields such as this could be a nerve-wracking experience. The ADD played a significant part in the reduction of Königsberg.

precautions. Lorries and tanks travelled to their positions with headlights blazing and radio messages were sent in clear. There was no need for secrecy as the Germans had little or nothing with which to hinder their enemy's preparations. Naturally the psychological effect of watching this steady flow of men and matériel on the other side of no-man's-land drained the morale of those who would soon be on the receiving end. All the Fritzes could do was wait for the inevitable.

Infantry teams similar to those used in Danzig were in place, trained and ready, by the morning of 6 April when Vasilevsky gave the order to begin the main phase of Operation 'Samland'. As the infantry went over the top the guns, which had already been firing for several days, moved on to targets deeper in the pocket. Throughout the morning the ground forces pushed ahead while overhead *Shturmoviks* and higher altitude machines kept the defenders under constant fire from rockets, bombs and cannon. With the valour borne of desperation

Above: A Soviet machine-gun team in East Prussia. The Maxim shown here is the pre-1943 model without the fluted water jacket and fluid port. In urban fighting the shield was often left in place to protect the gun crew from stone fragments when firing prone.

Above: NCOs and men of an unidentified Luftwaffe field division in their entrenchment near Königsberg. Unused to and ill-trained for the rigours of ground combat, these units were often raised as a result of the grotesque manpower auctions carried out to impress the Führer during the last months of the war.

long as possible so that the maximum number of refugees could be shipped out. On 13 April the last East Prussian battle started. For two days the Soviets attacked and by the end of 15 April Group Samland was reduced to 20,000 men. As the Kriegsmarine worked day and night to evacuate troops and equipment as well as civilians, the Red Air Force flew sortie after sortie to stop them. The last ships sailed on 21 April just as the Soviets overran the final defence line outside the port.

Gauleiter Koch was not among the POWs or the dead. He escaped from East Prussia on an icebreaker along with his baggage, papers and car. Koch was later captured but plea-bargained his life for the secrets of some art treasure and died in a Polish prison in the 1980s.

On Hitler's orders General Lasch was condemned to death for surrendering and his family imprisoned. Under interrogation Lasch described the significance of his defeat in the following way:

'The fall of Königsberg is the loss of the largest fortress and German outpost in the east. The effect on the morale of the German population and Army caused by the loss of Königsberg is hard to express. German casualties in personnel and weapons are very costly for Germany which now counts every soldier. The fall of Königsberg will expedite the final collapse . . .'

What was difficult for Hitler to absorb was the speed with which the city's defences had collapsed. Was it symptomatic of a growing malaise in the army and nation as a whole?

Controversy still surrounds the fate of two refugee ships, the *Wilhelm Gustloff* and the *Goya*, both of which were torpedoed by Soviet submarines. The circumstances have led to suggestions that these events were war crimes as the ships were carrying only civilians. Whatever the rights and wrongs the fact remains that they vie for the title of greatest maritime disaster of all time as over 6,000 souls perished aboard each vessel.

Slovakia

There had been little to note in 4th Ukrainian Front's area of responsibility in early 1945 as the major operations had been going on either to the north or the south. Petrov's forces had had little to do bar follow up as the Germans withdrew steadily towards the border of their Protectorate of Bohemia-Moravia.

However, in mid-February Petrov had been ordered to submit plans for a major offensive to clear the industrial zone of Moravska-Ostrava which lay some 240km (150 miles) east of Prague and 210km (130 miles) north of Bratislava dominating his front's route to either capital. It would be a

the German troops held on; at least now the waiting was over. The fighting continued through the night with barely a pause. Early the next day nearly 250 bombers of the ADD, covered by 125 fighters and accompanied by more than 200 ground-attack aircraft, ranged over the city bombing or strafing groups of defenders or buildings where the resistance was strong. In a nightmare of flaming ruins and noise the order to evacuate the city was given; civilians jostled to attach themselves to the groups of soldiers who were to lead the break-out. Unfortunately for these crowds Soviet observers saw them and called in artillery strikes, killing hundreds as they milled about in confusion. As the forward units of the two Soviet thrusts drew closer

together Lasch decided that the time had come to surrender. Vasilevsky accepted the garrison's capitulation at 21:30 hours on 9 April. A number of soldiers made their escape in the confusion, taking refuge in the Pillau area. Here they were renamed Group Samland and put under the command of Saucken who replaced Muller at the head of what had been Fourth Army.

The Samland Peninsula

By gathering the waifs and strays of Danzig and Königsberg, Saucken's Group Samland consisted, according to Soviet figures, of 65,000 men, 1,200 guns and 166 armoured vehicles. In keeping with Saucken's philosophy, the defence was to hold out for as

Above: A heavily damaged He-111H returns from a mission. By 1944–5 air support for the Wehrmacht was only possible on a limited, local scale due to the shortage of aviation fuel and the concentration of Luftwaffe resources on the Western Front.

difficult place to fight in as it was a heavily built-up area with a large number of factories. That Army Group Centre would abandon it was out of the question; the region was an important munitions production area therefore it would be defended for as long as possible. As *Stavka* had stipulated Prague as Petrov's ultimate destination, it was a complex problem. Simultaneously Tolbukhin would be going for Vienna and Malinovsky for Bratislava.

4th Ukrainian Front began its offensive on 10 March preceded by an artillery barrage but without air cover, as the weather was bad. The Soviet infantry made little headway, penetrating only 11km (7 miles). This was felt to be too narrow a gap to exploit by the insertion of V Guards Mechanised Corps' small tank forces.

Stavka had now reached the end of its patience as Petrov had once again failed to make any progress. Accused of failing to prepare adequately or to inform Moscow that the conditions were not good enough, Petrov was replaced by General A. I. Yeremenko. However, thanks to his political connections, Petrov reappeared as Konev's chief of staff at 1st Ukrainian Front later in the month.

With Yeremenko in place, 4th Ukrainian Front's attacks began again on 24 March with

Thirty-Eighth Army in the van. Now the Germans were driven back to the Oder River but the capture of the industrial zone eluded the Soviets. Nevertheless AGC had been prevented from transferring any of its forces from this region to bolster the defences in Hungary where the Soviets had just begun their offensive.

Yugoslavia

To the south the Bulgarians and Yugoslavians stood on the borders of Bosnia-Herzegovina. In early February Tito's forces had entered Herzegovina, capturing Mostar on 15 February after bitter fighting during which a Croatian division took heavy casualties. Concerned now for the fate of Sarajevo, the German commander of Army Group E, General Löhr, ordered the stiffening of regular Croatian units with Germans.

Using his tank brigade with air cover from attached Soviet formations under General A. N. Vitruk, Tito now moved forward with 40,000 men and 100 guns towards Sarajevo. The operation began on 17 March, its timing synchronised with that of Tolbukhin's

offensive to the north. Having thrown back a counter-attack by XV SS Cossack Corps and the *Prinz Eugen* Mountain Division, the Yugoslavs occupied the city several days later. The Germans and their allies began to pull back to Croatia and then withdraw from the region completely as the threat of Soviet encirclement with the possibility of capture by Tito's forces became increasingly likely.

The Croatian regime of Ante Pavelic was left to fend for itself. None of the multitude of armed militias, political factions, ethnic groups or the Croatian Army proved capable of holding Tito's well-organised and well-equipped divisions. The occupation of Croatia was undertaken at a steady pace to reduce casualties and to allow the factions to evacuate or destroy themselves. As an independent state Croatia was finished, Zagreb was reoccupied and Yugoslavia reborn amidst scenes of inter-ethnic violence that would be repeated half a century later.

But, as the final drama in the Balkans began to play itself out, Hitler's last gamble, Operation 'Spring Awakening', was about to commence.

41

Above: German mountain troops in action. The artillery piece is the 75mm Model 1936 mountain gun that had a range of 9,150 metres (10,000 yards). The shield was often omitted to allow for greater mobility. These weapons broke down into six loads for mule transport and weighed 726kg (1,600lb). A skid chassis for use in snow could replace the wheels.

Operation 'Spring Awakening'

Tolbukhin, commanding 3rd Ukrainian Front, had been positioned to the south of the Kursk salient in 1943 but had clearly absorbed the defensive lessons that had so effectively broken the back of Germany's armoured might. He was to draw on that experience in March 1945. Under orders from *Stavka* to prepare to fight a defensive battle, Tolbukhin had little time to prepare his battered and run-down forces.

The ground over which the battle would be fought was low-lying and saturated. The Soviet position backed onto the Danube River and was intersected with canals and streams that were all rising with the onset of the thaw. Three defensive lines were to be dug west of the Danube with the first, main, line being 5–6km (3–4 miles) deep, the second not far behind the first was thinner while the third was no more than 24km (15 miles) to the rear. Low hills were dotted here and there. Batteries of 100mm anti-tank

guns, capable of knocking out Tiger tanks at 1,500 metres (1,640 yards) were organised with specified fields of fire. Large numbers of smaller calibre anti-tank guns were positioned in concealed gun pits and carefully camouflaged. All the gun crews were reminded of the instructions on fighting Tigers, particularly the ranges at which the lighter weapons were effective:

'The front part of the Panzer VI is reliably penetrated by armour-piercing shells of 45mm, 57mm and 76mm guns from distances of 100–700 metres [110–770 yards]. By armour-piercing shells of 100mm and 122mm guns from 700–1,000 metres [770–1,100 yards]. Commanders of gun crews and gunners must carefully study and know the vulnerable places of the tank, as well as which shell from which gun from what distance kills the tank . . . Guns of all types fire the standard shells only at the suspension, turret base and gun . . . Commanders of gun crews and gunners must allow the tank to close up, as close as possible, and open fire from distances securing reliable destruction.' (from a Red Army pamphlet)

All this was similar to British infantry in the colonial wars being told to hold their fire until they could see the whites of their enemies' eyes. Apart from hindering movement the wet ground would also help to conceal the heavier anti-tank guns. These had muzzle brakes that raised clouds of dust when the gun fired. Damping the ground or covering it with a tarpaulin was the usual way of getting over this problem.

To the right and rear of the line was the armour. Numbering a little over 400 armoured fighting vehicles of all types, it was a mixed bag that consisted mainly of T-34s, heavy tank destroyers and self-propelled guns. There were only 15–20 of the latest IS-2 tanks. These formations would be held in reserve to seal off any breaches in the infantry and gun lines.

Weather and airfield conditions permitting, Seventeenth Air Army would provide air cover. Artillery support, although organised on the basis of local conditions, was to be ready to provide help for adjacent units should the need or opportunities arise. Special positions were dug to enable the *Katyusha* rocket launchers to fire their lethal volleys almost parallel to the ground — such drastic and dramatic measures had proved effective in the past. The engineers sowed thousands of

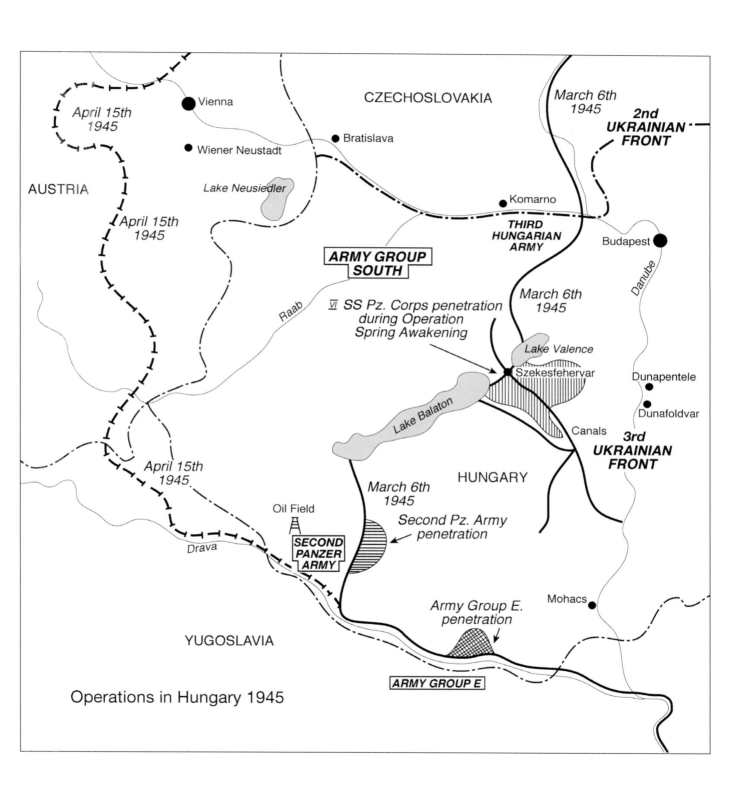

Operations in Hungary 1945

Above: Abandoned Tiger Is await transportation back to the USSR for display as trophies. Vehicle number 200 clearly shows its protective coating of Zimmerit anti-magnetic-mine paste. The Tiger I was produced between August 1942 and August 1944, 1,350 being delivered. It was the first German tank to use wide tracks, 72cm (28.5 inches), which made operating in snow or mud much easier.

anti-tank and anti-personnel mines where they would either disable the Panzers or force them to present their weaker side armour to the waiting anti-tank gunners. And everywhere the infantry dug while maybe lending half an ear to the exhortations of their political officers and possibly giving a moment's thought to joining the Communist Party, which guaranteed to inform the family if a member was killed in action.

Aware that this would be a battle of attrition, Soviet logistics officers ordered the construction of an aerial runway across the Danube that was capable of moving 1,200 tons of supplies a day as well as carrying a fuel pipeline for the armoured units. As the river was thawing so ice floes were washed along in the current causing the bridging troops to work around the clock to prevent their fragile charges from being damaged. If the defence system failed then these were almost the only routes back from disaster.

Tolbukhin visited Bulgarian First Army's HQ to satisfy himself that all was in order on his extreme left flank. At the same time he kept in constant touch with his right where it connected with Malinovsky's 2nd Ukrainian Front's left near Budapest. Malinovsky was due to begin his offensive to clear Hungary and move into Bohemia-Moravia no later than 17–18 March and Tolbukhin was scheduled to open his next offensive two days before that.

On the German side of the line reinforcements had been arriving steadily, including infantry replacements for those lost during the Hron operation of the previous month. However, not all of these were of the high standards previously demanded by the SS. Many were untrained Luftwaffe ground crew or Kriegsmarine sailors. The commander of the 9th SS Panzer Division *Hohenstaufen* had received immediately prior to its transfer to Hungary '20 replacements, unfortunately almost all old men from the Ukraine, some of whom neither speak nor understand German'.

By the beginning of March nearly all the men taking part were aware that Sixth SS Panzer Army would be mounting the main attack between the lakes. This operation would be supplemented by two weaker operations on the right. The first pitted Second Panzer Army against Fifty-Seventh Army and was called Operation 'Icebreaker'. The second, Operation 'Forest Devil', would involve units of Army Group E. These troops would strike at the junction of Bulgarian First Army and Yugoslav Third Army. This last operation would begin on 5 March. The lack of secrecy was to cost the Germans and their Hungarian allies dear.

Information from Hungarian deserters, combined with Yugoslav and Soviet intelligence, gave Tolbukhin warning of the direction of the three attacks. When

Operation 'Forest Devil' began theories were confirmed. Attacking across the Drava River, the ubiquitous XV SS Cossack Corps and several other divisions made some inroads into their opponents' positions but were stopped quite easily within a day or so. Operation 'Icebreaker' was equally unsuccessful. Although classified as a Panzer Army the Second had a mere 70 armoured vehicles to its name, the strongest formation being 16th SS Panzergrenadier Division *Reichsführer-SS*. However, it was the Sixth SS Panzer Army that was expected to smash through the Soviet front and it began operations on 6 March.

Following a short barrage and with a surprising amount of air cover, 356th Infantry and 1st and 3rd Panzer Divisions struck at the junction of Fourth Guards and Twenty-Sixth Armies while the *Leibstandarte* and *Hitler Jugend* Divisions, supported by Hungarian I Cavalry Corps, hit the right and centre of Twenty-Sixth Army. Bravely as the Soviet infantry and gunners fought, they were pushed back, but only a mere 3km (2 miles) and at a cost to the SS that was out of all proportion to the gains.

II SS Panzer Corps, which included the *Das Reich* and *Hohenstaufen* Divisions, both of which were relatively well-equipped and rested after the Battle of the Bulge, went into action the same day. The weather was unkind, with a temperature of 11 degrees Centigrade, and it was sunny and warm. Therefore the conditions were the worst possible for tank crews at this time of year — a sea of mud. In common with all the Panzer divisions *Hohenstaufen* found the going appalling. The

Above: Soviet engineers under fire cut their way through barbed wire entanglements. The soldier in the foreground has a PPS-43 sub-machine gun with its stock folded. Less well known than the other SMGs, the 43 had a box magazine which held 35 rounds. The camouflage suit shown here was only issued to elite front line units such as engineers and scouts.

commanding officer, Standartenführer Sylvester Stadler, noted:

'A massed Panzer attack is simply impossible. The entire landscape has turned to softened mud in which everything sinks. Obersturmbannführer Telkamp, a prudent Panzer commander, led the most advanced company personally and had to determine that his regiment could not be committed because the heavy vehicles sank into the mud. After two Panzers had disappeared into the filth up to their turrets the attack on a broad front by the advancing grenadiers could only still be supported by one Panzer company from the only highway in the attack sector. Since the Russians expected our attack, the regiment soon received heavy defensive fire from all weapons. Under these circumstances, the attack only went forward with difficulty.'

The Germans had ignored the Hungarians' warnings and were now paying the penalty in blood.

The following day was simply a repeat of the first, giving Tolbukhin a chance to move his reserves into place. The V Guards Cavalry Corps, with 10 tanks and a brigade of self propelled guns including 50 or more SU-100 tank destroyers, moved to support Twenty-Sixth Army. Artillery fire was concentrated on the attack lines and once more the SS advance could be measured in hundreds of metres.

Of *Hohenstaufen's* front Stadler wrote bitterly:

'The Russians attacked all day long in battalion and regimental strength from their well-constructed positions. Since they knew the terrain well, the support by artillery, heavy mortars and tanks was targeted and effective. Scarcely was an attack repulsed when the Russians appeared again in another place. The

Hohenstaufen kept up its high morale, as it, under the given circumstances, was able to hold off all the attacks and make them extremely costly for the enemy. Unfortunately, our own losses were equally high.'

This grinding battle of attrition continued. On 10 March a Hungarian infantry division was pushed forward to support I SS Panzer Corps and Sepp Dietrich came up to the front line to inspire the men of the *Leibstandarte*, his old command, to greater efforts. When two more Panzer divisions, 6th and 23rd, were committed the situation began to change in the Germans' favour. The breach in the Soviet lines was increased to 24km (15 miles). On 12 March elements of the *Leibstandarte* and *Hitler Jugend* managed to cross the Sio Canal, an important part of the Soviet defences, causing Tolbukhin to commit three armoured units from his fast diminishing reserve. These were XVIII and XXIII Tank Corps and I Guards Mechanised Corps with a combined strength of over 100 tanks (including 47 Shermans) and about 60 tank destroyers. As the armoured battle

Above: Hitching a ride on a StuG III assault gun in Hungary. The bars along the side of the superstructure are the mounting for the side armour, which has been removed to prevent clogging from mud.

swayed to and fro, the losses on both sides mounted. Fuel and ammunition shortages plagued the Germans who had difficulty organising resupply across the mine-strewn ground behind their forward positions. As at Kursk, isolated Soviet infantry groups stalked the German positions ambushing the unwary, particularly ration and ammunition parties. Rear security was often left to groups of Hungarian cavalrymen who patrolled the area with some caution as horse's hooves set off mines as well as a man or vehicle.

Mustering his last reserves, Army Group South's commander, General Wohler, made one last effort to break through the Soviets' last line of defence before the Danube. The attack failed. Sepp Dietrich now requested that the offensive be called off. However, events overtook the Germans as Tolbukhin launched his own operation, deploying Ninth Guards Army which was to be joined by Sixth Guards Tank Army transferred from 2nd Ukrainian Front. The Soviet intention was very straightforward: to attack the left flank and rear of Sixth SS Panzer Army. Then, having isolated it, destroy it with the assistance of Twenty-Sixth and Twenty-

Seventh Armies which would advance to the west. The offensive started on 16 March as per instructions.

The Road to Vienna

The Soviet offensive began well, German resistance was worn down and the northern flank of the salient created by their advance soon began to buckle under the pressure. AGS began to withdraw to its start lines of two weeks before but it was not a planned, orderly retreat. Furthermore, III Panzer Corps had been reduced to 40% of its armoured strength and Sixth SS Panzer Army to a little over one-third. The Red Air Force faced virtually no opposition from the Luftwaffe. The Soviet aircrews relished the freedom to shoot up the almost defenceless columns of German vehicles. Nor was there any chance of Wohler transferring reserves from quieter sectors of AGS — this possibility evaporated when 2nd Ukrainian Front began its own operation on 19 March. The Germans were pulling back across the ground between Lakes Balaton and

Velencze. The key to the escape corridor was the small town of Szekesfehervar. If the two Soviet fronts could link up there then Sixth SS Panzer Army would be encircled.

Amid scenes of desperate fighting four Panzer divisions, with infantry support, held open a gap less than 1.6km (1 mile) wide which enabled many of the troops to make their escape. Heavy equipment was abandoned as fuel ran out; everything was sacrificed to keep the tanks operational. Typical of the rapidly declining strength of the armoured troops was the return for the *Das Reich* Division which listed a total of five Panzer IVs, two Panthers and five Jagdpanthers as being fit for combat. Burnt out by the offensive and now reeling westwards, such formations as *Das Reich* were divisions in name only. There were no more men to pad out the ranks of the grenadier regiments and very few tanks left, around which they huddled. As the front collapsed SS battlegroups fought delaying actions around hamlets and fords in an effort to buy time for their fellow combatants to escape. The history of the *Wiking* Division paid tribute to one such effort:

> 'It must be remarked at this point [22 March] that the 9th SS Panzer Division *Hohenstaufen* played a decisive part in the fortunate break-out of *Wiking*. Contrary to orders, Stadler had pushed his front as far forward as possible to the northern part of Lake Balaton in order to hold the sector open for the Division.'

The Soviets were unable to close the trap and the SS escaped.

But this was as nothing in Hitler's eyes. As far as he was concerned the SS had failed him and cost Germany Hungary's oil. As punishment he ordered that the SS divisions, which wore cuff titles as a mark of their elite status, should forfeit the right to them. Ironically it was Himmler who had to transmit this order. Some sources claim that the *Leibstandarte* returned theirs in a chamber pot.

Nor was it only Germans who were involved in this collapse. The Hungarians, where they could, made for home. Realising that there was no alternative, thousands more surrendered. Here and there the more fanatical, especially men of the SS, fought on to the bitter end or retreated with their comrades in arms to fight another day. With Fifty-Seventh Army exerting the same pressure on Second Panzer Army Hungary was swiftly cleared. By the end of March AGS had been reduced to a shambles and 3rd Ukrainian Front stood poised along the Austrian border. Behind the lines NKVD security regiments rounded up thousands of German and Hungarian stragglers.

The plan for the capture of Vienna was predicated on *Stavka*'s belief that the city would be heavily fortified and fanatically defended, particularly as most of the remains of Sixth SS Panzer Army were heading in that direction. On 1 April the forces assigned to the Vienna operation were Forty-Sixth Army approaching from the east, Fourth and Ninth Guards Armies from the south and west with Sixth Guards Tank Army. Naturally Vienna had been designated a fortress and the local Volkssturm had been called out by the Gauleiter, Baldur von Schirach, a young half-American. But it was a fantasy fortress with a reluctant Volkssturm. Tolbukhin aimed to surround the city and pushed his infantry into the southern and eastern approaches whilst his tanks headed west. As German resistance stiffened, representatives of the Austrian underground proposed to the Soviets that they postpone their attack until the German defenders were subverted. However, the plan was betrayed and the resistance leaders' corpses were displayed on

Above: Street fighting in Vienna in April 1945. This machine-gun team has removed the gun's shield to reduce its weight. The man nearest the camera appears to be armed with a 7.62mm M 38 carbine. This gun had a barrel that was 213mm (8 inches) shorter than the standard infantry rifle and was therefore a less clumsy weapon for close combat.

the Floridsdorf Bridge. Karl Renner, an old socialist, who offered to form a provisional government, made another approach to the Soviets. After some consideration Stalin agreed to Renner's proposal.

Prior to the main attack Tolbukhin issued a declaration to the Viennese on 6 April in which he stated:

> 'The Red Army is waging war on the German aggressors and not on the inhabitants of Austria who may pursue their peaceful labour undisturbed . . . Citizens of Vienna! Help the Red Army to liberate the Austrian capital. Make your contribution to the cause of liberating Austria from the German fascist yoke!'

Although there had been fighting for several days it now began in earnest. Hampered by the bomb-damaged buildings, the Soviet infantry pressed towards the city centre. Landmarks such as the Ringstrasse and the amusement park were battered almost beyond recognition. To speed matters along tanks were committed to the fighting. A veteran officer of the Sixth Guards Tank Army recollected, 'We absolutely locked our hatches from inside . . . when we burst into Vienna they were throwing grenades at us from the upper floors of buildings. I ordered all the tanks to be parked under the archways of buildings and bridges.' Urban combat was not a healthy environment for armoured vehicles. Nevertheless the Guards' Shermans pushed on regardless of the losses they took from Panzerfausts or the odd enemy tank they encountered. By 8 April they were approaching the bridges over the Danube. Another Guardsman's reminiscence described the effect of a shot from an ISU-152 tank destroyer on a Panther (possibly one of the handful left with *Das Reich*):

'The ISU let loose and the impact knocked the Panther backward (for about 400–500 metres). Its turret separated from the hull and landed some metres away. But as a result of the shot broken glass fell from above . . . It was good thing we were all wearing helmets. This, my first experience of fighting in a large city, was sad indeed.'

The ISU-152 was known throughout the Red Army as the 'animal hunter' as its ability to deal with Tigers and Panthers was unquestionable.

The next day Stalin ordered that the northern escape route be blocked. For the next four days the pockets of resistance were worn down. *Das Reich* lost its last tanks on 13 April, the day the Soviets declared the city taken and in Moscow the celebratory volleys thundered out with what was almost becoming monotonous regularity.

Berlin and Moscow: Berlin

In February Hitler had declared Berlin a fortress and its Gauleiter, Minister of Propaganda Josef Goebbels, therefore assumed responsibility for the capital's defence. Remarkable as it may seem, one of the first soldiers from whom Goebbels sought advice was the leader of the ROA, General Vlasov. Goebbels sent an aide to find out what could be gleaned from Vlasov as he had had considerable experience as one of the defenders of Moscow during the winter of 1941–2. Apparently Vlasov was polite but unforthcoming. The day-to-day running of military affairs was left to General Helmut Reymann who took up his post on 6 March. Reymann found himself adrift in a sea of confusion and inter-agency rivalry. The propaganda machine had described the Berlin Defence District as a 'hedgehog position simply bristling with defences'. As Reymann discovered, this was arrant nonsense. The Nazi Party had called for the mobilisation of workers to build trenches, bunkers and anti-tank ditches but few reported and they lacked the equipment to do much more than scrape the surface. Earth-moving machinery had been sent elsewhere, lacked fuel or was controlled by some authority that would not sanction its release. Supplies were controlled by one set of bureaucrats who followed their own guidelines, and plans for the evacuation of civilians were purely theoretical. The garrison was almost non-existent, comprising some Volkssturm battalions, an anti-aircraft division and some ceremonial units. Reymann dutifully assembled a staff and allocated them tasks while he attempted to negotiate with Army Group Vistula for some experienced units.

The command of AGV had proved too much for the delicate sensibilities of the Reichsführer-SS who seems to have spent more time asleep or in the sanatorium than at his HQ. Consequently a face-saving formula was agreed whereby Himmler stepped down, on the grounds of overwork, to be replaced by General Gotthard Heinrici. Heinrici was an officer with a wealth of experience in defensive fighting against the Red Army. During the winter of 1941–2, when the future of Army Group Centre had hung in the balance, he had been responsible for developing the tactic of emptying his front line just before the Soviet barrage and then launching counter-attacks with relatively fresh troops. As Heinrici described it:

'It was like hitting an empty bag. The Russian attack would lose its speed because my men, unharmed, would be ready. Then my troops on sectors that had not been attacked would close in and reoccupy the original front lines.'

After falling out of favour in late 1943, Heinrici returned to command First Panzer and Hungarian First Armies as part of AGC in Slovakia in the autumn of 1944 where he demonstrated his skill against Petrov's 4th Ukrainian Front.

When Heinrici arrived at Zossen in March 1945 Guderian appraised him of the situation facing AGV in the following terms:

'The Russians are looking down our throats. They've halted their offensive to reorganise and regroup. We estimate that you'll have 3–4 weeks — until the floods go down — to prepare. In that time the Russians will try to establish new bridgeheads on the western bank and broaden those that they already have. They have to be thrown back. No matter what happens elsewhere, the Russians must be stopped on the Oder. It's our only hope.'

From the Baltic coast in the north to the confluence of the Oder and Neisse Rivers in Silesia where it joined Schörner's AGC, AGV's line ran for 280km (175 miles) along the Oder's banks. The Germans held three bridgeheads on the eastern bank: to the north at Stettin, in the centre and directly east of

Above: A female medic applies first aid to a casualty in the front line. Medics like this were expected to follow close on the heels of the assault troops. Women played a larger role in the Red Army than in any other. Each nurse carried material for dressing wounds, including iodine and bandages.

Berlin at Küstrin (Kostrzyn) and to the south at Frankfurt an der Oder. The two armies which constituted AGV were Third Panzer (General Hasso von Manteuffel) which defended the line from the coast for roughly 145km (90 miles) and the stronger Third (General Theodor Busse) which linked up with AGC and covered the direct approach to Berlin that lay along Reichsstrasse One. Used as he was to the conditions on the Eastern Front, the weakness of some of the units under his command came as a surprise to Heinrici as many were divisions on paper only. However, the worst discovery was that an attack had been insisted on by Hitler that was designed to eliminate the largest Soviet bridgehead by a pincer move out of the Frankfurt and Küstrin bridgeheads. This was almost underway when he took command on 22 March. Heinrici declared to Guderian, 'Our troops will be pinned with their backs to the Oder. It will be a disaster.'

In part Hitler's enthusiasm for this attack had been fuelled by the apparent success of a counter-attack by AGC against the town of Lauban (Luban), near its boundary with AGV, in early March. The Soviet Third Guards Tank Army had been caught off balance and driven back which encouraged Schörner to advance towards Breslau. These successes, accompanied by a propaganda fanfare, including the usual list of Soviet atrocities, and a personal visit from Goebbels himself, were to be short-lived. Nevertheless the Küstrin–Frankfurt attack was to go ahead. Unfortunately for AGV some of its units were caught whilst manoeuvring near Küstrin, defeated and the city cut off by elements of Soviet Eighth Guards Army. Despite furious German counter-attacks on 23 March Küstrin remained isolated. On 27 March the attack from Frankfurt was launched only to be stopped in its tracks by Soviet artillery and air strikes which confined it almost to its start line.

The following day, after an unprecedented row with Hitler, Guderian was ordered to take sick leave and he was replaced by General Hans Krebs who was unlikely to cause Hitler any concern over the condition of the Oder front as his reports were tailored to generate confidence. Fortress Berlin now came under AGV and life in the Führerbunker settled down into its last few weeks of surreal fantasy.

Hitler's mind was now occupied with thoughts of destruction and retribution. The conviction that the German people had proved unworthy of his ambitions grew to assume concrete form when Albert Speer, his Armaments Minister and as close to a kindred spirit as Hitler had, presented him with a report which predicted the collapse of the German economy in 'four to eight weeks'. Speer concluded that the collapse was inevitable. At that point Hitler declared, 'We can no longer afford to concern ourselves with the population.'

This chilling sentence was to presage what became known as the 'Nero Orders' which involved the evacuation of the population of western Germany and the wholesale destruction of the Reich's industrial, commercial and social fabric. Hitler went on to say:

'If the war is lost, the people will be lost also. It is not necessary to worry about what the German people will need for elemental survival. On the contrary, it is best to destroy even these things. For this nation has proved to be the weaker, and the future belongs to the stronger eastern nation. In any case, only those who are inferior will remain after the struggle, for the good ones have already been killed.'

To his lasting credit Speer spent the next few weeks hurrying about preventing this demonic retribution for, although Hitler changed his mind, there were still sufficient fanatics in positions of authority to carry it out come what may.

On 7 March American forces had captured the bridge over the Rhine River at Remagen. Incensed, Hitler had ordered the execution of several Wehrmacht officers who were deemed to be responsible. To discourage similar acts, supposedly of treachery, desertion or cowardice, a Führer Order was issued instituting drumhead courts martial with almost unlimited powers to execute any member of the SS, Heer, Kriegsmarine or Luftwaffe who was not where he should be regardless of the situation. Martin Bormann followed this line and empowered his Gauleiters to carry out similar justice. In a short space of time the rear areas of every army group were decorated with the hanging corpses of those who had allegedly betrayed the party, the people and the nation. Pensioners of the Volkssturm and teenagers of the Hitler Youth were not exempt from such punishment and passers-by could read the charge and verdict that was usually pinned to the victim's chest. In this climate of mistrust and fear the Third Reich prepared for the final battle.

Berlin and Moscow: Moscow

As the Red Army cleared the last pockets of resistance in East Prussia, moved up to the Oder and pushed into Austria and Czechoslovakia, Stalin considered his next move. Planning was already underway at *Stavka* for the offensive that would sweep into Berlin. However, the Supreme Commander of the Red Army had several areas of concern. First and foremost amongst these was the possibility that the Western Allies would, or already had, come to an arrangement with the Germans to fight a joint war against the USSR. Reports were reaching Moscow that the Anglo-American advance in the west was going ahead with little or no resistance and that German troops were surrendering in their thousands. The Soviet experience was almost the reverse — resistance in the east was grimly determined with many Germans preferring suicide to surrender. Stalin had been the leader of the USSR for years during which it had been viewed by the governments of the west as, at best, a pariah and to him such a war was a perfectly logical next step. Indeed the conditions for the Western Allies to wage such a war would be close to perfect, as the Red Army's supply lines would be stretched to their limit across a Poland that was nowhere near accepting of its new regime. Furthermore, there were two well-equipped Polish armies, albeit under Soviet command, on Polish soil that might turn their guns on their liberators. The move against Berlin would therefore have to be prepared down to the last bullet and carried out with as much speed as possible.

Stalin, for reasons noted earlier, did not trust Churchill one inch and, as the British were in the best position to advance on Berlin, having crossed the Rhine on 24 March, it seemed probable that they would get there first, denying that well-deserved glory to the USSR.

But there was more than simple glory, political kudos or industrial gold to Berlin; there was scientific treasure, more precisely the German atomic weapons research programme. This had produced a substantial quantity of uranium that the Soviets, despite their vast mineral resources, lacked. It was absolutely vital to Stalin's mind that the USSR catch up and keep pace with Anglo-American research in this field and capturing the German resources in Berlin was key to this. Operation 'Borodino' was the name given to the operation to secure this asset.

However, news reached Moscow on 30 March from Eisenhower's HQ which did much to allay Stalin's concerns. The Supreme Commander in the West outlined his plans for the next few weeks and they did not include Berlin, which Eisenhower regarded as relatively unimportant. The British would be moving towards Hamburg and Denmark, the Americans into central and southern Germany to link up with the Red Army on the Elbe River and pre-empt any German attempt to stage a last ditch defence in the mountains of Bavaria and Austria. The conquest of Berlin was therefore handed to the Soviets on a plate.

Naturally, British political leaders were displeased when they were told of Eisenhower's plans but there was nothing that could be done politically or militarily as President Roosevelt was dying and the orders had been issued.

Above: Two faces of defeat.

Chapter 9

Objective 105 – The Reichstag: April 1945

'To raise the banner of victory'. Marshal Zhukov on the eve of the Oder attack

Soviet Planning and Preparation

Stavka had been planning the Berlin operation for several weeks before Zhukov was summoned to Moscow at the beginning of March to make his contribution. Detailed planning then got underway. Returning to his HQ a couple of days later, Zhukov worked up his own plans in anticipation of the forthcoming offensive. The capture of Küstrin, by Eighth Guards Army on 30 March, allowed 1st Belorussian Front to expand its bridgehead thus easing the flow of supplies and the problem of storage.

At the end of March Zhukov and Konev both travelled to Moscow. 1st Ukrainian Front was now almost completely in line along the Neisse River and the two marshals were in good positions to go for Berlin. On 1 April Stalin asked them, 'Well now, who is going to take Berlin, we or the Allies?'

Konev was the first to affirm that his front was ready, rapidly followed by Zhukov. The general plan was then shown to them both. The offensive was to take place along the entire line from the Baltic Sea to Görlitz in Silesia and involve Rokossovsky's 2nd Belorussian Front as well as Konev's and Zhukov's fronts. The German line along the Oder and Neisse Rivers was to be broken, the defenders isolated and bypassed by the tank armies, which would head for Berlin itself leaving the mopping up to the infantry armies. 1st Ukrainian Front would have the job of cutting Army Group Centre off from Army Group Vistula and Berlin and linking up with the Americans on the Elbe taking Dresden on the way; 2nd Belorussian Front would perform a similar task against Third Panzer Army. 1st Belorussian Front would

Above: Female traffic controllers were a common sight along the Soviet lines of communication. Above the sign points out the distances to Berlin and Moscow. The lower sign shows the point to leave injured troops. Further along the information strikes a cautionary note and reads, 'Soldier, remember you are in Hitler's Germany.'

advance directly on Berlin through German Ninth Army.

Konev and Zhukov both presented their plans to Stalin who approved them with but one alteration. Stalin introduced an element of competition to spur his marshals on. The demarcation line between the two fronts was drawn so that it ended at the town of Lübben 60km (37 miles) south-east of Berlin. At that point, should the need arise, Konev was permitted to alter his line of advance from west to north-west and into Berlin. Therefore, should Zhukov run into difficulties, Konev would be in a position to take Berlin from the south, 'Whoever breaks in first, let him take Berlin', were Stalin's last words on the subject — it was to be a race.

The offensive was to begin no later than 16 April, leaving the two fronts a little over a fortnight to prepare. With that decided, the marshals left Moscow later that day.

When Konev and Zhukov had gone Stalin responded to Eisenhower's message outlining the Western Allies' plans. It was a carefully worded reply. Flattering Eisenhower by agreeing with his overall strategic concept, Stalin assured him that the Red Army's next major operation would be towards southern Germany. He admitted that some troops would be directed towards Berlin but with the rider that 'this plan may undergo certain alterations, depending on circumstances'. His order to his front commanders in fact stipulated that the operation had to be completed in no more than 15 days.

In East Prussia Rokossovsky merely received a directive from *Stavka* to 'redeploy westwards . . . and replace units of 1st Belorussian Front'. As Rokossovsky wrote:

'Only yesterday the troops had been facing eastwards; now they had to turn west and cover 300–350km [185–220 miles] in marching formation over country ravaged by the recent fighting . . . In view of the poor handling capacity of the railways we decided to use them only to transport tanks and other wheeled vehicles. The bulk of the troops proceeded in marching formation, using all available wheeled transport from trucks to horse carts. Infantry moved forward in waves, now on foot, now on wheels . . . There was not enough rolling stock on the railways and the track and bridges were in such a state that trains crawled along at walking speed.'

2nd Belorussian Front had to take over approximately 160km (100 miles) of Zhukov's front to allow his forces to concentrate to the south. As his men moved west, Rokossovsky visited Moscow to receive

Above: Soviet Guards cavalry officers pose near a recently captured German armoured train. Both sides used armoured trains extensively. The Wehrmacht's trains operated mainly against the partisans providing artillery support for the infantry or patrolling the supply lines. However, such units were extremely vulnerable to air attack despite mounting anti-aircraft guns.

his instructions. During this time he was granted four more days to position his troops; consequently his part in the Berlin operation would not start until 20 April. *Stavka* informed Rokossovsky that his front would have the job of cutting Third Panzer Army off from Berlin and pushing it back towards the coast so denying it the opportunity to escape to the west. On his return to Pomerania Rokossovsky visited the front line, which was forming along the Oder River. He described the view thus:

'The sight did not please us, however, at least from the tactical point of view. Between us and the enemy positions was the river, which forked here into two wide channels, the East and West Oder. The land between them was flooded at this time of the year, thus presenting us with a continuous water barrier 5 kilometres [3 miles] wide. The high western bank was hardly visible. It would have been simpler if it were all river, as we could then have crossed it in boats and pontoons.'

One of his officers commented, 'Our men call it "two Dniepers with a Pripyat in between", quite aptly I think.' This reference to the Dniepr River and the Pripyat Marshes showed that the Soviet troops did not hold this waterway in contempt as they usually did when comparing the rivers of eastern and central Europe. Rokossovsky ordered aerial reconnaissance of Third Panzer Army's

defences. This revealed machine-gun nests, and rifle pits along the river bank supported by the main system of trenches and bunkers to a depth of 10–11km (6–7 miles). To the west a similar line was being constructed along the Randow River 20km (12 miles) away. Rokossovsky's attack was to take place along a 45km (28-mile) front using Forty-Ninth, Sixty-Fifth and Seventieth Armies (infantry). When the break-through was made, tanks and cavalry would exploit it and advance to the west. The armies would attack simultaneously and wherever success was achieved then supporting arms would be introduced. As the assault troops moved into position the engineers busied themselves preparing and extemporising equipment to cross the rivers, the laying of corduroy roads and bridge building. Wherever possible the front line was advanced towards the German positions to reduce the distances that the attackers would have to cover.

Along Zhukov's front the preparations were equally impressive. To motivate and inform his army commanders Zhukov held a series of seminars and war games during 5–7 April. Having been put in competition with Konev, Zhukov now placed his own armies in a similar situation when he revealed a diorama of Berlin and posed the question, 'Who is going to be the first to reach the Reichstag?' This objective was numbered 105 and was the prime target as it was assumed Hitler would be found there. One Soviet general said, 'Just think. If I reach 107 and 108, I might grab Himmler and Ribbentrop together!'

Beautifully made as it was, the diorama could not convey the difficulties that fighting in a city of some 1,000 square kilometres (400 square miles) would entail.

During the next three days the army commanders were briefed on their roles in the offensive. The main attack was to take place in the darkness of early morning on 16 April and would be launched from the Küstrin bridgehead across a front of 44km (27 miles). To add to the Germans' surprise searchlights would illuminate the battlefield while dazzling the defenders and there would be a short but heavy barrage. According to Zhukov the searchlight stratagem was wargamed and, 'All participants unanimously agreed to their use.' Either no one recalled the failure of such a ploy during World War 1 or none had the courage to stand up to Zhukov when it was obvious that it was a double-edged tactic that would present the defenders with a beautifully lit field of fire. Nevertheless it was adopted.

Although there would be land attacks, many river crossings were also necessary. The first major obstacle, directly blocking the road to Berlin, was the Seelow Heights, the taking of which was assigned to Chuikov's Eighth Guards Army supported by Third and Fifth Shock Armies. When these forces had broken through, the armour of First Guards and Second Guards Tank Armies would drive towards the city itself. Zhukov, with Stalin's agreement, now altered the routes of the tank armies so that Berlin would be enveloped to north and south. First Guards Tank Army would now capture the eastern suburbs and then move south, Second Guards Tank Army would go north. The supporting attacks were to be made by four armies. First Polish and Sixty-First Armies in the north would advance to the Elbe and, until 2nd Belorussian Front began its attack, cover Zhukov's right flank from any counter-attack by Third Panzer Army. Thirty-Third and Sixty-Ninth Armies in the south would secure Frankfurt-on-Oder, complete the isolation of German Ninth Army by co-operating with Konev's left flank, and then move to the south of Berlin.

The army commanders were warned that Soviet intelligence had identified eight defence lines covering the approaches to the German capital. To crack these positions 1st Belorussian Front was allocated almost 9,000 guns and heavy mortars and hundreds of *Katyusha* rocket launchers with their expert Guards crews. As the senior officers dispersed to their command posts thousands of lorries poured supplies, guns and men into the concentration points. Hundreds of engineers laboured day and night in the freezing waters of the Oder to maintain and improve the 28 bridges that crossed the river behind the lines and on which the offensive depended.

Above: Although surrounded by members of his staff, Marshal Zhukov was well aware that his shoulders alone bore the responsibility for the success or failure of operations in Germany during the advance on Berlin. Following the end of the war he was rapidly marginalised by Stalin and spent years in military backwaters.

Luftwaffe attacks and German artillery strikes were unable to do more than cause a few hold-ups; the major difficulty was fitting everything into the rear positions. Despite the best efforts of the lady traffic controllers frantically waving their bats, jams inevitably built up as officers demanded priority. However, slowly the artillery moved into place. Row upon row of heavy guns took position in woods and forests ranked according to calibre and fire mission. Millions of shells piled up alongside the vehicles to distribute to them and wherever they could the infantry trained. Thousands of reserves, including a large percentage of paroled criminals from prisons and camps far inside the USSR, were brought in to fill up the ranks along with recently released POWs and ordinary conscripts. Activity on this scale did not go unnoticed by the Germans but, as one Soviet officer commented, 'No one seemed to give a damn what the Germans saw.' The more the enemy knew of the massive force assembling in front of him the more likely he was to be very, very afraid.

Having made themselves as comfortable as possible the infantry were, to use a modern phrase, 'psyched-up' by political officers and the press although this was later toned down by order of Moscow. Fear of a last minute use of chemical weapons generated the issue of

orders regarding gas masks and other precautions. Tank crews were reminded of the order to keep their hatches open to reduce the effect of a hit on the fighting compartment by a hollow-charge round. Bed springs and thin metal sheets were attached to the tank's hulls to absorb the impact of anti-tank fire. Veteran armoured troops preferred to keep their hatches shut rather than risk a mine, grenade or Molotov Cocktail being dropped into their vehicle. 'Horseless Tankers', as those members of tank units without tanks were known, painted the white crosses and bands, prescribed by inter-Allied agreement for air recognition, on the tank's turrets. Naturally rumours abounded and there were many ordinary soldiers who were well aware of when the offensive would begin, as no security precaution was ever watertight.

To the south Konev was already incorporating the move on Berlin into his plans in line with Stalin's earlier suggestion. In his orders for the forthcoming offensive Konev wrote, 'Berlin to be attacked from the south by a tank corps (from Third Guards Tank Army) reinforced with a rifle division of the Third Guards Army.' As his 7,000 guns deployed on the east bank of the Neisse and his bridge-building and engineering units laboured to construct rafts and any other vessel they could to supplement the pontoons and Lend-Lease amphibians that appeared daily, Konev briefed his senior commanders on their units' roles. The main attack would involve Third and Fourth Guards Tank Armies which would exploit the break-throughs made by Third and Fifth Guards and Thirteenth Armies. Elements of these forces would then swing towards Berlin and the north-west. The right flank would co-operate with Zhukov. Second Polish and Fifty-Second armies were to advance on Dresden and the Elbe. On the way they would be engaging Fourth Panzer Army, part of AGC.

The Neisse was fast-flowing and over 120 metres (130 yards) wide and the German defences were well provided with solid gun and machine-gun emplacements. Lacking a foothold on the steep western bank, Konev had opted for a long bombardment followed by an assault covered by smoke. This smoke-screen was to be laid by aircraft and extend, to quote Konev again, 'along a front 390km [240 miles] long, no more no less'. To increase his infantry strength Konev was given Twenty-Eighth and Thirty-First Armies, but they would not be available until the offensive was in progress as they had to travel from East Prussia.

The Soviets were massing 2,000,000 men, 41,000 guns and heavy mortars, 6,250 armoured fighting vehicles and almost 8,000 aircraft. If nothing else it was a monumental piece of staff work.

German Planning and Preparation

If the Soviet commanders faced deadlines, their German counterparts had to contend with a lunatic strung out on various drugs and surrounded by a court of sycophants who consistently fed his brain with drivel and false hopes. Tucked away in his bunker under the Reich's Chancellery Hitler existed in a dream world insulated by several metres of earth and concrete. In early April Heinrici kept an appointment with the Führer at which he was to brief him on the situation facing Army Group Vistula and his men's condition. This was the commander of AGV's first trip to the capital in two years and he likened the destruction he passed to 'a sea of rubble'. The conference was attended by all the Third Reich's grandees who, had they but known it, were directly under objective 106 on Zhukov's diorama. Heinrici was given the floor to enable him to return to his HQ as soon as possible.

He began, 'My Führer, I must tell you that the enemy is preparing an attack of unusual strength and unusual force . . . the main attack will hit Busse's Ninth Army . . . and the southern flank of Third Panzer Army.' Having outlined the forces available to Busse he declared Ninth Army to be 'in better shape than it was'. But, 'Third Panzer Army is in no state to fight at all . . . We can accept Third Panzer's weak condition only as long as the Oder remains flooded', but then 'The Russians will not fail to attack there too.' In a similarly candid vein Heinrici requested that the garrison of Frankfurt-on-Oder be withdrawn. Having briefly agreed with this suggestion Hitler then changed his mind. An argument ensued until finally Heinrici said, 'I do not believe that the forces on the Oder front will be able to resist the extremely heavy Russian attacks that will be made upon them.' To emphasise the point he continued, 'The fact is that, at best, we can hold out for just a few days. Then it will all come to an end.' At that point offers flooded in from the Luftwaffe and the Kriegsmarine as the representatives of both services vied with each other to provide more untrained, ill-equipped, inexperienced

Above: A weary anti-tank gunner puts the finishing touches to his emplacement. The weapon is a captured, converted Soviet field gun with the German designation 76.2mm PaK 36(r).

men as infantry for AGV. Heinrici then requested the return to his army group of the four armoured divisions that had been transferred to Schörner's Army Group Centre on 5 April. Hitler had authorised the move as he was convinced that the next major Soviet offensive would be directed at Prague. Hitler was also convinced that 'Army Group Vistula should be well able to withstand the secondary attacks.' Heinrici then stated, 'I cannot guarantee that the attack can be repelled.' Hitler, incandescent with rage, let Heinrici know that he and his men must have 'belief — then you will achieve victory, and the greatest success of the war'. With those words ringing in his ears and the promise of 150,000 reinforcements from the other services, Heinrici left the bunker for his HQ.

The condition of AGV had not been exaggerated. Ninth Army consisted of four corps, on the left CI and LVI Panzer, XI SS Panzer in the centre and V SS Mountain around Frankfurt. Defences had been dug to take skilful advantage of the terrain. The most formidable of these was the system based on the Seelow Heights facing 1st Belorussian Front. Seelow Heights was a horseshoe shaped plateau to the west of Küstrin that varied in height from 30–60 metres (100–200 feet) and overlooked the swampy Oderbruch (or Oder valley). Seelow Heights was the key to the German defence line and as such it had been lined with artillery including dozens of 88mm anti-aircraft/anti-tank guns taken from the Berlin air defence network. Volunteers from Eastern Europe, including several hundred Ukrainians, provided the crews for many of these guns. Heinrici hoped to turn the Oderbruch into a killing ground for his artillery and the armoured support that was held in the area.

Following the transfer of the tank divisions to AGC, AGV was left with only 700 armoured fighting vehicles. Few of these were manned by veterans, most of whom were now fighting for their lives around Vienna or were surrendering in the west as their fuel ran out. The two Panzer corps were armoured in name only. One of the tank divisions, *Müncheberg*, a part of LVI Corps, had only 50 tanks fit for action on 13 April. The division had been formed on 8 March 1945 but only included one tank regiment. There is some evidence that the division was to be issued with tanks, probably Panthers, which had been equipped with the revolutionary infra-red night firing devices.

The major armoured unit in XI SS Panzer Corps was the 502nd SS Heavy Tank Battalion that had taken delivery of some of the last Tiger IIs produced in late March. The greater part of the armoured strength was made up of assault guns and tank destroyers that were based on obsolete tank chassis such

Above: A Wehrmacht Panzer officer keeps watch.

as the Hetzer. In theory each infantry division had an assault gun component such as the 920th Assault Gun Brigade with 303rd Infantry Division *Döberitz*, part of XI SS Panzer Corps.

Amongst the infantry units was one of the ROA's two divisions, the 1st, also known by its German designation of 600th Panzergrenadier Division. On 13 April, at the personal request of General Vlasov, 1st Division went into action against the Red Army. A lack of air and artillery support, due to fuel and ammunition rationing, was blamed for the Russians' lack of success in this action. Their attack made little ground but the presence of the ROA generated several

hundred deserters from Soviet units. The division's commander, General S. K. Bunyachenko, deferring to no one but Vlasov, withdrew his men and marched off towards Czechoslovakia. On the way south various German commanders attempted to enlist the division's aid but Bunyachenko ignored them all and such was the condition of the Wehrmacht that no one seriously tried to stop him.

Manteuffel's Third Panzer Army comprised XXXIII and XVLVI Panzer Corps and the 3rd Marine Division made up of sailors and commanded by an admiral with a mainly naval staff. Foreign troops, experienced SS men, formed a significant part of Manteuffel's infantry although these units were nowhere near their titular divisional strengths.

In order to gain a clearer picture of the Soviet forces and a feel for the situation Heinrici flew over their lines almost every day. When Heinrici landed he and his staff would analyse the reports from the intelligence services and the information gleaned from prisoner interviews in the hope of predicting the date of the enemy attack. Finally, during the evening of Sunday 15 April, Heinrici decided that now was the time to withdraw to the second line of defence, as the Soviet guns would start their preliminary bombardment the following day. The Battle for Berlin was about to begin.

The Soviet order of the day that was read to all units prior to the offensive told them:

'The time has come to draw up the balance sheet of the abominable crimes perpetrated on our soil by the Hitlerite cannibals and to punish those responsible for these atrocities. The time has come to inflict the final defeat on the enemy and to draw this war to a victorious conclusion.'

Hitler's order of the day tapped into a different psychological vein and was heavily larded with threats and lies:

'You soldiers in the east already know the fate which threatens . . . German women, girls and children. The old men and children will be murdered; women and girls will be reduced to army camp whores. The remainder will go to Siberia . . . since January everything has been done to build up a strong front . . . The enemy is confronted by a tremendous amount of artillery . . . Losses in our infantry have been filled in with countless new units . . . Anyone ordering you to retreat, unless you know him very well, is to be taken prisoner on the spot no matter what his rank may be . . . At this moment when fate has removed from the earth the greatest war criminal of all time, the turning point of this war will be decided.'

Roosevelt was the 'greatest war criminal' and his death on 12 April had given Hitler wild hopes of a rift between the Western Allies and the USSR. Needless to say nothing came of this.

The Battle for Berlin — 1st Belorussian Front

'Now, Comrades. Now!' was Zhukov's simple command and, precisely at 05:00 hours Moscow time, 03:00 hours Berlin time, the very moment Hitler had gone to bed, three red flares soared into the sky and the Soviet guns began to fire. For the next 30 minutes thousands of tons of high explosive crashed onto the German front line where the token garrison huddled shivering as the earth around them erupted and shook. The Soviet infantry attack began, illuminated by the beams of the searchlights, just before the guns shifted targets. Eyewitnesses remember that being released into the attack seemed to have generated a sense of berserker fury in the men of the first waves who screamed and howled as if experiencing a collective release of tension. After waiting close to such an intense barrage and having had their emotions worked on by the political officers for days before, it is hardly surprising that they wanted to get on with the business in hand. In the centre

Above: Carrying the usual complement of passengers IS-2 tanks of 1st Belorussian Front move through an undamaged Pomeranian village. The turret is reversed and the main gun supported on a travelling bracket. On roads the IS-2 was capable of 37km/h (23mph); off road this was reduced to 17km/h (11mph).

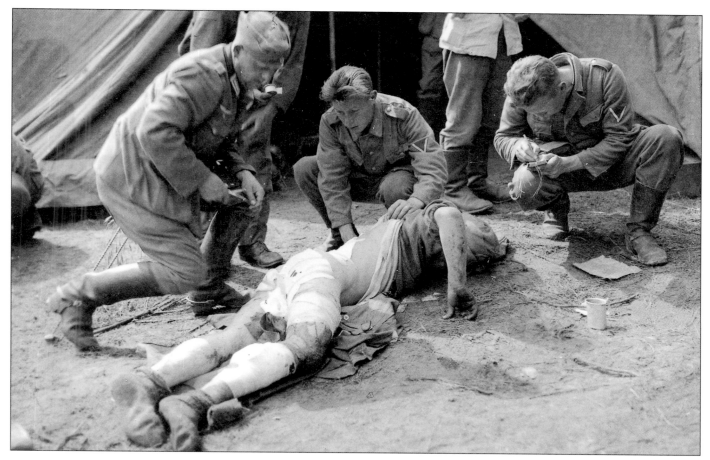

Above: A badly wounded infantryman receives help at a casualty clearing station behind the lines. The NCO to the right is writing out the ticket that will allow the casualty to be evacuated. Passes such as these were essential as detachments of field police were continually on the look-out for malingerers and lack of documentation frequently led to summary execution.

Chuikov's Guardsmen went forward out of the Küstrin bridgehead. Away to the right First Polish and Sixty-First Armies crossed the Oder in amphibians, pontoons and rafts while to the left Thirty-Third and Sixty-Ninth Armies advanced to isolate Frankfurt.

At first Eighth Guards Army made good progress but not, according to Chuikov, thanks to the searchlights:

'The searchlights were periodically turned on and off, and it seemed to the attackers that they were confronted by obstacles; they lost their orientation. After all, human vision is not adapted to sudden changes from darkness to light . . . In many sectors the sub-units stopped before the brooks and canals which intersected the Oder Valley deciding to wait for the dawn in order to examine the obstacles they would have to cross.'

Crossing a smoking lunar landscape, with the noise of the guns still ringing in their ears, the constant fear of German tracer and the overhead roar of aircraft, shells and rockets must have been enough to shred the nerves of experienced men let alone the newly arrived recruits. Heinrici received a report, which

informed him that 'annihilating fire had practically destroyed our front line fortifications'. Nevertheless his withdrawal the previous night had saved many of his men from the worst of the shelling. Now they must fight, but what they were lacking was artillery ammunition as Ninth Army had only had enough for two and a half days and a lucky shot on an ammunition dump had reduced the stock even further.

However, the Soviet attack was beginning to bog down in the Oderbruch. The torn ground and shattered trenches were proving to be an unforeseen obstacle and the German guns on the Seelow Heights were pouring fire into the tanks and self-propelled guns that were piling up on the banks of a canal. The sacrificial waves of the Soviet penal battalions had made considerable inroads into the minefields but there was still insufficient room for the vehicles to manoeuvre and a traffic jam was building up. Zhukov had moved up his supporting units too quickly and they were now paying the price for not waiting until the infantry had cleared the way.

By midday things were obviously not going according to plan and Zhukov therefore ordered another bombardment of the Seelow Heights to be followed by an attack involving 1,300 armoured vehicles of First Guards Tank Army. Second Guards Tank Army would attempt to cross to the Oderbruch. Both units took heavy casualties from German armoured formations that seemed to appear from nowhere and disappear almost as quickly into the smoke and confusion. The 1st Battalion of the *Müncheberg* Panzer Regiment proved particularly effective in this role. By late afternoon Chuikov's troops had fought their way to the outskirts of the town of Seelow where two important roads and a railway intersected. But once again they found their way blocked by infantry and armour. Nudged on by their own tanks the infantry tried to advance but made little headway and once more traffic snarl-ups exacerbated the inevitable confusion of battle. Zhukov, enraged at the lack of progress, ordered that the fighting continue into the night. Katukov, commanding the First Guards Tank Army, noted that he had 'never seen such resistance in the whole course of the war'.

At his HQ Heinrici received a telephone call from Krebs at Zossen, who appeared pleased, 'Well, we have good reason to be satisfied.' Heinrici was more sanguine and suggested they wait before commenting too optimistically. Across the river Zhukov was not a happy man; he had promised Stalin that the Seelow Heights would be taken by 17 April and that date was fast approaching. On the line from Moscow that night Stalin had indicated that he and *Stavka* were considering ordering Konev to head for Berlin with both his tank armies and had instructed Rokossovsky to incline his operation towards the north of Berlin in support of 1st Belorussian Front. Now that the competition was out in the open Zhukov would have to step up the pressure on his commanders.

The forces of 1st Belorussian Front around the Seelow Heights were redeployed during the night of 16/17 April in preparation for another assault.

From 10:00 hours on the 17th Zhukov's gunners hammered the German lines while aircraft of the ADD dropped hundreds of tons of bombs and ground-attack aircraft attacked any Panzer they could find. Fifteen minutes after the bombardment started the Eighth Guards Army stormed forward supported by First Guards Tank Army. Despite a counter-attack by German armour, Seelow was surrounded. As the German artillery began running out of ammunition an increasing number of the newly transferred Luftwaffe 'infantry' began to crack under the strain and slip away from the front line. Later that day Seelow fell but somehow the Ninth Army managed to hang on to most of its positions on the heights.

Aware of Konev's progress to the south, Stalin authorised him to make for Berlin. When Zhukov was notified of this he ordered his army commanders to renew their efforts. To the south around Frankfurt and to the north the progress had been equally slow; it was along the sandy slopes of the Seelow Heights that the break-through had to be made.

On the morning of 18 April, following another heavy artillery and air strike, the Guards attacked once more. Chuikov remembered:

'That day the German command committed two fresh motorised divisions, the *Kurmark* and the *Müncheberg*, and an SS infantry division under General Seifert. There was fierce fighting as the enemy undertook a series of counter-attacks, notably on the Army's left flank. In the Diedersdorf area the Germans attempted to cut the Küstrin–Berlin highway, along which XXIX Guards Rifle Corps and First Guards Tank Army were bringing up their combat vehicles and logistics. To remove this threat the commander of XXVIII Guards Rifle Corps was ordered to commit the second echelon 39th Guards Rifle Division.'

The SS infantry division was probably the remains of the 23rd Panzergrenadier Division *Nederland*, which included a regiment named *General Seyffarth*. Along with the 11th SS Panzer Division *Nordland*, *Nederland* was moved south from Third Panzer Army where these two divisions comprised much of the strength of III SS Panzer Corps commanded by Obergruppenführer Felix Steiner. *Nordland*'s transport column had suffered heavily from repeated attacks by *Shturmoviks* during the course of its move, although its tank battalion, *Hermann von Salza*, seems to have survived intact. In this action the Germans claimed to have destroyed 50 Soviet tanks; 17 of these were credited to one crew. Attached to the *Kurmark* Panzergrenadier

Above: An abandoned German Wespe (Wasp) self-propelled gun in a town in eastern Germany. The Wespe was a combination of a 105mm howitzer and a Panzer II chassis that provided mobile artillery support for the Panzer divisions. This vehicle has been left when it, like so many others, ran out of fuel.

Above: An IS-2 tank moves into a German town. The heavy DShK anti-aircraft machine gun has been removed as they often snagged in telephone or similar cables. The replacement is the lower profile DT weapon. Tank platoons (four tanks) engaged in street fighting operated in pairs moving and firing alternately along both sides of the street. The vehicle to the right appears to be a German command caravan.

Division was 502nd SS Heavy Tank Battalion, the Tiger IIs of which took a similarly heavy toll of the Guards' tanks. Interestingly, *Nordland* was the last known unit to which the 50 or so British traitors of the Britisches Freikorps or Legion of St George who joined the Waffen-SS were known to have been attached.

At midday Busse contacted Heinrici declaring, 'Today is the day of crisis.' However, it was to be another 24 hours before Ninth Army's third line of defence finally broke and a gap of 72km (45 miles) opened in front of 1st Belorussian Front. Ninth Army began to break up, LVI Corps under Weidling retreated west towards Berlin and XI SS Panzer Corps to the south. The following day, 20 April, was Hitler's 56th birthday and, apparently by coincidence, that was the day on which, at 11:00 hours, the artillery of 1st Belorussian Front opened fire on Berlin itself. Zhukov's tanks broke out into easier country spurred on by his order, 'To break through to Berlin first and to raise the banner of victory.' The German front line east of Berlin was in tatters but the situation to the south was even worse.

The Battle for Berlin — 1st Ukrainian Front

Success had attended Konev's efforts from almost the moment his artillery and air forces began their destruction of the German defences on the western bank of the Neisse River. As Konev observed to one of his army commanders, 'Our neighbours use searchlights, for they want more light. I tell you . . . we need more darkness.' The artillery barrage had started at 06:10 hours on 16 April and the first infantry began to cross, at 150 selected points, 45 minutes later. The smoke-screen worked to perfection, as there was little wind to disperse it. Led by the men of 6th Guards Rifle Division, part of Thirteenth Army, three waves of assault troops launched themselves onto the icy water frantically rowing or paddling almost anything that would float. Less than 30 minutes later the first bridgeheads had been established. Infantry casualties were lower than anticipated due to the smoke. Then it was the turn of the engineers to brave the freezing temperatures. As ferries were drawn

back and forth by cable, hundreds of engineers struggled in the water to build bridges capable of bearing tanks and heavy artillery. In scenes reminiscent of Napoleon's heroic engineers at the Berezina crossings in 1812, the bridges were built and maintained despite German artillery and Luftwaffe strikes. To suppress German fire from the surviving bunkers 200 machine guns were deployed as were light guns firing over open sights, 'just to keep their heads down', as the commander of Thirteenth Army recalled.

At 08:45 hours, when the Soviet artillery stopped firing, Konev was informed that 133 crossings along the 80km (50 miles) front had been secured and that Third Guards Tank and Thirteenth Armies were pushing west followed closely by Fourth Guards Tank Army. By midday the engineers had several 30- and 50-ton bridges operational and, as the tanks rolled westward, columns of POWs crossed to the east, many still dazed by the severity of the bombardment and the speed of the Soviet advance. The Second Polish Army was also making good progress en route to Dresden.

Above: Soviet infantry follow rapidly in the wake of their artillery's bombardment. Going into action with the minimum of equipment was a Soviet tradition, extra ammunition and grenades were usually the limit. The sweat on the men's backs is testament to their efforts.

By the end of the first day the Neisse bridgehead was 14km deep and 27km wide (9 miles by 17 miles) and, despite several counter-attacks which Schörner had cobbled together, Fourth Panzer Army was forced to retreat. Like Zhukov, Konev drove his men on through the night, I Guards Cavalry Corps was ordered to move into the German rear and soon the cry of 'der Kosaken kommen' was to cause as much panic in 1945 as it had in 1914.

The next major river barrier was the 45–55 metre (50–60 yard) wide Spree. Luckily for the Soviets it was less than a metre deep and the tanks rolled straight across it. That evening Konev spoke to Stalin who told him of Zhukov's slow progress and suggested 1st Belorussian Front's armoured units be routed through Konev's front. Having discussed the difficulties this move would cause, Stalin then gave his permission for Konev to, 'Turn your tank armies on Berlin.' This sweep to the north would take them through Zossen, the nerve centre of the German High Command that was less than 80km (50 miles) away. Orders went out to the tank armies to reach the suburbs of Berlin by 20 April avoiding any serious defensive positions and insisting on 'boldness of manoeuvre and swiftness of operations'. However, as the Guards tank armies raced away the men of Polish Second Army, marching to the west, crossed the old Napoleonic battlefield of Bautzen unaware that they were about to be hit by what was

virtually the last Panzer attack to be mounted in any strength.

Hitler, now aware that 1st Ukrainian Front was not moving on Prague, had ordered Fourth Panzer Army to launch a counter-attack. Unfortunately Schörner's AGC lacked the wherewithal to carry out a grand operation against an entire Soviet army group, therefore the group moving on Dresden was chosen. The *Grossdeutschland* Panzer Corps was to strike from the south and LVIII Panzer Corps' 20th Panzer Division and the Paratroop Panzer Division *Hermann Göring* from the north. Headed by over 100 tanks, the attack hit the junction of Fifty-Second and Second Polish Armies. The Poles were caught unawares and the German armour pushed into their rear some 25km (16 miles), causing havoc in their transport lines and bringing the advance to a halt as I Polish Tank Corps was pulled back to deal with the problem. The Germans managed to relieve the garrison at Bautzen but the attack came to an end on 24 April as the fuel ran out and powerful Soviet reinforcements, with strong air support, began to arrive.

On 21 April Zossen was abandoned and the majority of the staff transferred to keep communications systems and command structures in being. That afternoon units of Third Guards Tank Army arrived to be met by signs advising them to be careful with the equipment, as it would be 'valuable to the Red Army'. The only member of the skeleton

staff who remained sober told his final caller, 'Ivan is almost at the door. I'm closing down now.' But the tank thrust was slowing down so, to re-energise it, Konev issued his next instruction which read, 'Personal to Comrades Rybalko and Lelyushenko [commanding Third and Fourth Guards Tank Armies respectively]. Order you to break into Berlin tonight. 20.4.45.' Although there was a gap of 32km (20 miles) between the two tank armies, the Germans had nothing left to throw in and by the following day the attack had cut the Berlin Ring Road and Third Guards Tank Army was moving up to prepare for the next phase of the operation. Fourth Guards Tank Army had almost reached Potsdam while several advanced units were only 40km (25 miles) from 1st Belorussian Front's Forty-Seventh Army coming around the north of Berlin.

The remarkable pace of Konev's advance left in its wake thousands of refugees and German soldiers, few if any of whom had any fight left in them. This was not an attitude that would have pleased their former commander who had been mercilessly enthusiastic in carrying out Hitler's orders regarding supposed cowards and deserters. Around the town of Cottbus on the Spree a strong German force held out but the largest group, encircled by units of both 1st Belorussian and 1st Ukrainian Fronts, was what remained of Busse's Ninth Army and Fourth Panzer Army in the Spree forests.

Above: A Katyusha battery opens fire. This is the Model BM-13-16 mounted on a Lend-Lease American manufactured Studebaker chassis.

Above: The wreckage of Busse's Ninth Army marked its passage to the west. Throughout the war much of Germany's equipment was horse-drawn and these beasts of burden have paid the ultimate price.

A number of German units, such as Weidling's LVI Corps, disappeared for several days to re-emerge either with Busse or in Berlin. Naturally this gave rise to considerable communications problems and to a misleading idea as to the size of these formations that retained their titles but with much reduced strengths. Indeed Weidling was condemned to death when his corps vanished. He and his men resurfaced close to Berlin within a couple of days having fought a series of vicious rearguard actions on the way.

As Zhukov's armies moved into position around Berlin, Konev's tank armies drew up along the banks of the Teltow Canal and prepared to attack. On 23 April Stalin issued his definitive order regarding the capture of Berlin. The demarcation line was drawn 140 metres (150 yards) to the west of the Reichstag, which placed the parliament building in Zhukov's area of operations. It was now the job of the men of 1st Belorussian Front to capture 'the lair of the fascist beast' and raise the Red Flag over the ruins of his capital.

2nd Belorussian Front

However, at least Konev's men would be in at the death; to the north Rokossovsky's troops would not be included in the final glory. On 19 April Rokossovsky informed Stalin that all was ready. The guns opened fire at 06:00 hours along the main axis of operations. A smoke-screen provided cover along the 47km (29-mile) front. Aided by a provident mist, the assault began well and bridgeheads were established quickly. A diversionary attack down-river caused Manteuffel to withhold his reserves until it was clear which were the major thrusts. Seventieth Army was making reasonable progress as was Sixty-Fifth, but Forty-Ninth was getting nowhere and taking heavy casualties. Consequently Rokossovsky decided to exploit the situation on Sixty-Fifth Army's front where two 16-ton bridges had been moved into position thus enabling light self-propelled guns and artillery to cross and support the infantry against the counter-attacks of 27th SS Grenadier Division *Langemarck*'s Flemish infantry. By the

following evening the Sixty-Fifth Army's bridgehead had increased to 26 square kilometres (10 square miles) but it was exposed to fire from the heavy artillery in Stettin and ships of the Kriegsmarine.

Slowly but surely reinforcements were moved into the bridgehead and with the cancellation of the Berlin order on 23 April, 2nd Belorussian Front reverted to its original mission. Forty-Ninth and Seventieth Armies were now both more or less bogged down when Sixty-Fifth began to attack from its bridgehead. The weather had improved sufficiently for the Red Air Force to provide 'flying artillery' support for the advancing tanks. This was vital if the move was to be effective as the roads were mainly laid along the tops of the dykes that criss-crossed this marshy region. Losses amongst the mine-clearing engineer teams were inevitably high, particularly from well-concealed snipers, often local Volkssturm men whose knowledge of the terrain made them formidable opponents.

Eventually, on 25 April, Third Panzer Army began to withdraw to its defence line along the Randow River. Rokossovsky described the

Above: Elderly German replacements take their place in the line. Although they are well-dressed, weapons seem to be scarce.

fighting of the next day as continuing 'as fiercely as ever'. What his men were now encountering were local battalions of recently activated Volkssturm and scratched-together rearguards. Forty-Ninth Army moved to cut off Manteuffel's communications with Berlin and other formations were sent to guard the coast to prevent any landings by German units from AGN or the Samland Peninsula. Several battalions were ordered to clear the islands in the Oder River estuary. In fact Heinrici himself had instructed Manteuffel to retreat, ordering him to abandon the Stettin fortress at the same time. Two days later Keitel travelled from Berlin to meet with both generals. Having berated Heinrici, Keitel removed him from command of Army Group Vistula, telling him to 'return to your HQ and await your successor'. Heinrici waited and then drove to Plön, where Himmler and Dönitz had their HQ, which he reached on 1 May just in time to hear the broadcast announcing Hitler's death.

2nd Belorussian Front spent the last week of the war rounding up the stragglers of Third Panzer Army who were unable to reach the Elbe River where the British waited. On 3 May the Soviets met up with British Second Army and proceeded to clear the last German garrisons from the Baltic islands near the Danish coast.

In Berlin

For many Berliners the critical situation on the Oder was brought home to them with a vengeance on 16 April when they awoke to the roar of Zhukov's artillery causing the sky to light up and the earth to shudder. It was the latest event in a month that had already seen Budapest, Vienna and Königsberg fall to the Soviets and now it seemed that the capital's turn had come. Their fears were confirmed when the eight o'clock news announced that, 'Heavy Russian attacks continue on the Oder front.' Hitler slept on, content in his mind that Roosevelt's death would have a calamitous effect on the Allied cause. He was unaware of the order that had gone out to the Allied armies in the west that they should advance no further than the Elbe River although there would be a powerful thrust to link up with the Red Army in the Danube Valley. Berlin was to be left to the Soviets. The Red Air Force had already given notice of its arrival in the skies over Berlin on 28 March when it had carried out an early morning raid. Although most Berliners carried on as normally as possible, the next few weeks would change their lives out of all recognition. But, for all the noise of the guns, the city was pervaded by the false calm that precedes a thunderstorm.

Goebbels's Propaganda Ministry was working all-out to inspire the city's population to retain its faith in the ultimate victory. Slogans appeared on the walls of bomb-blasted buildings that seemed grotesquely optimistic, 'Vienna will be German again', 'Ein Volk, Ein Reich, Ein Führer' and the unfortunately worded, 'Who believes in Hitler believes in victory'. The irony of the latter was not lost on those who read it, for many Berliners had never been enthusiastic about Hitler or Nazism, not even in the glory days early in the war. Now, in what were obviously the last weeks of the war, fewer believed than ever before. However, their city was a fortress about to be besieged; consequently it was sensible to lay in as much food as possible and to carry on working as if nothing would change. Factories continued to produce munitions; the Volkssturm paraded; there had been no attempt to evacuate the ministries or the population; all in all therefore maybe the situation was not too bad? But behind the fortress propaganda there was little substance, as General Reymann well knew.

Berlin had been divided into three concentric defence rings the longest, around the outskirts being 100km (60 miles), the second 40km (25 miles) and the inner ring 11km (7 miles). Radiating out from the inner ring the city was divided into eight slices labelled clockwise from the Weissensee district in the east A–H. The inner ring was known as Zentrum or Zitadelle. Z sector enclosed all the government offices numbered on Zhukov's diorama and, for those who noticed such things, Zitadelle had been the code name for the disastrous German offensive at Kursk in 1943. The defence lines had been fortified with anything to hand. General Max Pemsel, the fortification expert who had constructed the Atlantic Wall, had arrived in Berlin on 12 April but had been sent away for arriving too late. On his way to the airport he noted the deplorable condition of the defences and 'thanked God for allowing this bitter chalice to pass me by'. Some effort had been made to dig trenches, erect anti-tank barriers and build barricades across the wider streets to link up ruined buildings but it was too little too late. Reymann commented, 'According to Goebbels we'll get everything we want if Berlin is encircled.' Even his attempts to create a runway along the East-West Axis to provide an emergency airstrip ran into opposition from Albert Speer, who also tried to prevent the destruction of the city's bridges. However, the S-Bahn, Berlin's elevated railway, provided a solid line of embankments and the rivers and canals were themselves formidable barriers, particularly in Z sector where they were overlooked by the massively strong ministerial buildings. Although the garrison was weak in veteran

Above: Young recruits undergo training with Panzerfaust anti-tank equipment. The instructor is holding the projectile for a Model 60M. The number refers to the range which was 60 metres (65 yards). The fins opened out as the projectile left the tube and it armed in-flight within 5 metres. Although it was theoretically a single-shot weapon the tubes were usually recycled. The figure on the left has an egg grenade hanging from his belt.

infantry, the Hitler Youth and Volkssturm had access to thousands of Panzerfausts but the majority of their other weapons gave the impression of coming from the collection of an antique weapons buff. On 18 April Reymann was ordered to send the Volkssturm to the Oder along with a considerable number of 88mm guns. As they tramped off the Nazi Party paper reported on the Soviet offensive and declared, 'Each Soviet tank which a grenadier, a Volkssturm man or a Hitler Youth destroys is worth more today than at any other time in this war. The hour of decision demands the last, the greatest, effort.'

As the Oder line crumbled Hitler got ready to celebrate his birthday on 20 April. Himmler, Goebbels, Keitel, Admiral Dönitz and Bormann all arrived to present their best wishes. The Führer emerged from the bunker, and during his last photo call presented some decorations to SS men and squeezed the cheeks of selected Hitler Youths. Göring was late, having spent the morning supervising the demolition of his palace behind Third Panzer Army's lines. When the daily situation report had ended Hitler ordered that, in the event of the Soviets linking up with the Western Allies, the north

of Germany would be controlled by Dönitz and the south by Field Marshal Albert Kesselring. The various ministries were then ordered to leave Berlin. This instruction gave rise to what was dubbed 'the flight of the golden pheasants', as senior party officials were popularly known due to their gaudy uniforms. Only Goebbels and Bormann of the top-rank Nazis remained with Hitler in the bunker. At this briefing it was pointed out that the Soviets were west of Vienna, the British almost in Hamburg, the French in Bavaria and the Americans on the middle Elbe. Jodl recalled that Hitler told him he would 'fight as long as the faithful fight next to me and then I shall shoot myself'. For the ordinary Berliners the Führer's birthday meant a larger ration than usual and what was probably the last general display of red Nazi flags that still retained the swastika. Very soon the party symbol would be removed in an attempt to make the flag acceptable to the new masters.

The next day, 21 April, was the last day on which the British and Americans bombed Berlin but by now the sound of the Soviet guns was almost constant. As Ninth Army pulled itself together in the forests to the south-east of Berlin some of its detached units began to arrive on the outskirts of Berlin. Hitler had sent instructions to Obergruppenführer Steiner's III SS Panzer Corps to attack the right wing of 1st Belorussian Front later that day. On paper it looked a splendid idea, in practice it was impossible, as Steiner's divisions had already been committed three days earlier and all he now commanded were a few 'regiments' of infantry and some stragglers. Hitler promised Steiner that he would be reinforced by Göring's bodyguard troops and 'every available man between Berlin and the Baltic Sea up to Stettin and Hamburg'. The written order that followed threatened officers, including Steiner, with death if they fell back to the west as, 'The fate of the Reich capital depends on the success of your mission.' Although he faced execution, Steiner did nothing as he realised that there was nothing to be done. No relief expedition was launched from the north. That night Weidling replaced Reymann as Berlin's military chief. Weidling arrived at the Führerbunker to clarify the matter of his death sentence as the remains of his LVI Panzer Corps joined the motley groups preparing to defend the city. The garrison had increased to roughly 45,000 Wehrmacht and SS men and a similar number of Volkssturm with about 50 operational armoured vehicles.

On 22 April, when Hitler discovered that Steiner's forces had not moved, he became almost hysterical and, having declared that the war was lost, announced that he would remain in Berlin and take his own life. Hitler was informed the next day of Göring's announcement that he was now head of state. For this presumption Göring's arrest was promptly ordered.

As the Soviets gathered to the south of Berlin, Hitler summoned another force to its rescue, Twelfth Army. Commanded by General Walther Wenck, Twelfth Army was

holding the Elbe against the Americans. Keitel visited Wenck's HQ on 23 April and simply announced, 'We must save the Führer.' Keitel then showed Wenck and his staff how they should relieve Berlin. As Keitel left Wenck decided that he would send a token force towards Berlin, leave a screen facing the Americans and use the bulk of his troops to break through and open up an escape route to the west for the remains of Busse's Ninth Army, which had been completely cut off the day before. Wenck visited his men and appealed to them to support his move, which they appear to have done with few dissenters. A couple of days later an announcement was made to the population of Berlin that, 'General Wenck's army has just joined up with the Americans. They are attacking towards Berlin. Hold up your courage!'

With relief on the way and Reymann's replacement more of a 'fighting general', Hitler felt somewhat more comfortable about the city's position. But beyond the dank confines of his bunker people's lives were changing. Shelling was now taken as a matter of course; queuing for food had become more dangerous due to the randomness of the

Above: A Tiger I moves through a German town towards the end of the war. The vehicle nearest the camera is a Volkswagen Schwimmwagen, the amphibious version of the Kubelwagen. Fuel shortages seem to have been localised with some regions plentifully supplied while others were almost dry.

Above: An abandoned Luftwaffe airfield that was overrun towards the end of April 1945. The Fw 190s and Stukas all appear to have parts removed, possibly to repair similar types. By this stage of the war very few Luftwaffe squadrons were operational.

Above: Here a heavy gun, a 152mm Model 1935, prepares to fire on a German position in Berlin. The other members of the crew have taken cover in the buildings to the left of the gun as the devastating effect of the explosion at close range was likely to cause 'friendly' casualties. The crane for lifting the 48-kg (106-lb) shot is to the left of the breech.

explosions; and bands of field police and SS men combed the streets hunting for deserters or traitors. Those they found were usually executed in public and left to dangle from the nearest lamp post or tree to 'encourage' the others. Services began to break down as workers absented themselves from their jobs or were rounded up to man the barricades.

A final message reached the Berlin telegraph office from Tokyo which read, 'Good luck to you all.'

The Last Days

1st Belorussian Front conducted a softening-up propaganda campaign against Berlin's defenders at the same time as its assault teams pushed deeper into the suburbs. As well as leaflets being dropped, trusted German POWs were allowed to pass into the city in an attempt to counter Goebbels's

hair-raising tales of Soviet behaviour in occupied Germany. Their efforts seem to have achieved some success. On 22 April Zhukov ordered his men to keep going day and night and two days later Eighth Guards Army was ordered to cross the Spree River. On the same day at 06:20 hours 1st Ukrainian Front opened its attack on the Teltow canal. An incredible 650 guns per kilometre (1,100 yards), with barely enough space for the crews to operate, fired for almost an hour. Unsurprisingly the German defences collapsed as 203mm shells gutted buildings and bunkers indiscriminately. After crossing the canal under cover of this hurricane of fire, the Soviet infantry secured several bridgeheads and very soon tanks were rolling across newly established pontoon bridges. Later that day Rybalko, commanding Third Guards Tank Army, made his way to Chuikov's HQ and formally announced the arrival of 1st Ukrainian Front to Zhukov. Outside Berlin the two fronts met up and completed the city's encirclement at midday on 25 April at roughly the same time as Konev's Fifth Guards Army made contact with the

Americans near Torgau on the Elbe.

That night Hitler summoned Weidling to the bunker where he told him that:

'The situation must improve, from the south-west the Twelfth Army of General Wenck will come to Berlin, and together with Ninth Army, will deliver a crushing blow to the enemy. The troops commanded by Schörner will come from the south. These blows should change the situation to our advantage.'

It was complete nonsense but reinforcements did arrive by air, two battalions of naval cadets, reportedly in their parade uniforms. Tempelhof airport was now the scene of heavy fighting so Gatow airfield was used instead. Indeed some intrepid flyers landed on the East-West Axis, the old parade route through the city centre.

As the Soviets moved inexorably towards sector Z they faced a remarkable selection of defenders. Although the Volkssturm usually tried to surrender or make their way home, the men of the European Waffen-SS fought on. These 'crusaders against Bolshevism' knew

they had little chance of survival as POWs and most of them fought to the bitter end. There were few Germans amongst them. Alongside the Scandinavians of the *Nordland* Division there were Russian, Latvian, French, Dutch, Belgian, Spanish and Hungarian volunteers. Any semblance of central command and control was disappearing fast as the men of the Red Army cleared block after block, showing little mercy to soldier or civilian alike. Tanks, heavy artillery and *Katyushas* were used at point-blank range simply to flatten any building that appeared to offer resistance. No soldier was prepared to take any unnecessary chances with victory so close. Flame-throwers were used to scour rooms, cellars and air raid shelters and, as the defensive zone grew smaller, so the resistance became more fanatical. In the midst of all this carnage the civilians just sat tight and prayed for it to end.

In his eagerness to take the Reichstag Zhukov had committed two tank armies but these formations took heavy losses from the Panzerfaust-armed tank-hunting teams. The handful of German tanks and assault guns mounted the occasional counter-attack to some effect but the lack of fuel caused many of them to be used as static gun positions.

Hitler had refused Weidling's suggestion of a break-out stating, 'I am staying and I will fall at the head of my troops.' He was at the head of his forces physically as the bunker was in the heart of sector Z where the last major groups of defenders gathered. Psychologically he was in a different world altogether. By 28 April Soviet infantry were within 1,500 metres (1,640 yards) of the Reichstag but none was aware that the 'fascist beast' was in the process of making his mistress an honest woman. Remarkably, in the midst of all the chaos, Goebbels had managed to find the appropriate official to conduct the ceremony. The Hitlers' reception lasted for 20 minutes and the registrar was killed making his way back to his unit. The bridegroom spent his wedding night composing his will and political testament so that these documents could be smuggled out of his doomed capital.

In the early hours of 29 April 301st Rifle Division took the Gestapo HQ on the Prinz Albrecht Strasse and later that day Eighth Guards Army crossed the Landwehr canal and took the Potsdamer bridge to reach the Tiergarten, within a stone's throw of Weidling's HQ. That night Weidling made his last report to Hitler. SS Brigadeführer Mohnke, commanding sector Z and Weidling were in accord that the fighting in Berlin would end within 24 hours. Keitel confirmed that Twelfth Army had failed to reach Berlin and that Ninth Army was surrounded.

The next morning, 30 April, the assault on the Reichstag began. However, the building and its defenders hung on despite a concentrated bombardment. While the Soviets moved in, Hitler and his wife killed themselves. Later that evening Zhukov's troops finally hoisted their flag over the Reichstag despite the fact that fighting was still going on in many of the offices below. That night Krebs, with the permission of Goebbels, the new Chancellor, approached Chuikov's HQ to ask for an armistice.

Above:
Part of a squadron of Il-2 *Shturmoviks* flies over a residential area of Berlin in April 1945. On closer inspection the bomb-damaged buildings can be clearly seen. The rear gunner was armed with a 12.7mm UBT machine gun. Removing the rear canopy to improve visibility was a common practice.

Opposite top:
Not eager to lose their lives with the end of the war so close, this Soviet infantry section moves cautiously towards the entrance of an underground station on Frankfurter Allee. Thousands of German soldiers and civilians took refuge in these tunnels and underground waterways and many were still inclined to resist to the death. The sign gives directions to an overground air raid shelter.

Opposite:
With casualties mounting rapidly and Berlin's hospitals taxed beyond their capacity medical staff worked where they could. This open-air facility is typical of such overflow wards.

Right:
The air superiority enjoyed by the Allies made any missions undertaken by the Luftwaffe almost suicidal. This FW 190 was brought down by Soviet ground fire during the spring of 1945.

Chapter 10

The Last Days of the Reich: May 1945

'Everything in Berlin was quiet.'
Marshal Chuikov's memoirs

Krebs arrived at Chuikov's HQ at 22:00 hours on 30 April to arrange a separate armistice with the Soviets. Chuikov contacted Zhukov who in turn spoke to Stalin and was told that nothing less than unconditional surrender was acceptable. A German staff officer returned to the bunker to present these terms to Goebbels. There then began hours of fruitless discussion during which both Krebs and Chuikov reiterated their positions. The journey between both HQs was not an easy one as few soldiers on either side were aware of the negotiations and there were those in the German ranks who were not prepared to

surrender and would shoot anyone they suspected of entering into such discussions whatever their rank. Zhukov had given the Germans a deadline, 10:15 hours on 1 May, by which, if they did not agree to an unconditional surrender, 'We'll blast Berlin into ruins.' As Goebbels refused to accept these terms when Krebs returned to the bunker, the Soviet guns did precisely what Zhukov expected of them. As the Moscow garrison marched across Red Square in the usual May Day celebrations, the *frontoviki* of Eighth Guards Army once more launched themselves at the Reichstag's other floors in another attempt to flush out the last SS men who retreated to the cellars.

In the Tiergarten the defenders of the

massive flak tower were approached to surrender which they did later that night. Soviet loudspeaker vans toured the front lines broadcasting an appeal to the defenders in all areas to lay down their arms. Many did so.

In the bunker itself the remaining group of Hitler's disciples prepared themselves. Bormann and Mohnke organised their own break-out with the aid of men of the *Nordland* Division while Goebbels and his wife organised their suicides. Having murdered their children, they then took their own lives. At 21:30 hours Hamburg Radio broadcast the news to those who could receive it that Hitler, 'In the battle against Bolshevism . . . fought to the last breath before his death at the head of his troops.' During the early

Above: An interesting trio of vehicles, headed by an SU-76M self-propelled gun loaded with infantry, passes through a German town during April 1945. Next to the main armament is a Maxim machine gun on its wheeled carriage. The open cab of the SU-76 made it very vulnerable to enemy attack. The second vehicle is a Lend-Lease amphibious Jeep, and behind that an American lorry.

Above: Marked with air-recognition stripes, a column of Soviet armour drives along the Unter den Linden with the Brandenburg Gate to their rear.

Above: Zhukov's prime objective was the Reichstag and the honour of capturing it spurred Chuikov's Guardsmen to make almost suicidal attacks. Here Soviet infantry winkle out some of the building's last defenders from the cellars with grenades dropped through the ceilings.

hours of the morning of 2 May the last SS men in the Reichstag capitulated. Later that day Axis forces in Italy surrendered.

Shortly after midnight on 2 May Weidling's LVI Panzer Corps contacted Chuikov to arrange their surrender and six hours later Weidling crossed into the Soviet zone, wary to the last of SS men who might decide to obey Goebbels's order to shoot deserters in the back. In other parts of the city various groups, responding to wild rumours of escape routes, attempted to leave the capital. Amongst them were Bormann, Mohnke and Artur Axmann, the leader of the Hitler Youth. Their attempt failed and Bormann was almost certainly amongst the thousands who died that night. Very few slipped through the Soviet lines and reached the west but two of Hitler's secretaries were amongst them.

After some discussion Weidling wrote out the surrender order to the Berlin garrison which read:

Above: As the original Soviet caption says, 'Here it is the fucking Reichstag!' As the prime objective of the Soviet forces in Berlin it is unsurprising that the delight in its capture should be so vehemently expressed.

Above: Finally the Red Banner, mounted on the Reichstag roof, flies over the ruins of Berlin.

'On 30 April 1945 the Führer took his own life and thus it is that we who remain — having sworn him an oath of loyalty — are left alone. According to the Führer's order you, German soldiers, were to fight on for Berlin, in spite of the fact that ammunition has run out and in spite of the general situation, which makes further resistance on our part senseless. My orders are: to cease resistance forthwith.'

This order was broadcast by Doctor Hans Fritsche, Goebbels's deputy at the Propaganda Ministry, who according to Chuikov was 'brought in on a self-propelled gun'. At 15:00 hours on 2 May the fighting in Berlin officially ended. As the Red Army began to celebrate and organise the surviving enemy troops into POW columns, the NKVD and SMERSH set about ferreting out the whereabouts of Hitler's corpse and other such tasks including organising the security cordon around the atomic weapons research facility at Dahlem. At Dahlem the Kaiser Wilhelm Institute for Physics had been a prime objective for the stocks of uranium it held. The uranium, the laboratories and the scientists were promptly shipped back to the USSR to be used in the Soviets' own atomic

Above: Many myths have grown up around the planting of the Red Flag on the Reichstag. These two NCOs, M. Kantaria and M. Yegorov, have just returned from re-enacting the event for the benefit of the camera. The damage done to the building can be clearly seen behind them.

Above: The charred remains of Josef Goebbels and his wife Magda and the bodies of their poisoned children. Goebbels was identified by his orthopaedic shoe.

research programme. As Chuikov, the victor of Stalingrad and now effective conqueror of Berlin wrote, 'Everything was quiet in Berlin.'

As thousands of Berliners emerged from the rubble and attempted to come to terms with their new situation, the men of Wenck's Twelfth and Busse's Ninth Armies were still fighting for their lives to the south of the city.

Escape to the Elbe

Sources disagree radically, from 40,000 to over 200,000, on the number of troops and civilians that had gathered themselves around the remains of Ninth Army. It is a figure, much like the casualty statistics for the Berlin operation, which will remain forever speculative.

Wenck and Busse had been in communication and agreed that their two armies would rendezvous at the old Wehrmacht training ground near Kummersdorf. From there they would retire to the Elbe and dig in to allow time for the evacuation of as many troops and civilians as possible to the safety of the American lines.

Zhukov and Konev were aware of the German armies but for the moment their attention was focussed on the situation in Berlin. Intelligence reports indicated to Konev that German Twelfth Army consisted

Above: Underfoot a portrait of Hitler, nearby a shattered eagle. Nazi symbols such as these were often the first targets for Soviet troops celebrating victory.

Above: The marking at the rear of the lorry is the Red Army's tactical sign for a motorised artillery unit. The gun's camouflage appears to be more symbolic than practical. It is a 122mm howitzer M1937 M-30, one of the most commonly used Soviet guns.

of two Panzer corps, XLI and IIL, along with XX and XXXIX Corps. When Twelfth Army began to show signs of heading east, Konev's forces in its path, which were mainly units of V Guards Mechanised Corps and Thirteenth Army (supplemented by thousands of recently released POWs) began to dig in. To the east Third, Thirty-Third, and Sixty-Ninth Armies along with II Guards Cavalry Corps from 1st Belorussian Front were mustering to deal with Busse.

It was Wenck who struck first. Twelfth Army's Panzer force, benefiting from the concentration of supply units that had fled to the region from all over Germany, had a good supply of fuel and ammunition. But the terrain over which they attacked, on 24 April, was not good tank country, being quite heavily wooded. The first assault, headed by a scratch division named *Theodor Korner*, failed to make much impression on the Soviet lines. The following day a stronger force supported by an assault-gun brigade began to drive the Soviets back, forcing Konev to commit reserves to hold the line.

To the east Ninth Army was almost ready to move. The rearguard was formed from V SS Mountain Corps and XI SS Panzer Corps, although neither bore much resemblance to its title. The advanced guard was composed of

two Panzer divisions, 21st and the *Kurmark* with 712th Infantry Division. Between them the two Panzer divisions mustered roughly 30 tanks, mainly Panthers and Tiger IIs, which had been fuelled by draining the last drops from surplus vehicles. However, survivors remembered their anger at staff officers who kept their vehicles moving no matter what the situation. The break-through to Kummersdorf was timed for 08:00 hours on 26 April. However, the rearguard was by that time involved in the first of a series of running battles with units of 1st Belorussian Front that had been ordered into action earlier that morning. Zhukov's intention was to split Ninth Army up and link up with 1st Ukrainian Front to destroy the Germans piecemeal. Konev had ordered his units to redeploy to meet the threat from the east but the move was carried out lethargically. Ninth Army's armoured group struck the junction of Third Guards and Twenty-Eighth Armies, which had been subjected to a barrage that lasted until the German gunners ran out of ammunition. Busse's men fought with grim resolution, as they were all well aware of the

odds against them. Konev praised their efforts saying they fought 'purposefully and desperately'. By 10:00 hours some men had crossed the Dresden–Berlin autobahn which was the main supply route for the two Soviet armies. However, counter-attacks and heavy bombing took their toll and confused fighting lasted all day. Hitler, aware of Busse's change of direction reminded both him and Wenck that their mission was 'not only . . . [to] save Ninth Army but principally to save Berlin'. These orders fell on deaf ears. Wenck did have a small force advancing towards Potsdam where the garrison, now grandly titled Army Group Spree, still held out. Such flagrant disobedience and lack of communication coming so hard on the heels of Steiner's passivity must have been much like a slap in the face for Hitler who even a week before could have had Busse executed within a matter of hours.

On 27 April the Germans attacked again and, thanks to the sterling work of the rearguard in holding off Zhukov's forces, Ninth Army's armoured spearhead pushed further west. Unfortunately Ninth Army was

Above: Camouflaged under a netting pyramid to avoid tell-tale shadows, this gun crew prepares to fire. This is a 152mm M1937 ML-20 howitzer. It could throw a 44-kg (97-lb) shell to a maximum of 17,230 metres (18,840 yards) and was served by nine men.

beginning to lose cohesion as the Red Air Force and artillery pounded its columns mercilessly. Busse described his army and its thousands of civilians as 'pushing west like a caterpillar'. As food distribution broke down the hungry mass ate what it could find. When vehicles were damaged their fuel was siphoned off, and any useful parts cannibalised. Every day there were fewer and fewer soldiers and civilians, as the butcher's bill grew steadily longer. The wounded were often left to fend for themselves unless lucky enough to be picked up by a rare vehicle that was not too grossly overloaded. The Soviets had no problem in tracing Ninth Army's route, as it was, by many accounts, difficult in places to avoid walking on dead or wounded Germans.

By late April 1st Ukrainian Front had established three lines of defence between Wenck and Busse. Even though they were insubstantial they had to be broken through.

Sandwiched between the two German forces was V Mechanised Corps that was fighting both ways at once.

Finally the two armies began to link up; at first a small party from the advanced guard got through but soon the numbers increased. As Wenck recalled, 'The men of the Ninth Army were so tired, so worn out, in such terrible shape, that it was unbelievable . . .' that they should have got so far. Out of this mass appeared General Busse to whom Wenck simply said, 'Thank God you're here.' Other senior officers were not so enthusiastically received, particularly the commander of XLI Panzer Corps who had abandoned his men and hurried west with his wife and horses. To the east Soviet cavalrymen hunted for survivors in the shattered forests or

amongst the debris of smashed vehicles. Occasionally the eerie silence that had descended was broken by the crack of a carbine as the most seriously wounded were put out of their misery.

Both forces now moved towards the Elbe where a bridgehead was established roughly 25km long and 18km deep (16 by 11 miles). It was not only the remains of Twelfth and Ninth Armies that packed into this space but a flood of refugees drawn by the chance of safe passage to the west. Soviet attacks were rare and unenthusiastic as the infantry left the job of speeding the Germans on their way to the artillery. The German perimeter held until late in the afternoon of 7 May when Wenck and his staff crossed the river into American captivity.

Above: German infantry enter a slit trench. The last man appears to have a flame-thrower over his left shoulder.

Above: An interesting contrast in capitalism and communism as the Red Army marches past a smouldering branch of the Deutsche Bank. The simplicity of the men's equipment is clear although one has liberated a guitar.

Above: The Allied commanders meet in Berlin for the German surrender. From left to right, Montgomery, Eisenhower, Zhukov and France's de Lattre de Tassigny.

Above: Berliners queue for jobs as hostesses at a nightclub in Soviet-occupied Berlin shortly after the end of hostilities. The poster at the left of the image gives some idea of their duties.

Czechoslovakia

On 28 April Konev had been instructed to move units of his command out of Berlin for use against Dresden and Prague. As this left the final operations and glory in Berlin to Zhukov there was naturally a feeling of resentment throughout the 1st Ukrainian Front; nevertheless an order was an order. In practical terms it did simplify matters for the troops in Berlin as there was only one voice commanding and losses to friendly fire fell as problems with demarcation lines were reduced and the combat zone became more confined.

Army Group Centre under Field Marshal Schörner had been cut off from Army Group South by the Soviet counter-offensive south of Budapest in March. Schörner had then been cut off from contact with Army Group Vistula and lost one of his corps when Konev's armour had swept across the Neisse River. Although some efforts had been made to re-establish contact, by late April AGC was effectively isolated in Czechoslovakia. One of Hitler's last orders was to reward Schörner with command of the German Army. Schörner was as determined as ever to do his

Below: The ISU-122 was properly classified as a heavy assault gun. Occasionally these guns were used for indirect fire missions, but during urban operations they were simply used in the close-range building- and bunker-busting role. They were organised in five-gun batteries with an additional vehicle for the unit commander. These two are parked near central Berlin.

duty and fight on 'until the last man and the last bullet'.

As the Soviets swept over the border into Austria, Malinovsky's 2nd Ukrainian Front and Yeremenko's 4th Ukrainian Front were heavily engaged with AGC in Slovakia and Bohemia-Moravia. Malinovsky had been ordered to move there when he had cleared the German forces from his route out of Hungary. Re-crossing the Hron River in late March Malinovsky turned his attention to Bratislava, the Slovakian capital, and detailed 1st Guards Mechanised Group and Seventh Guards Army to take the city.

However 4th Ukrainian Front's progress was still slow. Therefore on 3 April *Stavka* increased Yeremenko's strength to 250,000 men and 300 tanks and ordered him to push ahead into the Moravska-Ostrava region. Although Yeremenko requested further time to prepare for what he anticipated would be a long, gruelling struggle he was ordered to:

'. . . mount his main attack with Sixtieth and Thirty-Eighth Armies, plus two Breakthrough Artillery Divisions and XXXI Tank Corps towards the western bank of the Oder River with the immediate objective of occupying, not later than 12–15 April Oprava, Moravska-Ostrava and . . . Olomouc, thus linking up with . . . 2nd Ukrainian front.'

Malinovsky was ordered to 'link up with 4th Ukrainian Front'.

Before Yeremenko lay the old Czechoslovakian defences which had been recently improved by Schörner's engineers. Elsewhere, as Malinovsky advanced towards Bratislava, the Slovakian fascists left the defence to others. Hitler had had great faith in the locally recruited (*Volksdeutsche*) 31st SS Grenadier *Bohmen-Mahren* Division; however, it was little more than a regiment in strength. When the Danube Flotilla's gunboats opened fire most of the Bratislava garrison made good their escape and the city fell to the Soviets on 5 April.

Moravska-Ostrava

The Soviet offensive was timed to coincide with the breaching of the Oder line and began on 15 April. Sixtieth and Thirty-Eighth Armies opened the attack along an 11km (7-mile) front. It became obvious within a matter of days that the operation had run into difficulties. The German lines were penetrated, but at such a snail's pace that the defenders had little or no trouble in sealing off the attackers. Heavy artillery or self-propelled guns had to brought up to the front line to smash the bunkers from point-blank range, which was inevitably a time-consuming process. Although there were several cracks in AGC's defences the integrity of the system was not imperilled. Under

increasing pressure from *Stavka* to take Moravska-Ostrava, Yeremenko realigned First Guards, Thirty-Eighth and Sixtieth Armies, modifying his plan which now called for a series of attacks around the German positions aiming to squeeze them out with a minimum of damage to the industrial and mining infrastructure. It was a similar strategy to that employed by Konev in Silesia and proved to be equally effective. By the afternoon of 30 April the Germans were in full retreat.

Brno was the next important city that stood between the Soviets and Prague and it too was the centre of a large military–industrial complex. This operation was to be carried out by 2nd Ukrainian Front's woefully under-strength Second Guards Tank Army that had been reduced to just over 150 armoured fighting vehicles. The addition of First Guards Mechanised Group doubled the armoured strength of Second Guards Tank Army. On 23 April Soviet artillery blasted a hole in the

German lines, the infantry then followed up and the tanks pushed on to outflank Brno from the north and east. Twenty-four hours later the assault on the city began. Although 10 per cent of the Soviet armour was knocked out in street fighting, Brno fell to Malinovsky on 27 April. AGC now pulled back towards Prague in the face of the combined power of 2nd and 4th Ukrainian Fronts.

Prague: Rebellion and Liberation

The dramatic shrinkage of the Third Reich increased the political wrangling between the USSR and the Western Allies. Much to Churchill's displeasure, Eisenhower decided to advance only a short distance into Czechoslovakia, thus allowing the Red Army a free hand to liberate Prague and deal with the remains of Schörner's forces to the west of the city. Konev had already begun his redeployment and it came as no surprise when, on 1 May, the entirety of 1st

Above: The last two rockets are loaded on to the launching frame of a *Katyusha* BM-13H mounted on a Lend-Lease Studebaker US6 lorry. The contrast between the undamaged buildings in the background and the destructive power about to be unleashed is noticeable.

Ukrainian Front was ordered to give its full attention to the situation in northern Czechoslovakia and the encirclement of AGC. Zhukov's forces were the only Soviet troops now fighting in Berlin other than those in the ranks of the Wehrmacht. Malinovsky was instructed to occupy positions to the south of Prague and take it by no later than the middle of May. 4th Ukrainian Front would move from the east and complete the perimeter around AGC.

The strength of the Soviet forces now moving into place was overwhelming and included 2,000 armoured vehicles, 4,000 aircraft and over 24,000 guns and mortars. Compacted as AGC now was, it was incapable of matching this concentration of power or of a prolonged resistance.

Amongst the flotsam of Germany's collapse that washed up in Prague were General Andrei Vlasov and the ROA. Vlasov had arrived from Dresden on 16 April, anticipating that the 1st ROA Division (General S. K. Bunyachenko) would join him. The 2nd ROA Division, which had been refitting around Linz in Austria, was also on its way north in company with XV SS Cossack Corps. However, it was unable to reach Vlasov. Bunyachenko's men had left the Oder front before the final collapse and marched south. They avoided being mustered into AGC despite a personal visit from Schörner himself. The Russians assured Schörner that they would not turn against their former allies. The Czech resistance, which had failed to come to an arrangement with Vlasov regarding the liberation of Prague, turned to Bunyachenko who was more amenable but this led to a rift between Vlasov and his general.

With his dreams rapidly turning to nightmares and virtually no control over the ROA Vlasov fell into a decline, seeking to alleviate his depression with alcohol. His melancholy was compounded when the ROA's tiny air force flew off to surrender to the Americans who had been ordered to halt some 120km (75 miles) west of Prague. The Czech resistance was unaware of the American–Soviet demarcation line.

Konev's forces, having redeployed with admirable skill, were to begin operations north of Prague on 6 May and Dresden was to be taken by Fifth Guards Tank Army.

However, on 4 May the citizens of Prague spontaneously rose up and, with virtually no German opposition in the capital, almost liberated themselves. During the course of the following day barricades sprang up and broadcasts for help were made in English and Russian. The German protectorate of Bohemia-Moravia was declared to be at an end. Schörner's response was uncharacteristically lethargic but eventually a

few tanks and some SS units were despatched to regain control of the city. This move provoked the Czechs to appeal to Bunyachenko for support, as they had received no reply from the Soviets. The ROA men took the airport and radio station from the Germans and Vlasov appealed in person to the German forces to surrender. Unfortunately for Vlasov's troops the hastily-assembled Czech National Council, which included many communists, decided to wash its hands of the Russian renegades and told them to leave Prague. Although many of the Russians marched west, some did not receive the order and found themselves forced to fight alongside the Germans to save their own skins.

As the last shots were fired, representatives of AGC met with the Czechs to discuss capitulation. Soviet tanks were closing in from all directions and it was preferable to surrender to the Czechs. Caught incompletely prepared by the Prague uprising, *Stavka* ordered Malinovsky and Konev into action on 6 May. It was on that day that Fortress Breslau finally surrendered after a siege of almost 100 days.

While Schörner's men prepared to fight their last battles, the German High Command was travelling to Berlin. Field Marshal Keitel signed the formal surrender document in the presence of Marshal Zhukov, Britain's Air Chief Marshal Tedder as Eisenhower's deputy and representative and France's General de Lattre de Tassigny. When the deed was accomplished Zhukov dismissed Keitel and his entourage and the celebrations began. It was 8 May.

Endings

Konev ordered this news to be broadcast to the Germans opposite his lines and allowed them three hours to comply. As no answer was forthcoming the Soviets resumed their offensive with a mighty artillery barrage. By the early hours of 9 May T-34s were making their way into Prague where, shortly after midday, the men of 1st and 2nd Ukrainian Fronts met up.

Less than a week later Vlasov and his entourage were caught by the Red Army, others surrendered to Americans who handed them over to the Red Army, who proceeded to exact a terrible revenge on these traitors to the USSR. A similar fate was in store for the Cossack corps and other *Osttruppen*.

The Ukrainian units in German service fared somewhat better. On 12 March Shandruk had finally obtained from the German government terms similar to those of the KONR but, of course, by then it was only a pipe dream. Nevertheless Shandruk travelled to Austria where he took command of the *Galizien* Division which was to become

1st Ukrainian Division of the Ukrainian National Army. Although *Galizien* had been heavily involved in fighting the Soviets as a part of IV SS Panzer Corps, it was taken out of the line for a swearing-in ceremony on 25 April when it technically ceased to be part of the Waffen-SS. A second Ukrainian division was destroyed almost before it was fully established during the last fighting in Czechoslovakia. The Ukrainians had decided, in the event of Germany surrendering, to head west. That is exactly what they did, from where, with Papal intervention as they were Catholics, they were allowed to emigrate to the Americas or Britain.

To the south the men and their families of the Croatian Army gave themselves up to the British rather than to Tito's forces, whose treatment of them was unlikely to be lenient. The remaining German units under General Saucken at the mouth of the Vistula River capitulated to Vasilevsky's 3rd Belorussian Front during the course of the second week of May.

Army Group Courland, having kicked its heels for months, began to surrender on 8/9 May. The situation in Courland was rather more complicated as there were several formations recruited from Baltic nationals who were not inclined to go quietly. The majority of the Baltic SS men had been evacuated earlier in the year but those who remained slipped away into the forests to carry on the fight against the USSR. Guerrilla warfare continued in the Baltic states, the Ukraine and in the Carpathian Mountains until the late 1950s.

From October 1944 the Germans had made a half-hearted attempt to organise a guerrilla movement. Known as Werewolves, members were generally recruited from the Hitler Youth. Their task was to commit acts of sabotage behind enemy lines. The movement carried out isolated acts of terrorism, including assassination, and vandalism such as painting pro-Nazi graffiti on buildings. However, the Soviet security forces took the threat seriously and treated suspected Werewolf members mercilessly. In reality there was little substance to the Werewolf movement and its activities faded away within weeks of the war's end.

By the end of the second week of May the Red Army had established itself along most of the east–west demarcation line and rounded up the majority of the German troops unaccounted for or still attempting to flee to the west. In the final analysis the Third Reich had not dragged the world down 'in flames' as Hitler had anticipated.

As the Soviet news agency Novosti laconically announced on 15 May, 'The reception of Nazi men and officers taken prisoner was completed on all fronts.'

Bibliography

Beevor, A., *Berlin: The Downfall 1945*,
Viking Penguin, London 2002

Bialer, Seweryn (ed), *Stalin and his Generals*,
Souvenir Press, 1970

Boyd, A., *The Soviet Airforce*,
Macdonalds and Jane's, London 1977

Carell, P., *Scorched Earth*,
Schiffer Publishing 1994

Clark, A., *Barbarossa 1941-45*,
Macmillan London, 1965

Dallin, A., *German Rule in Russia 1941-45*,
Macmillan London, 1957

Duffy, C., *Red Storm on the Reich*,
Routledge London, 2000

Erickson, J., *The Road to Berlin*,
Weidenfeld and Nicholson, 1983

Glantz, D. and House, J. M.,
When Titans Clashed, University of Kansas (reprint), 1998

Glantz, D. and Orenstein, H., *Belorussia 1944: The Soviet General Staff Study*, Frank Kass, 2004

Guderian, H., *Panzer Leader*,
Futura, reprinted 1974

Konev, I., *Year of Victory*,
Progress Press, Moscow 1970

Lee Ready, J., *The Forgotten Axis*,
McFarland, 1987

Lucas, J. and Cooper, M., *Hitler's Elite*,
Macdonalds and Jane's, London 1975

Nierhorster, L., *The Royal Hungarian Army 1920-45*,
Axis Europa Books, New York 1998

Rokossovsky, K., *A Soldier's Duty*,
Progress Press, Moscow 1970

Ryan, C., *The Last Battle*,
Collins, London 1966

Sajer, G., *The Forgotten Soldier*,
Cassell, London 2001 (reprint)

Shtemenko, S., *The Last Six Months*,
William Kimber, London 1978

Ungvary, K., *Battle for Budapest*,
I. B. Tauris, London 2005

Various contributors, *Slaughterhouse: The Handbook of the Eastern Front*, The Aberjona Press, 2004

Zaloga, S., *Operation Bagration*,
Osprey, 1996

Zhukov, G., *The Memoirs of Marshal Zhukov*,
Progress Press, Moscow 1985

Ziemke, E. F., *Stalingrad to Berlin: The German Defeat in the East*,
University of the Pacific Press, Washington 2002 (reprint)

Index